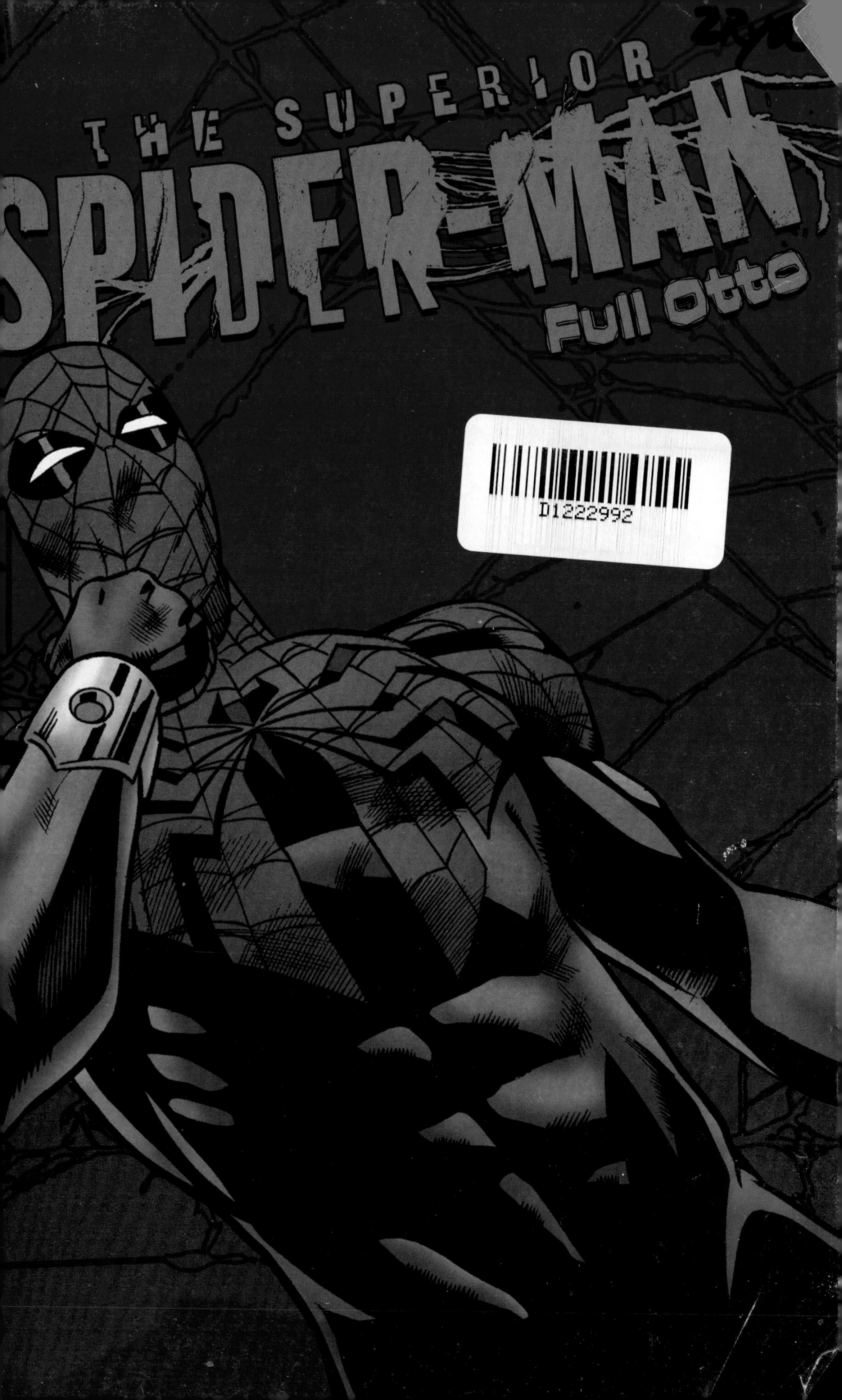
THE SUPERIOR
SPIDER-MAN
Full Otto

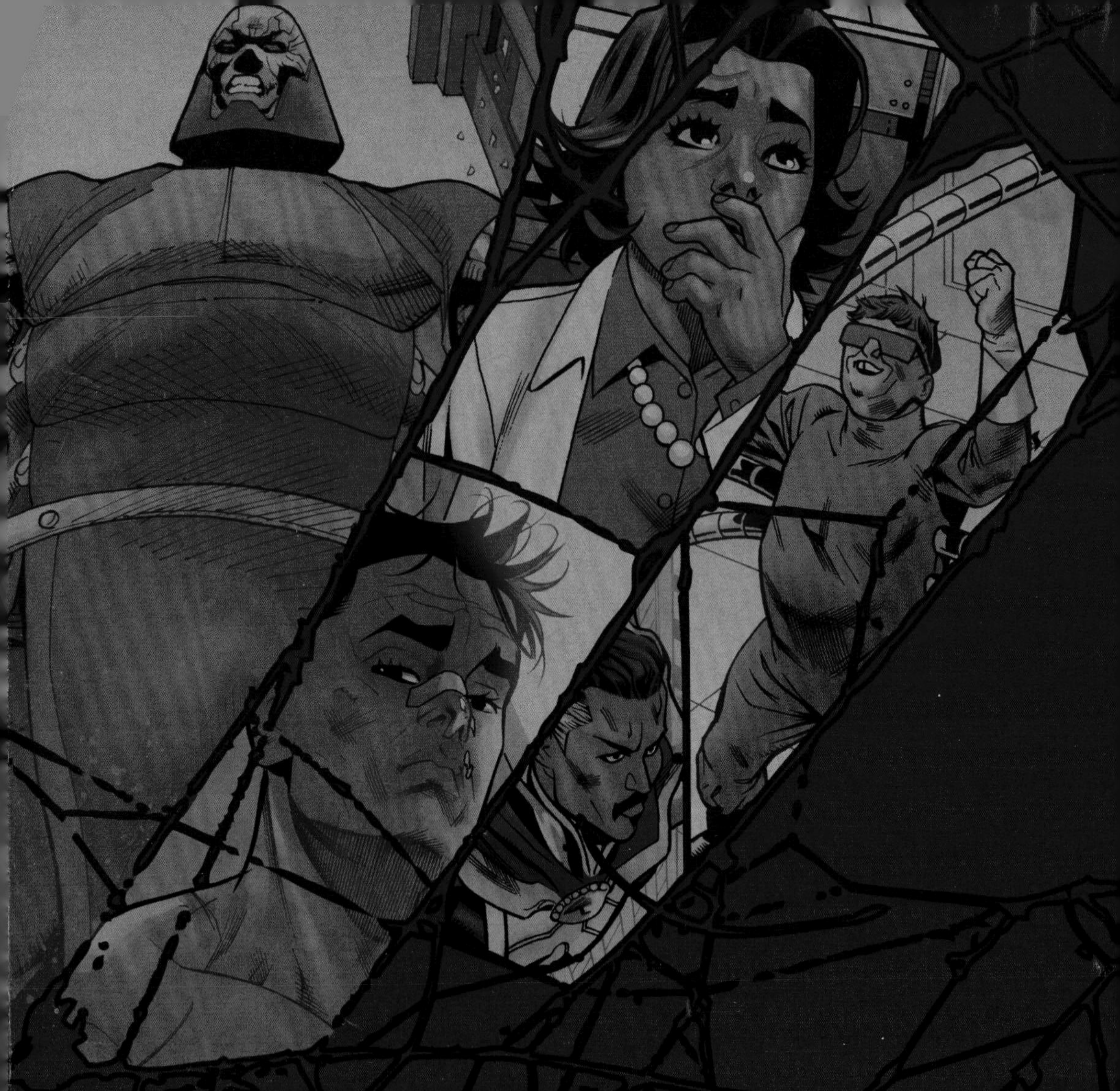

DOCTOR OTTO OCTAVIUS! KNOWN FOR MANY YEARS AS DOCTOR OCTOPUS, OCTAVIUS HAD A LIFE-ALTERING EXPERIENCE WHEN HE SWAPPED MINDS WITH HIS SWORN ENEMY, SPIDER-MAN! BY TAKING ON SPIDER-MAN'S MISSION, OCTAVIUS ALSO ABSORBED HIS SENSE OF RESPONSIBILITY. HE REDEDICATED HIMSELF TO SELFLESS ACTS ON BEHALF OF INNOCENTS, BUT HIS SENSE OF SUPERIORITY MADE OTTO A DIFFERENT KIND OF HERO.

AFTER HEROICALLY GIVING UP SPIDER-MAN'S BODY TO SAVE THE WOMAN HE LOVES AND TAKING A NEW BODY AND THE ALIAS ELLIOT TOLLIVER, OTTO HAS BEGUN A NEW LIFE. A PROFESSOR AT HORIZON UNIVERSITY BY DAY AND VIGILANTE BY NIGHT, OTTO (WITH THE PAID HELP OF THE NIGHT SHIFT, A TEAM OF SUPER VILLAINS) PROTECTS THE CITY OF SAN FRANCISCO AS THE SUPERIOR SPIDER-MAN!

SPIDER-MAN CREATED BY STAN LEE & STEVE DITKO

COLLECTION EDITOR **JENNIFER GRÜNWALD** • ASSISTANT EDITOR **CAITLIN O'CONNELL** • ASSOCIATE MANAGING EDITOR **KATERI WOODY**
EDITOR, SPECIAL PROJECTS **MARK D. BEAZLEY** • VP PRODUCTION & SPECIAL PROJECTS **JEFF YOUNGQUIST** • BOOK DESIGNER **SALENA MAHINA**

SVP PRINT, SALES & MARKETING **DAVID GABRIEL** • DIRECTOR, LICENSED PUBLISHING **SVEN LARSEN**
EDITOR IN CHIEF **C.B. CEBULSKI** • CHIEF CREATIVE OFFICER **JOE QUESADA**
PRESIDENT **DAN BUCKLEY** • EXECUTIVE PRODUCER **ALAN FINE**

SUPERIOR SPIDER-MAN VOL. 1: FULL OTTO. Contains material originally published in magazine form as SUPERIOR SPIDER-MAN #1-6. First printing 2019. ISBN 978-1-302-91480-6. Published by MARVEL WORLDWIDE, INC., a subsidiary of MARVEL ENTERTAINMENT, LLC. OFFICE OF PUBLICATION: 135 West 50th Street, New York, NY 10020. © 2019 MARVEL No similarity between any of the names, characters, persons, and/or institutions in this magazine with those of any living or dead person or institution is intended, and any such similarity which may exist is purely coincidental. **Printed in Canada.** DAN BUCKLEY, President, Marvel Entertainment; JOHN NEE, Publisher; JOE QUESADA, Chief Creative Officer; TOM BREVOORT, SVP of Publishing; DAVID BOGART, Associate Publisher & SVP of Talent Affairs; DAVID GABRIEL, SVP of Sales & Marketing, Publishing; JEFF YOUNGQUIST, VP of Production & Special Projects; DAN CARR, Executive Director of Publishing Technology; ALEX MORALES, Director of Publishing Operations; DAN EDINGTON, Managing Editor; SUSAN CRESPI, Production Manager; STAN LEE, Chairman Emeritus. For information regarding advertising in Marvel Comics or on Marvel.com, please contact Vit DeBellis, Custom Solutions & Integrated Advertising Manager, at vdebellis@marvel.com. For Marvel subscription inquiries, please call 888-511-5480. **Manufactured**

THE SUPERIOR SPIDER-MAN

Full Otto

CHRISTOS GAGE
WRITER

MIKE HAWTHORNE
PENCILER

WADE VON GRAWBADGER
WITH **VICTOR OLAZABA** (#2) & **ANDY OWENS** (#5)
INKERS

JORDIE BELLAIRE
COLORIST

VC'S CLAYTON COWLES
LETTERER

TRAVIS CHAREST (#1-4) & **JORGE COELHO** (#5)
COVER ART

**KATHLEEN WISNESKI
& ANNALISE BISSA**
ASSISTANT EDITORS

**NICK
LOWE**
EDITOR

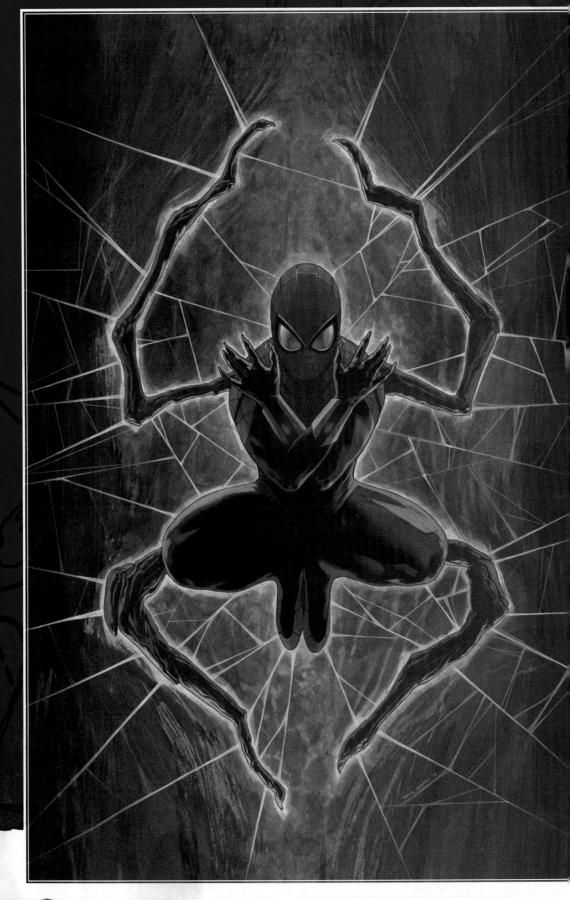

1

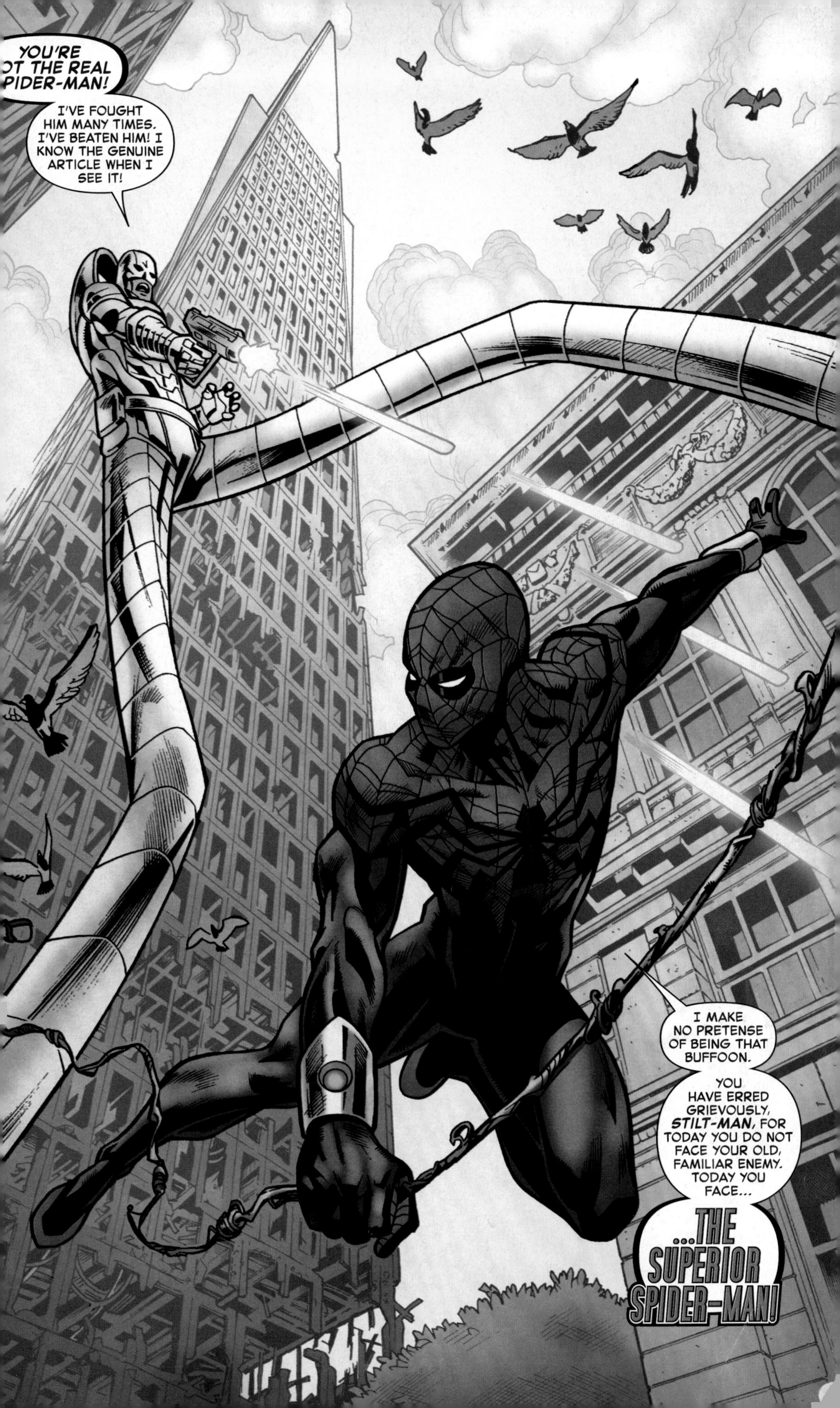
YOU'RE OT THE REAL SPIDER-MAN!
I'VE FOUGHT HIM MANY TIMES. I'VE BEATEN HIM! I KNOW THE GENUINE ARTICLE WHEN I SEE IT!
I MAKE NO PRETENSE OF BEING THAT BUFFOON.
YOU HAVE ERRED GRIEVOUSLY, STILT-MAN, FOR TODAY YOU DO NOT FACE YOUR OLD, FAMILIAR ENEMY. TODAY YOU FACE...
...THE SUPERIOR SPIDER-MAN!

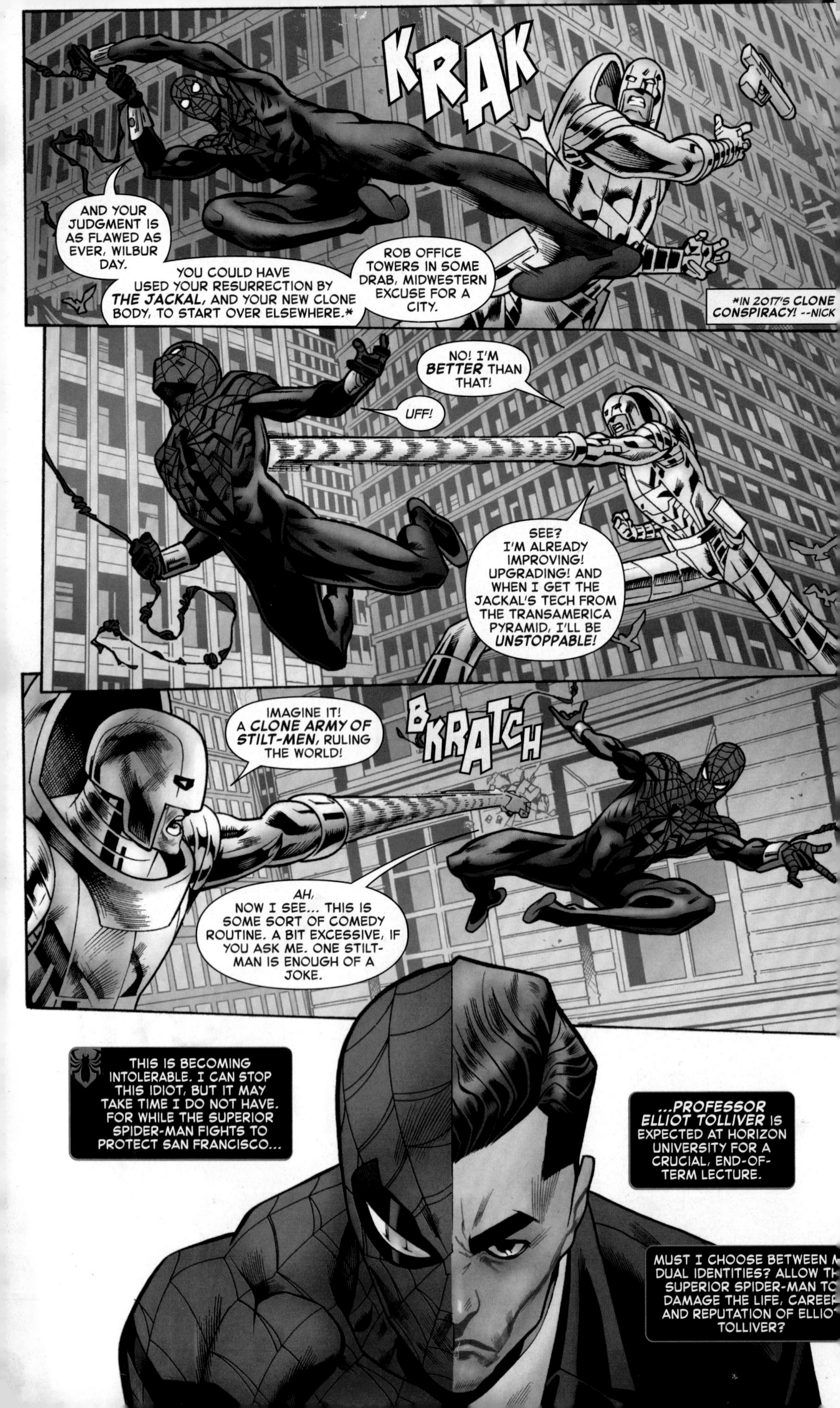

KRAK
AND YOUR JUDGMENT IS AS FLAWED AS EVER, WILBUR DAY.
YOU COULD HAVE USED YOUR RESURRECTION BY THE JACKAL, AND YOUR NEW CLONE BODY, TO START OVER ELSEWHERE.*
ROB OFFICE TOWERS IN SOME DRAB, MIDWESTERN EXCUSE FOR A CITY.
*IN 2017'S CLONE CONSPIRACY! --NICK
NO! I'M BETTER THAN THAT!
UFF!
SEE? I'M ALREADY IMPROVING! UPGRADING! AND WHEN I GET THE JACKAL'S TECH FROM THE TRANSAMERICA PYRAMID, I'LL BE UNSTOPPABLE!
IMAGINE IT! A CLONE ARMY OF STILT-MEN, RULING THE WORLD!
BKRATCH
AH, NOW I SEE... THIS IS SOME SORT OF COMEDY ROUTINE. A BIT EXCESSIVE, IF YOU ASK ME. ONE STILT-MAN IS ENOUGH OF A JOKE.
THIS IS BECOMING INTOLERABLE. I CAN STOP THIS IDIOT, BUT IT MAY TAKE TIME I DO NOT HAVE. FOR WHILE THE SUPERIOR SPIDER-MAN FIGHTS TO PROTECT SAN FRANCISCO...
...PROFESSOR ELLIOT TOLLIVER IS EXPECTED AT HORIZON UNIVERSITY FOR A CRUCIAL, END-OF-TERM LECTURE.
MUST I CHOOSE BETWEEN M DUAL IDENTITIES? ALLOW TH SUPERIOR SPIDER-MAN TO DAMAGE THE LIFE, CAREEF AND REPUTATION OF ELLIO TOLLIVER?

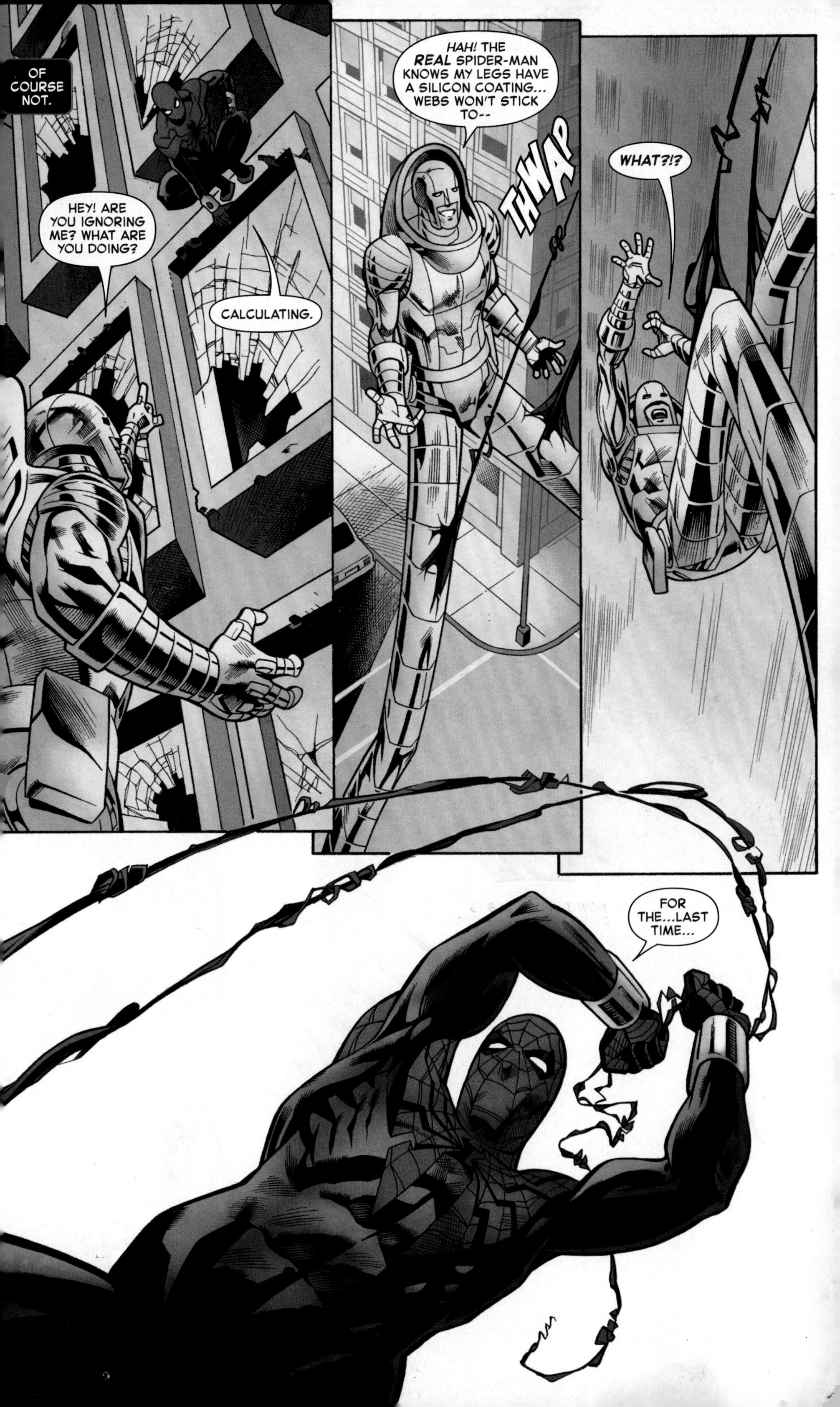
OF COURSE NOT.
HEY! ARE YOU IGNORING ME? WHAT ARE YOU DOING?
CALCULATING.
HAH! THE REAL SPIDER-MAN KNOWS MY LEGS HAVE A SILICON COATING... WEBS WON'T STICK TO--
THWAP
WHAT?!?
FOR THE...LAST TIME...

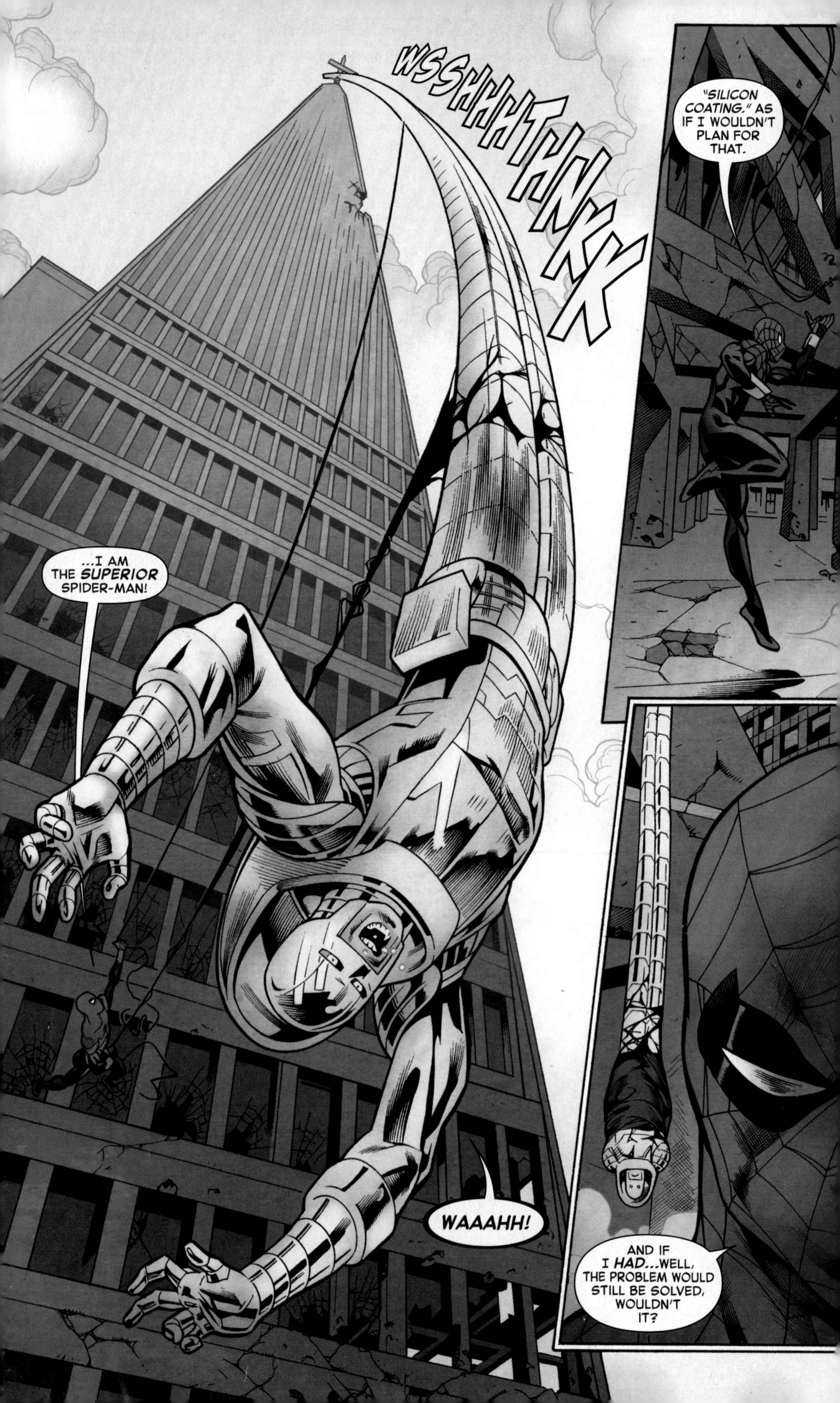

WSSHHHTHNKK
...I AM THE SUPERIOR SPIDER-MAN!
WAAAHH!
"SILICON COATING." AS IF I WOULDN'T PLAN FOR THAT.
AND IF I HAD...WELL, THE PROBLEM WOULD STILL BE SOLVED, WOULDN'T IT?

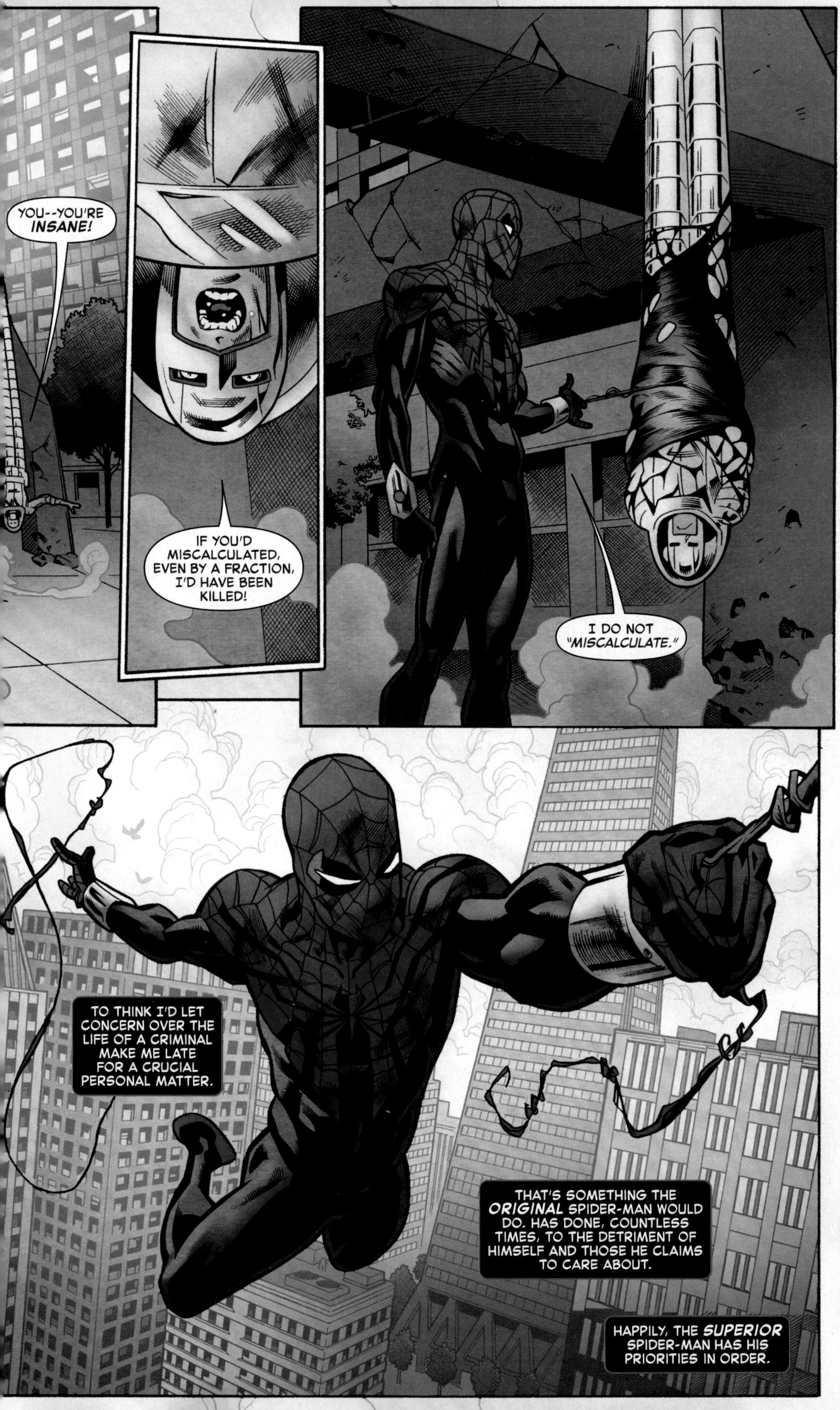
YOU--YOU'RE INSANE!
IF YOU'D MISCALCULATED, EVEN BY A FRACTION, I'D HAVE BEEN KILLED!
I DO NOT "MISCALCULATE."
TO THINK I'D LET CONCERN OVER THE LIFE OF A CRIMINAL MAKE ME LATE FOR A CRUCIAL PERSONAL MATTER.
THAT'S SOMETHING THE ORIGINAL SPIDER-MAN WOULD DO. HAS DONE, COUNTLESS TIMES, TO THE DETRIMENT OF HIMSELF AND THOSE HE CLAIMS TO CARE ABOUT.
HAPPILY, THE SUPERIOR SPIDER-MAN HAS HIS PRIORITIES IN ORDER.

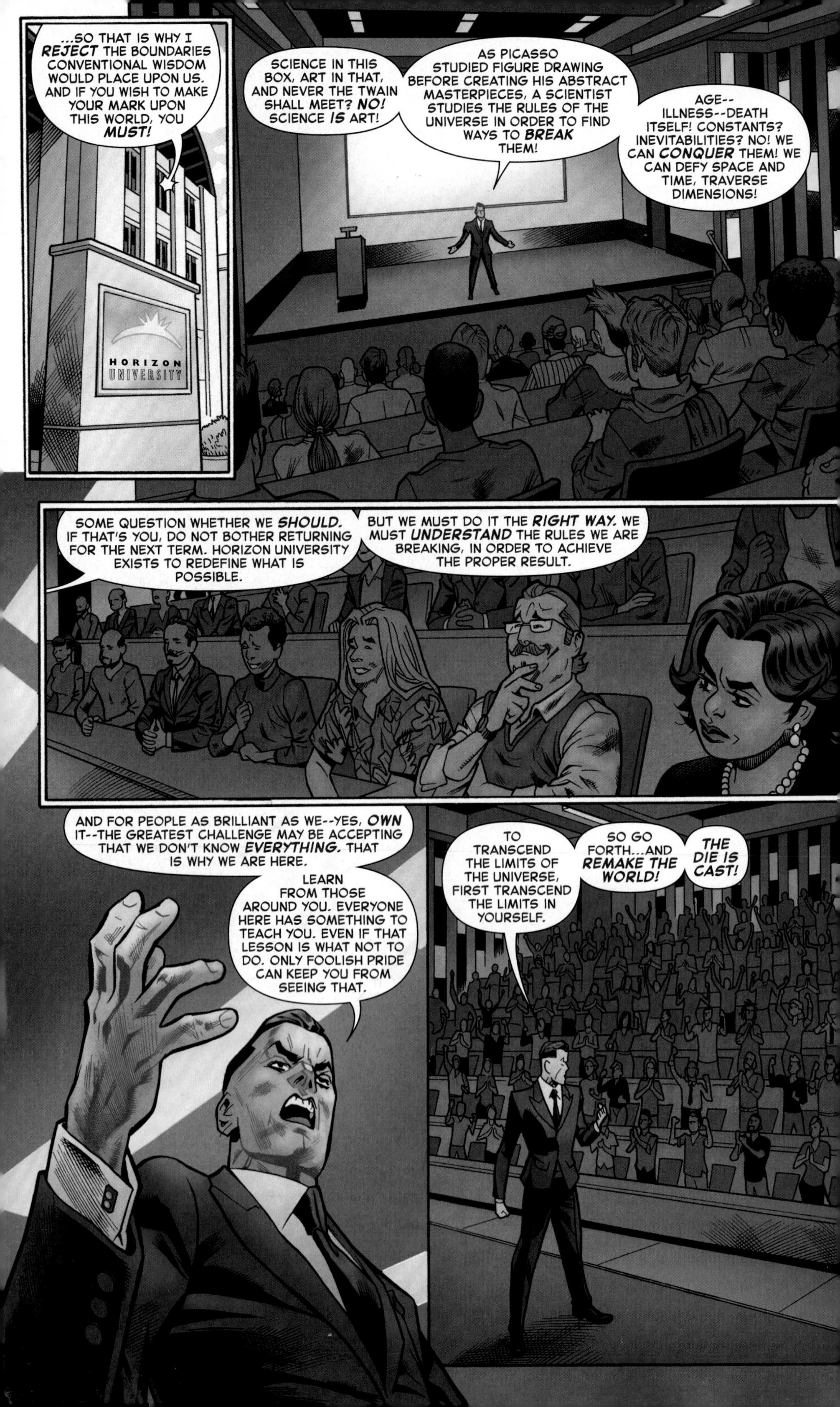
...SO THAT IS WHY I REJECT THE BOUNDARIES CONVENTIONAL WISDOM WOULD PLACE UPON US. AND IF YOU WISH TO MAKE YOUR MARK UPON THIS WORLD, YOU MUST!
HORIZON UNIVERSITY
SCIENCE IN THIS BOX, ART IN THAT, AND NEVER THE TWAIN SHALL MEET? NO! SCIENCE IS ART!
AS PICASSO STUDIED FIGURE DRAWING BEFORE CREATING HIS ABSTRACT MASTERPIECES, A SCIENTIST STUDIES THE RULES OF THE UNIVERSE IN ORDER TO FIND WAYS TO BREAK THEM!
AGE--ILLNESS--DEATH ITSELF! CONSTANTS? INEVITABILITIES? NO! WE CAN CONQUER THEM! WE CAN DEFY SPACE AND TIME, TRAVERSE DIMENSIONS!
SOME QUESTION WHETHER WE SHOULD. IF THAT'S YOU, DO NOT BOTHER RETURNING FOR THE NEXT TERM. HORIZON UNIVERSITY EXISTS TO REDEFINE WHAT IS POSSIBLE.
BUT WE MUST DO IT THE RIGHT WAY. WE MUST UNDERSTAND THE RULES WE ARE BREAKING, IN ORDER TO ACHIEVE THE PROPER RESULT.
AND FOR PEOPLE AS BRILLIANT AS WE--YES, OWN IT--THE GREATEST CHALLENGE MAY BE ACCEPTING THAT WE DON'T KNOW EVERYTHING. THAT IS WHY WE ARE HERE.
LEARN FROM THOSE AROUND YOU. EVERYONE HERE HAS SOMETHING TO TEACH YOU. EVEN IF THAT LESSON IS WHAT NOT TO DO. ONLY FOOLISH PRIDE CAN KEEP YOU FROM SEEING THAT.
TO TRANSCEND THE LIMITS OF THE UNIVERSE, FIRST TRANSCEND THE LIMITS IN YOURSELF.
SO GO FORTH...AND REMAKE THE WORLD!
THE DIE IS CAST!

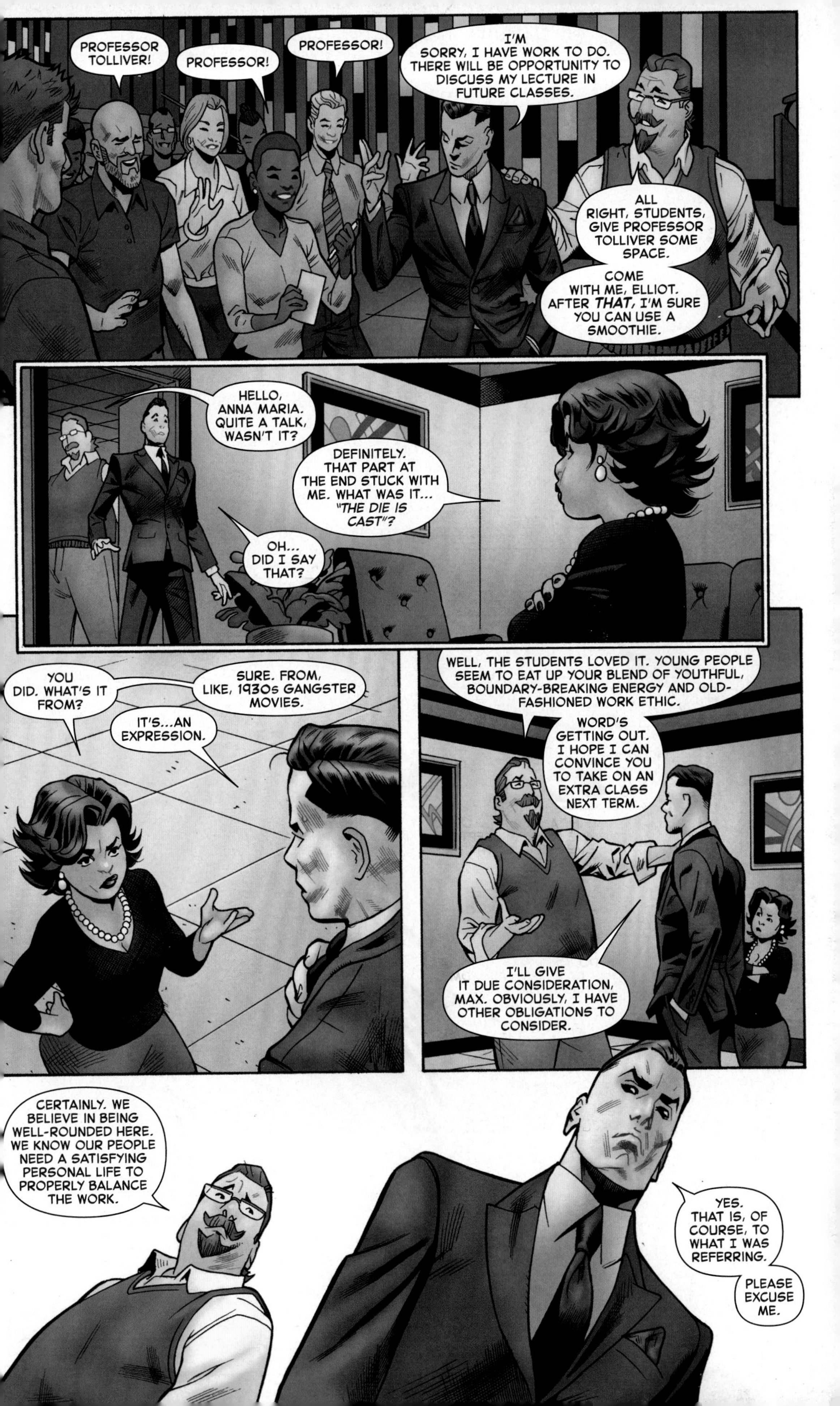
PROFESSOR TOLLIVER!
PROFESSOR!
PROFESSOR!
I'M SORRY, I HAVE WORK TO DO. THERE WILL BE OPPORTUNITY TO DISCUSS MY LECTURE IN FUTURE CLASSES.
ALL RIGHT, STUDENTS, GIVE PROFESSOR TOLLIVER SOME SPACE.
COME WITH ME, ELLIOT. AFTER *THAT,* I'M SURE YOU CAN USE A SMOOTHIE.
HELLO, ANNA MARIA. QUITE A TALK, WASN'T IT?
DEFINITELY. THAT PART AT THE END STUCK WITH ME. WHAT WAS IT... *"THE DIE IS CAST"?*
OH... DID I SAY THAT?
YOU DID. WHAT'S IT FROM?
IT'S...AN EXPRESSION.
SURE. FROM, LIKE, 1930s GANGSTER MOVIES.
WELL, THE STUDENTS LOVED IT. YOUNG PEOPLE SEEM TO EAT UP YOUR BLEND OF YOUTHFUL, BOUNDARY-BREAKING ENERGY AND OLD-FASHIONED WORK ETHIC.
WORD'S GETTING OUT. I HOPE I CAN CONVINCE YOU TO TAKE ON AN EXTRA CLASS NEXT TERM.
I'LL GIVE IT DUE CONSIDERATION, MAX. OBVIOUSLY, I HAVE OTHER OBLIGATIONS TO CONSIDER.
CERTAINLY. WE BELIEVE IN BEING WELL-ROUNDED HERE. WE KNOW OUR PEOPLE NEED A SATISFYING PERSONAL LIFE TO PROPERLY BALANCE THE WORK.
YES. THAT IS, OF COURSE, TO WHAT I WAS REFERRING.
PLEASE EXCUSE ME.

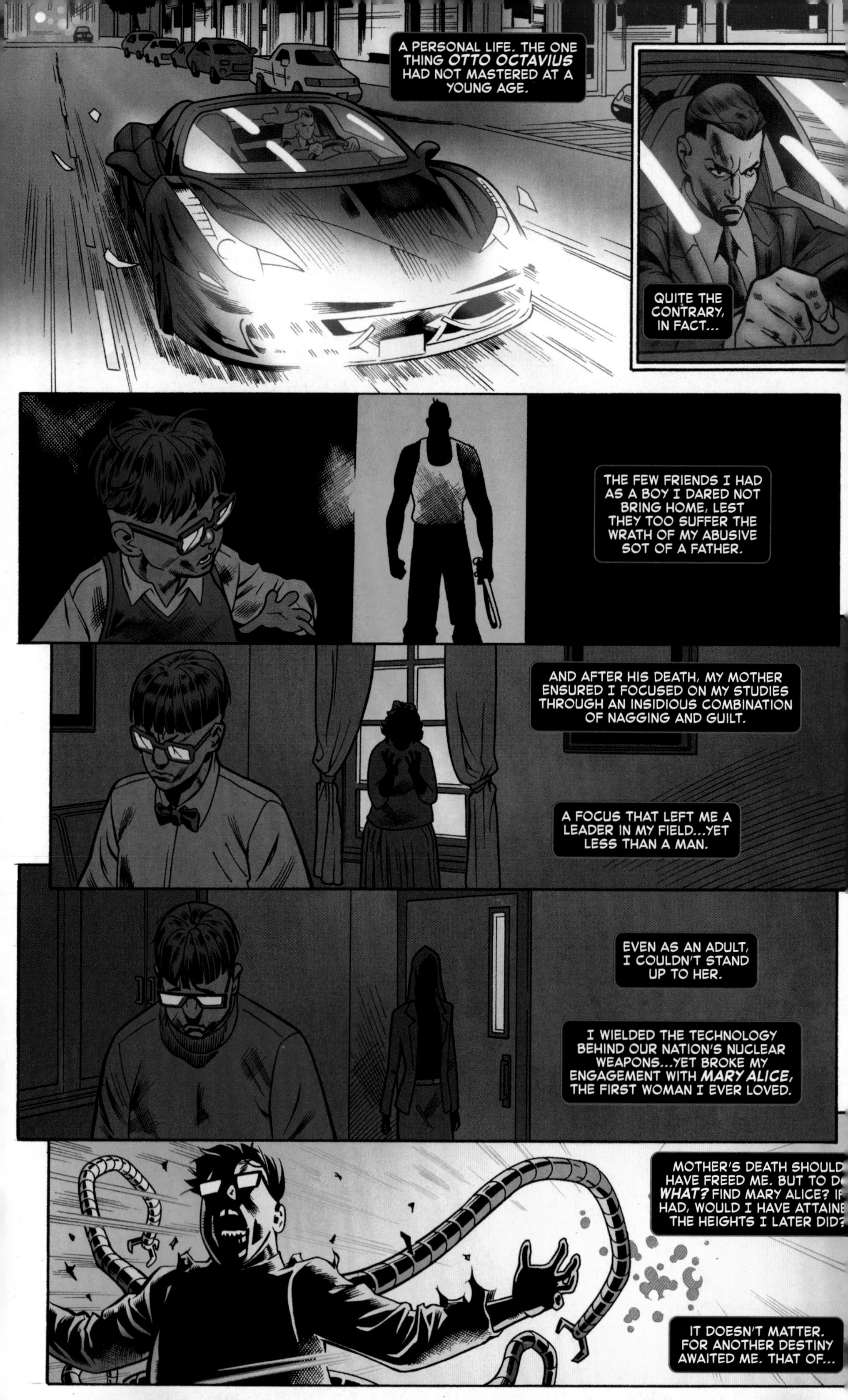

A PERSONAL LIFE. THE ONE THING OTTO OCTAVIUS HAD NOT MASTERED AT A YOUNG AGE.
QUITE THE CONTRARY, IN FACT...
THE FEW FRIENDS I HAD AS A BOY I DARED NOT BRING HOME, LEST THEY TOO SUFFER THE WRATH OF MY ABUSIVE SOT OF A FATHER.
AND AFTER HIS DEATH, MY MOTHER ENSURED I FOCUSED ON MY STUDIES THROUGH AN INSIDIOUS COMBINATION OF NAGGING AND GUILT.
A FOCUS THAT LEFT ME A LEADER IN MY FIELD...YET LESS THAN A MAN.
EVEN AS AN ADULT, I COULDN'T STAND UP TO HER.
I WIELDED THE TECHNOLOGY BEHIND OUR NATION'S NUCLEAR WEAPONS...YET BROKE MY ENGAGEMENT WITH MARY ALICE, THE FIRST WOMAN I EVER LOVED.
MOTHER'S DEATH SHOULD HAVE FREED ME. BUT TO D WHAT? FIND MARY ALICE? I HAD, WOULD I HAVE ATTAIN THE HEIGHTS I LATER DID?
IT DOESN'T MATTER. FOR ANOTHER DESTINY AWAITED ME. THAT OF...

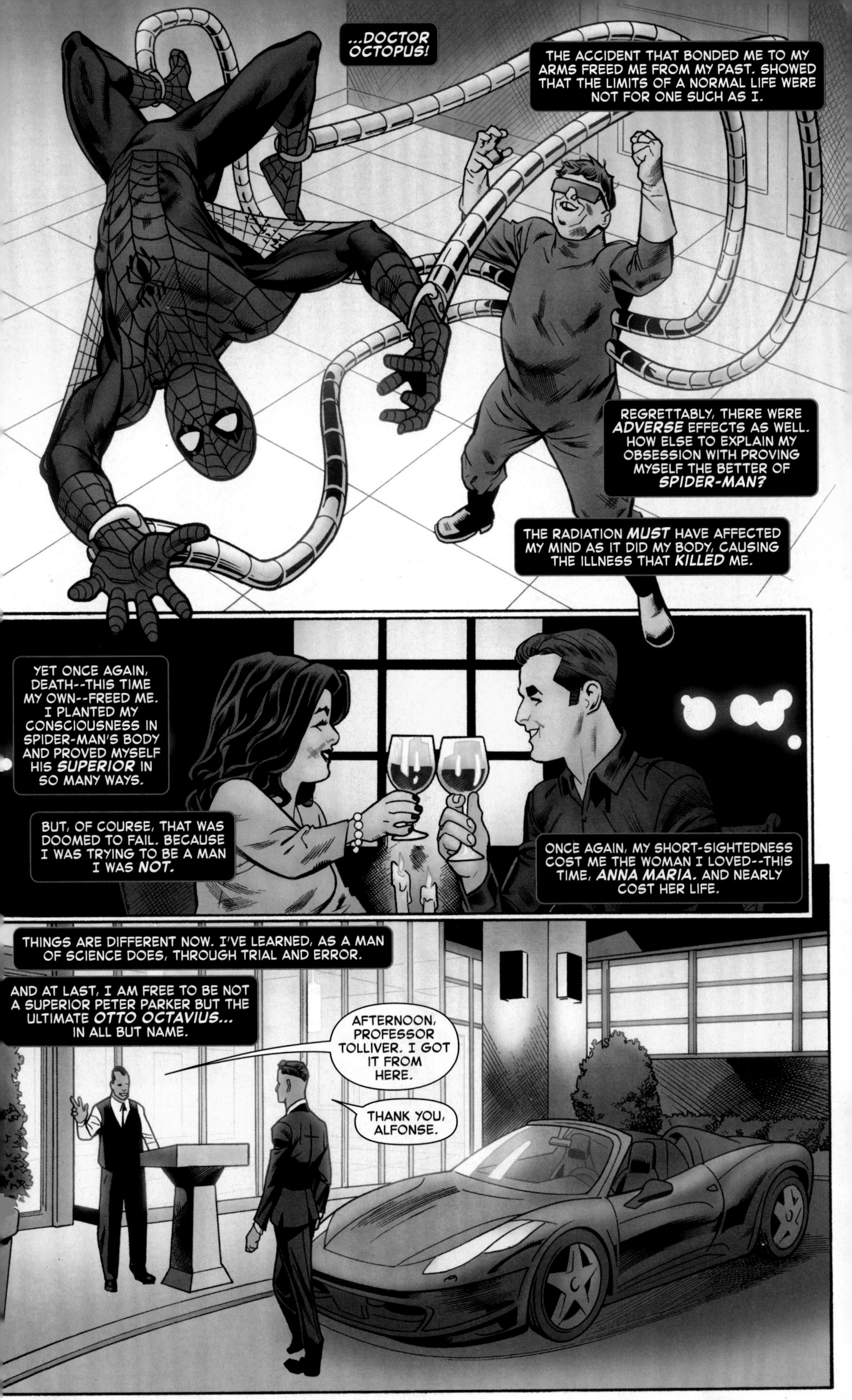
...DOCTOR OCTOPUS!
THE ACCIDENT THAT BONDED ME TO MY ARMS FREED ME FROM MY PAST. SHOWED THAT THE LIMITS OF A NORMAL LIFE WERE NOT FOR ONE SUCH AS I.
REGRETTABLY, THERE WERE ADVERSE EFFECTS AS WELL. HOW ELSE TO EXPLAIN MY OBSESSION WITH PROVING MYSELF THE BETTER OF SPIDER-MAN?
THE RADIATION MUST HAVE AFFECTED MY MIND AS IT DID MY BODY, CAUSING THE ILLNESS THAT KILLED ME.
YET ONCE AGAIN, DEATH--THIS TIME MY OWN--FREED ME. I PLANTED MY CONSCIOUSNESS IN SPIDER-MAN'S BODY AND PROVED MYSELF HIS SUPERIOR IN SO MANY WAYS.
BUT, OF COURSE, THAT WAS DOOMED TO FAIL. BECAUSE I WAS TRYING TO BE A MAN I WAS NOT.
ONCE AGAIN, MY SHORT-SIGHTEDNESS COST ME THE WOMAN I LOVED--THIS TIME, ANNA MARIA. AND NEARLY COST HER LIFE.
THINGS ARE DIFFERENT NOW. I'VE LEARNED, AS A MAN OF SCIENCE DOES, THROUGH TRIAL AND ERROR.
AND AT LAST, I AM FREE TO BE NOT A SUPERIOR PETER PARKER BUT THE ULTIMATE OTTO OCTAVIUS... IN ALL BUT NAME.
AFTERNOON, PROFESSOR TOLLIVER. I GOT IT FROM HERE.
THANK YOU, ALFONSE.

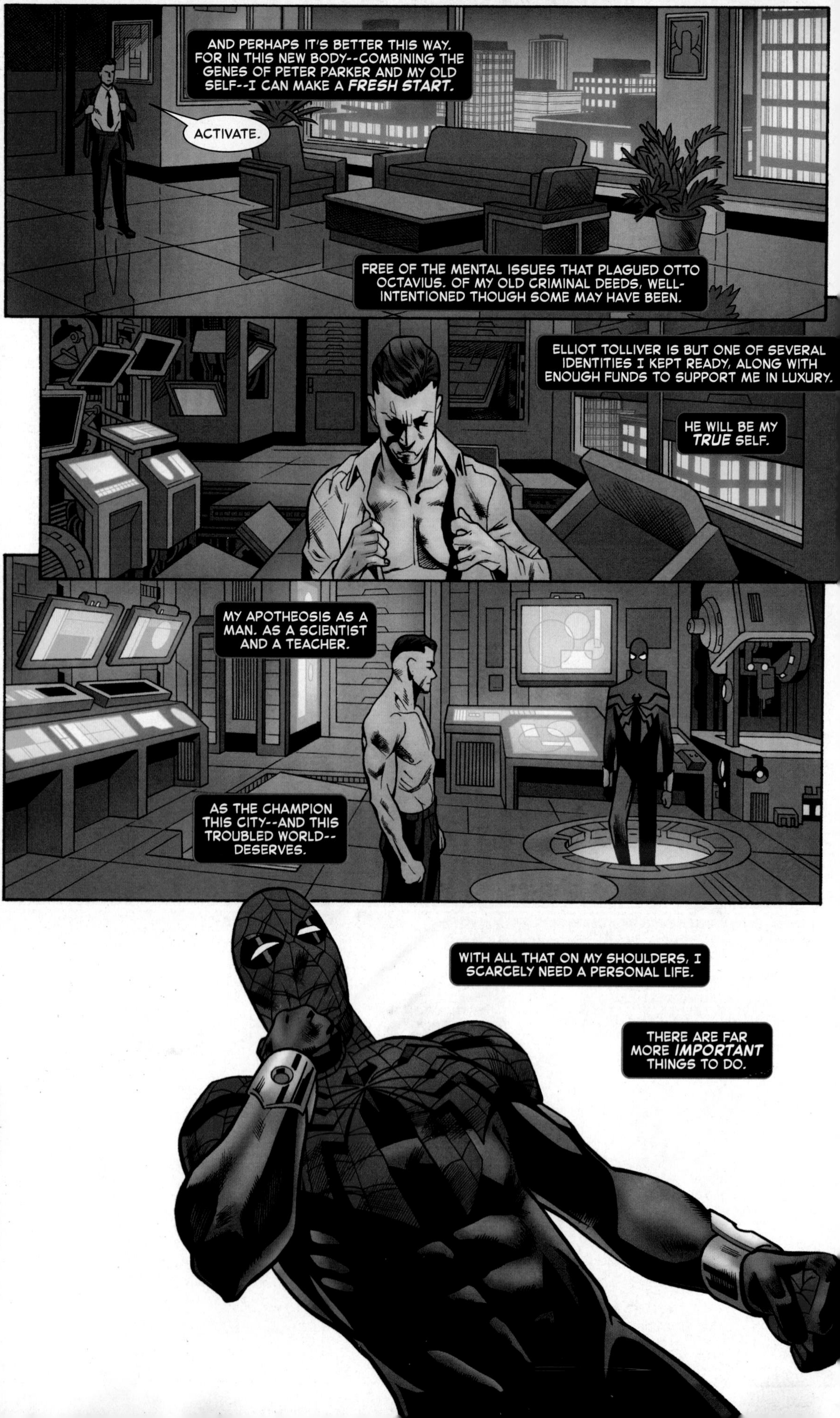
AND PERHAPS IT'S BETTER THIS WAY. FOR IN THIS NEW BODY--COMBINING THE GENES OF PETER PARKER AND MY OLD SELF--I CAN MAKE A FRESH START.
ACTIVATE.
FREE OF THE MENTAL ISSUES THAT PLAGUED OTTO OCTAVIUS. OF MY OLD CRIMINAL DEEDS, WELL-INTENTIONED THOUGH SOME MAY HAVE BEEN.
ELLIOT TOLLIVER IS BUT ONE OF SEVERAL IDENTITIES I KEPT READY, ALONG WITH ENOUGH FUNDS TO SUPPORT ME IN LUXURY.
HE WILL BE MY TRUE SELF.
MY APOTHEOSIS AS A MAN. AS A SCIENTIST AND A TEACHER.
AS THE CHAMPION THIS CITY--AND THIS TROUBLED WORLD--DESERVES.
WITH ALL THAT ON MY SHOULDERS, I SCARCELY NEED A PERSONAL LIFE.
THERE ARE FAR MORE IMPORTANT THINGS TO DO.

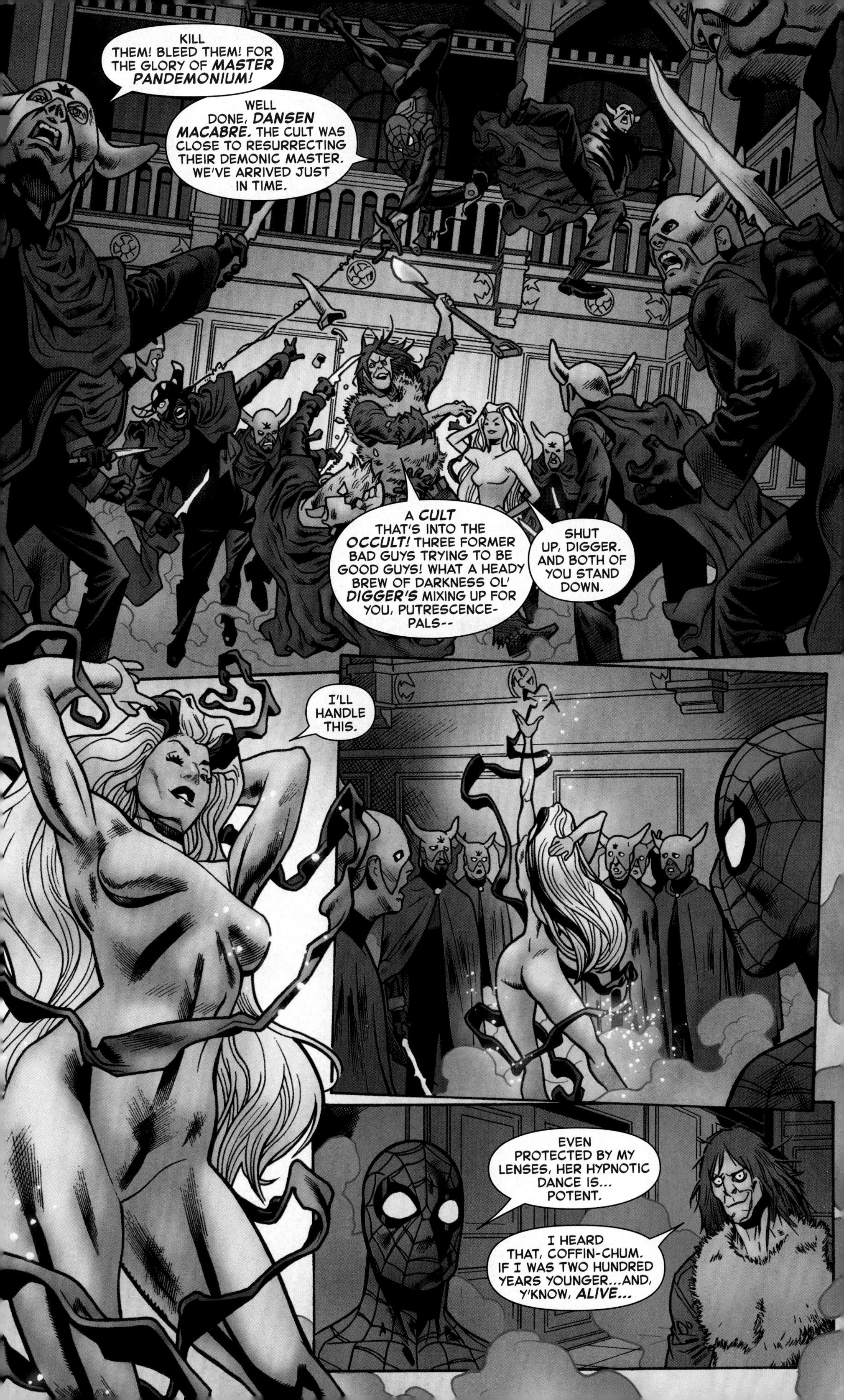
KILL THEM! BLEED THEM! FOR THE GLORY OF MASTER PANDEMONIUM!
WELL DONE, DANSEN MACABRE. THE CULT WAS CLOSE TO RESURRECTING THEIR DEMONIC MASTER. WE'VE ARRIVED JUST IN TIME.
A CULT THAT'S INTO THE OCCULT! THREE FORMER BAD GUYS TRYING TO BE GOOD GUYS! WHAT A HEADY BREW OF DARKNESS OL' DIGGER'S MIXING UP FOR YOU, PUTRESCENCE-PALS--
SHUT UP, DIGGER. AND BOTH OF YOU STAND DOWN.
I'LL HANDLE THIS.
EVEN PROTECTED BY MY LENSES, HER HYPNOTIC DANCE IS... POTENT.
I HEARD THAT, COFFIN-CHUM. IF I WAS TWO HUNDRED YEARS YOUNGER...AND, Y'KNOW, ALIVE...

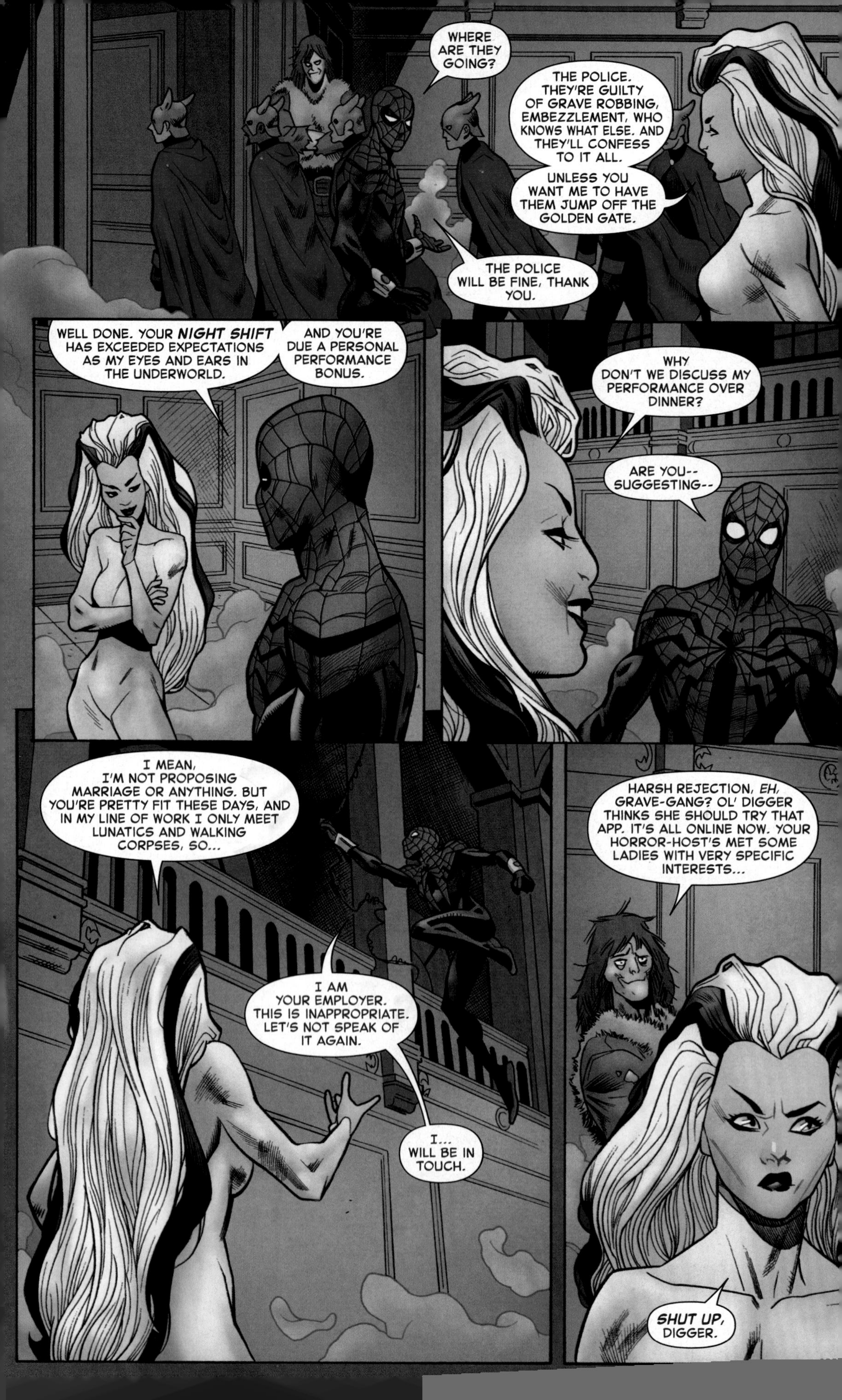

WHERE ARE THEY GOING?
THE POLICE. THEY'RE GUILTY OF GRAVE ROBBING, EMBEZZLEMENT, WHO KNOWS WHAT ELSE. AND THEY'LL CONFESS TO IT ALL.
UNLESS YOU WANT ME TO HAVE THEM JUMP OFF THE GOLDEN GATE.
THE POLICE WILL BE FINE, THANK YOU.
WELL DONE. YOUR NIGHT SHIFT HAS EXCEEDED EXPECTATIONS AS MY EYES AND EARS IN THE UNDERWORLD.
AND YOU'RE DUE A PERSONAL PERFORMANCE BONUS.
WHY DON'T WE DISCUSS MY PERFORMANCE OVER DINNER?
ARE YOU-- SUGGESTING--
I MEAN, I'M NOT PROPOSING MARRIAGE OR ANYTHING. BUT YOU'RE PRETTY FIT THESE DAYS, AND IN MY LINE OF WORK I ONLY MEET LUNATICS AND WALKING CORPSES, SO...
I AM YOUR EMPLOYER. THIS IS INAPPROPRIATE. LET'S NOT SPEAK OF IT AGAIN.
I... WILL BE IN TOUCH.
HARSH REJECTION, EH, GRAVE-GANG? OL' DIGGER THINKS SHE SHOULD TRY THAT APP. IT'S ALL ONLINE NOW. YOUR HORROR-HOST'S MET SOME LADIES WITH VERY SPECIFIC INTERESTS...
SHUT UP, DIGGER.

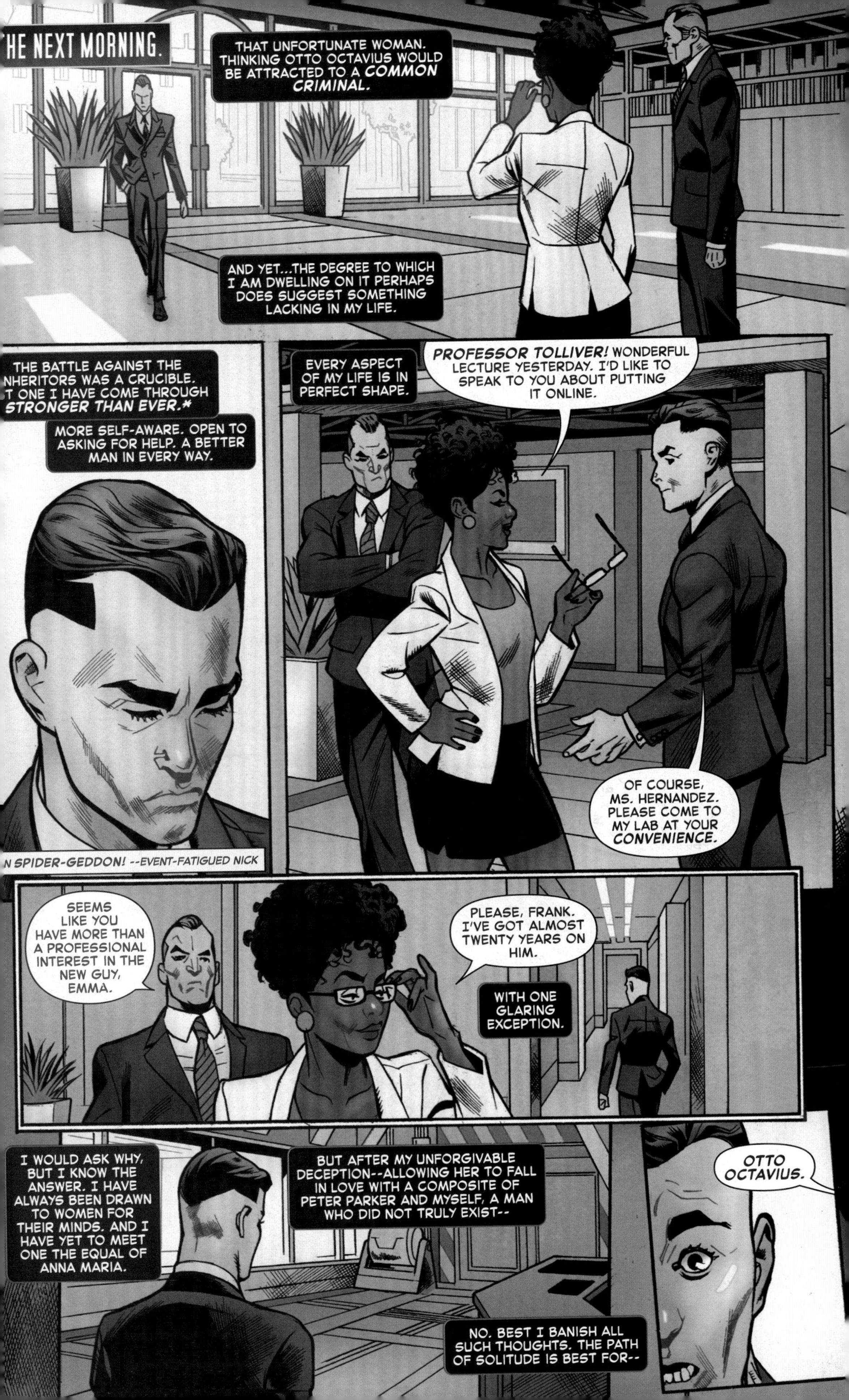

HE NEXT MORNING.
THAT UNFORTUNATE WOMAN. THINKING OTTO OCTAVIUS WOULD BE ATTRACTED TO A COMMON CRIMINAL.
AND YET...THE DEGREE TO WHICH I AM DWELLING ON IT PERHAPS DOES SUGGEST SOMETHING LACKING IN MY LIFE.
THE BATTLE AGAINST THE NHERITORS WAS A CRUCIBLE. T ONE I HAVE COME THROUGH STRONGER THAN EVER.*
MORE SELF-AWARE. OPEN TO ASKING FOR HELP. A BETTER MAN IN EVERY WAY.
N SPIDER-GEDDON! --EVENT-FATIGUED NICK
EVERY ASPECT OF MY LIFE IS IN PERFECT SHAPE.
PROFESSOR TOLLIVER! WONDERFUL LECTURE YESTERDAY. I'D LIKE TO SPEAK TO YOU ABOUT PUTTING IT ONLINE.
OF COURSE, MS. HERNANDEZ. PLEASE COME TO MY LAB AT YOUR CONVENIENCE.
SEEMS LIKE YOU HAVE MORE THAN A PROFESSIONAL INTEREST IN THE NEW GUY, EMMA.
PLEASE, FRANK. I'VE GOT ALMOST TWENTY YEARS ON HIM.
WITH ONE GLARING EXCEPTION.
I WOULD ASK WHY, BUT I KNOW THE ANSWER. I HAVE ALWAYS BEEN DRAWN TO WOMEN FOR THEIR MINDS. AND I HAVE YET TO MEET ONE THE EQUAL OF ANNA MARIA.
BUT AFTER MY UNFORGIVABLE DECEPTION--ALLOWING HER TO FALL IN LOVE WITH A COMPOSITE OF PETER PARKER AND MYSELF, A MAN WHO DID NOT TRULY EXIST--
OTTO OCTAVIUS.
NO. BEST I BANISH ALL SUCH THOUGHTS. THE PATH OF SOLITUDE IS BEST FOR--

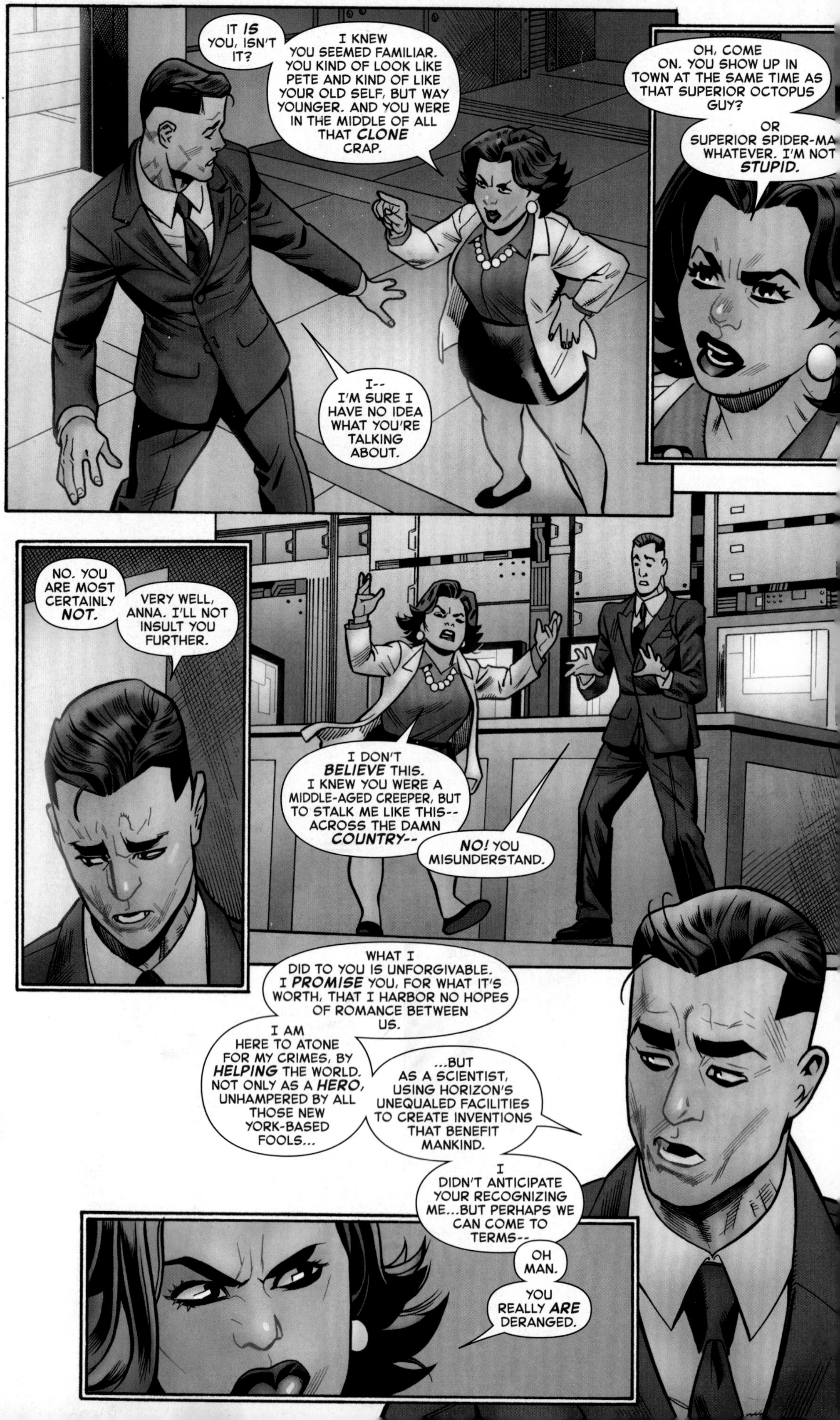
IT IS YOU, ISN'T IT?
I KNEW YOU SEEMED FAMILIAR. YOU KIND OF LOOK LIKE PETE AND KIND OF LIKE YOUR OLD SELF, BUT WAY YOUNGER. AND YOU WERE IN THE MIDDLE OF ALL THAT CLONE CRAP.
I-- I'M SURE I HAVE NO IDEA WHAT YOU'RE TALKING ABOUT.
OH, COME ON. YOU SHOW UP IN TOWN AT THE SAME TIME AS THAT SUPERIOR OCTOPUS GUY?
OR SUPERIOR SPIDER-MA WHATEVER. I'M NOT STUPID.
NO. YOU ARE MOST CERTAINLY NOT.
VERY WELL, ANNA. I'LL NOT INSULT YOU FURTHER.
I DON'T BELIEVE THIS. I KNEW YOU WERE A MIDDLE-AGED CREEPER, BUT TO STALK ME LIKE THIS-- ACROSS THE DAMN COUNTRY--
NO! YOU MISUNDERSTAND.
WHAT I DID TO YOU IS UNFORGIVABLE. I PROMISE YOU, FOR WHAT IT'S WORTH, THAT I HARBOR NO HOPES OF ROMANCE BETWEEN US.
I AM HERE TO ATONE FOR MY CRIMES, BY HELPING THE WORLD. NOT ONLY AS A HERO, UNHAMPERED BY ALL THOSE NEW YORK-BASED FOOLS...
...BUT AS A SCIENTIST, USING HORIZON'S UNEQUALED FACILITIES TO CREATE INVENTIONS THAT BENEFIT MANKIND.
I DIDN'T ANTICIPATE YOUR RECOGNIZING ME...BUT PERHAPS WE CAN COME TO TERMS--
OH MAN.
YOU REALLY ARE DERANGED.

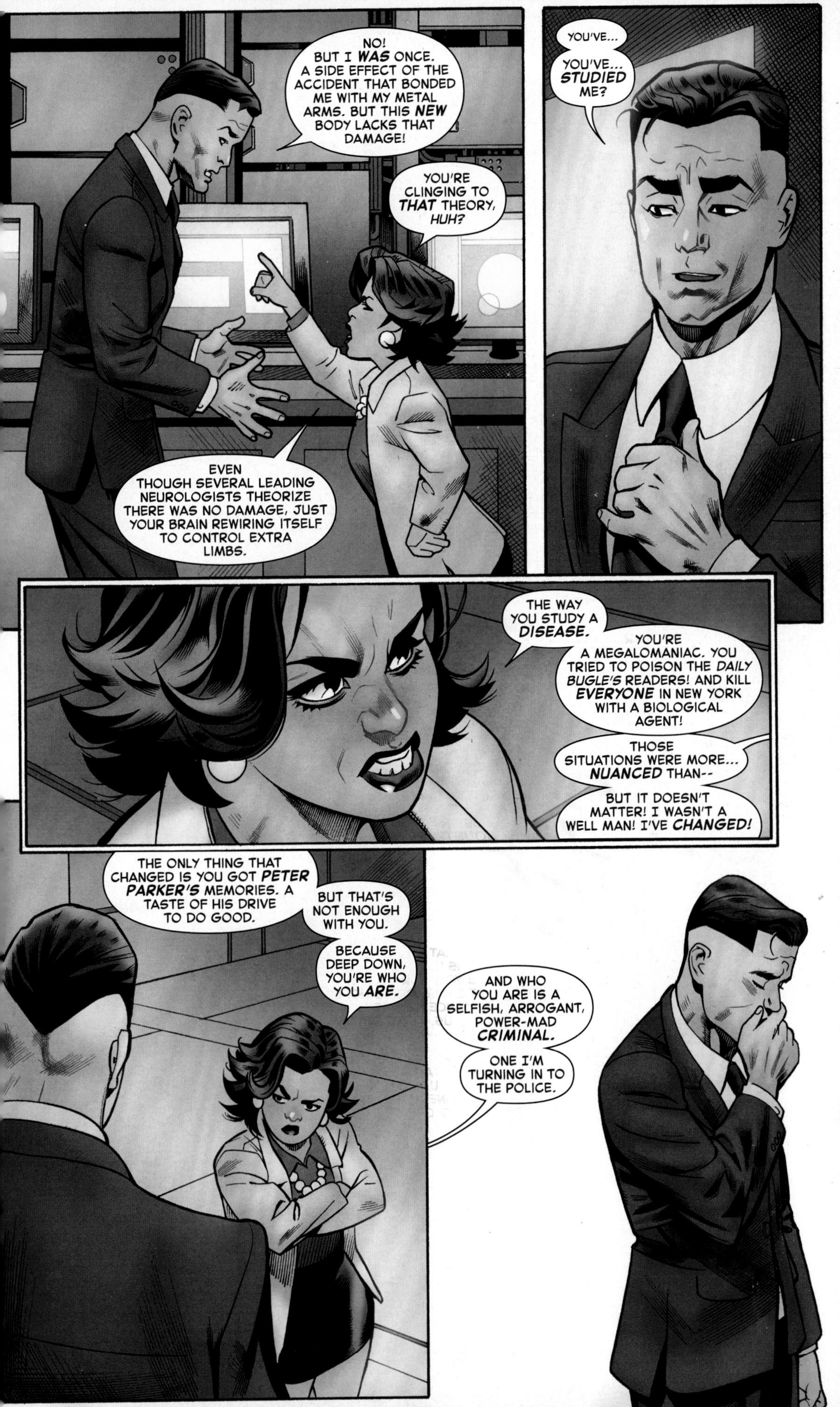
NO! BUT I WAS ONCE. A SIDE EFFECT OF THE ACCIDENT THAT BONDED ME WITH MY METAL ARMS. BUT THIS NEW BODY LACKS THAT DAMAGE!
YOU'RE CLINGING TO THAT THEORY, HUH?
EVEN THOUGH SEVERAL LEADING NEUROLOGISTS THEORIZE THERE WAS NO DAMAGE, JUST YOUR BRAIN REWIRING ITSELF TO CONTROL EXTRA LIMBS.
YOU'VE...
YOU'VE... STUDIED ME?
THE WAY YOU STUDY A DISEASE.
YOU'RE A MEGALOMANIAC. YOU TRIED TO POISON THE DAILY BUGLE'S READERS! AND KILL EVERYONE IN NEW YORK WITH A BIOLOGICAL AGENT!
THOSE SITUATIONS WERE MORE... NUANCED THAN--
BUT IT DOESN'T MATTER! I WASN'T A WELL MAN! I'VE CHANGED!
THE ONLY THING THAT CHANGED IS YOU GOT PETER PARKER'S MEMORIES. A TASTE OF HIS DRIVE TO DO GOOD.
BUT THAT'S NOT ENOUGH WITH YOU.
BECAUSE DEEP DOWN, YOU'RE WHO YOU ARE.
AND WHO YOU ARE IS A SELFISH, ARROGANT, POWER-MAD CRIMINAL.
ONE I'M TURNING IN TO THE POLICE.

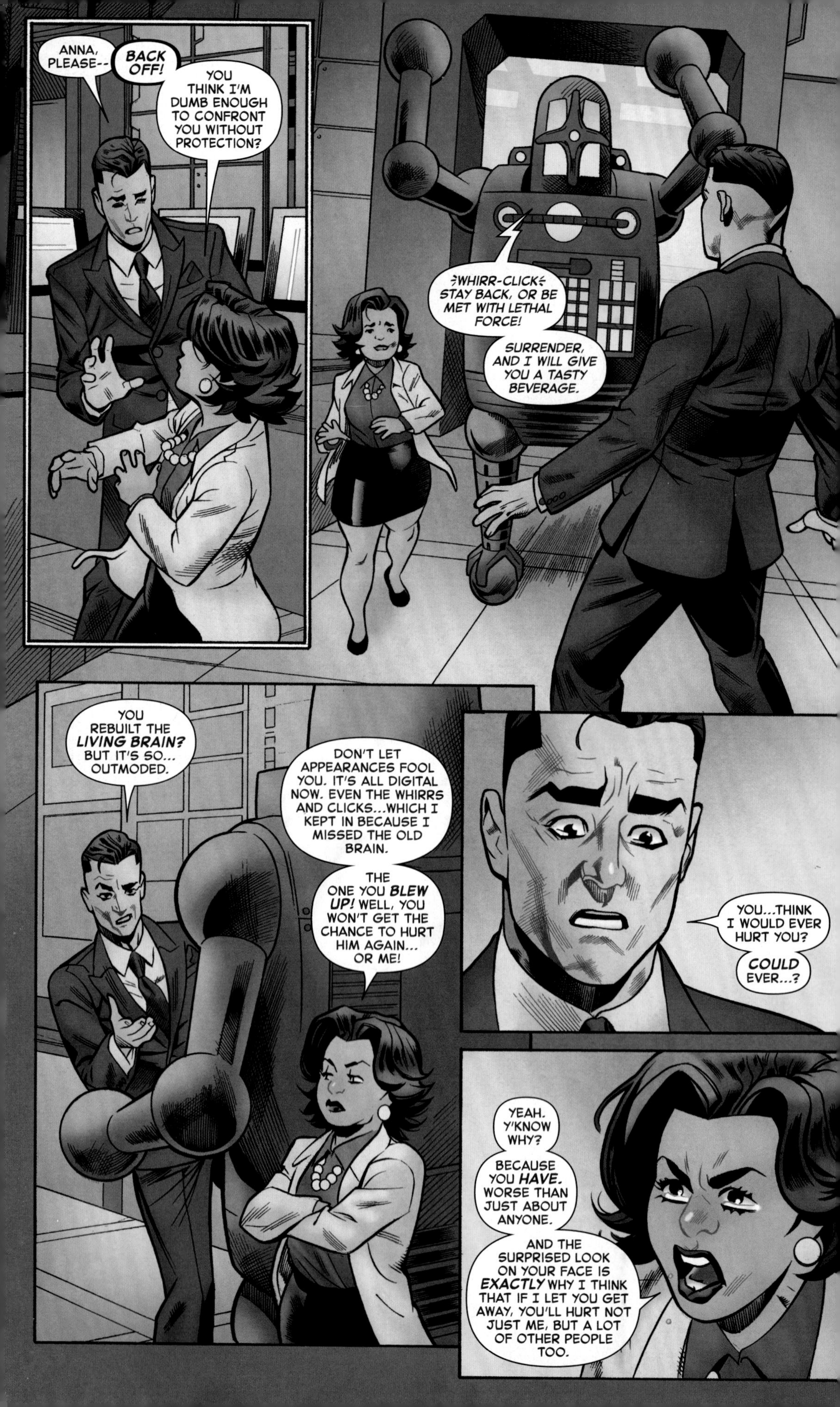
ANNA, PLEASE--
BACK OFF!
YOU THINK I'M DUMB ENOUGH TO CONFRONT YOU WITHOUT PROTECTION?
WHIRR-CLICK STAY BACK, OR BE MET WITH LETHAL FORCE!
SURRENDER, AND I WILL GIVE YOU A TASTY BEVERAGE.
YOU REBUILT THE LIVING BRAIN? BUT IT'S SO... OUTMODED.
DON'T LET APPEARANCES FOOL YOU. IT'S ALL DIGITAL NOW. EVEN THE WHIRRS AND CLICKS...WHICH I KEPT IN BECAUSE I MISSED THE OLD BRAIN.
THE ONE YOU BLEW UP! WELL, YOU WON'T GET THE CHANCE TO HURT HIM AGAIN... OR ME!
YOU...THINK I WOULD EVER HURT YOU?
COULD EVER...?
YEAH. Y'KNOW WHY?
BECAUSE YOU HAVE. WORSE THAN JUST ABOUT ANYONE.
AND THE SURPRISED LOOK ON YOUR FACE IS EXACTLY WHY I THINK THAT IF I LET YOU GET AWAY, YOU'LL HURT NOT JUST ME, BUT A LOT OF OTHER PEOPLE TOO.

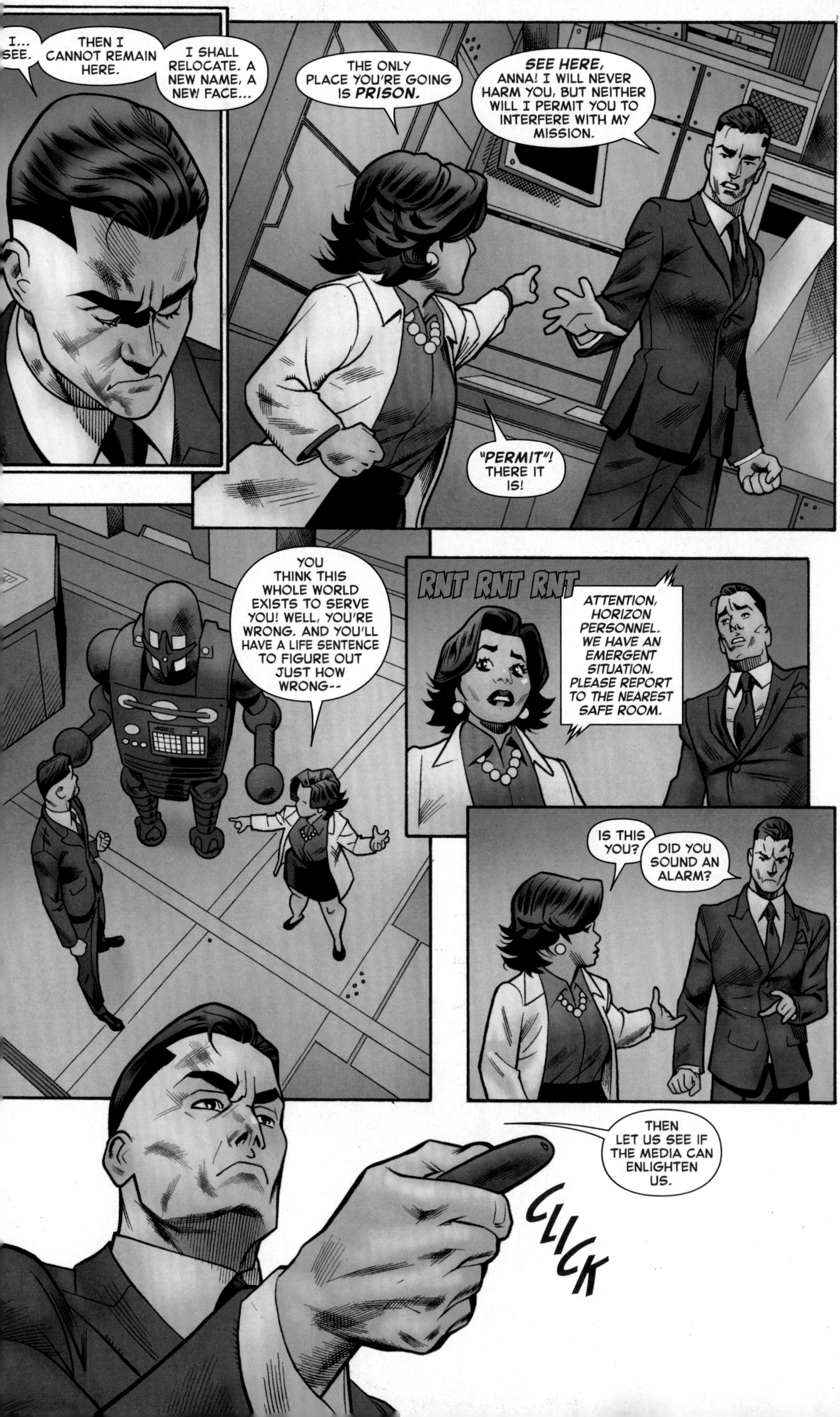
I... SEE.
THEN I CANNOT REMAIN HERE.
I SHALL RELOCATE. A NEW NAME, A NEW FACE...
THE ONLY PLACE YOU'RE GOING IS PRISON.
SEE HERE, ANNA! I WILL NEVER HARM YOU, BUT NEITHER WILL I PERMIT YOU TO INTERFERE WITH MY MISSION.
"PERMIT"! THERE IT IS!
YOU THINK THIS WHOLE WORLD EXISTS TO SERVE YOU! WELL, YOU'RE WRONG. AND YOU'LL HAVE A LIFE SENTENCE TO FIGURE OUT JUST HOW WRONG--
RNT RNT RNT
ATTENTION, HORIZON PERSONNEL. WE HAVE AN EMERGENT SITUATION. PLEASE REPORT TO THE NEAREST SAFE ROOM.
IS THIS YOU?
DID YOU SOUND AN ALARM?
THEN LET US SEE IF THE MEDIA CAN ENLIGHTEN US.
CLICK

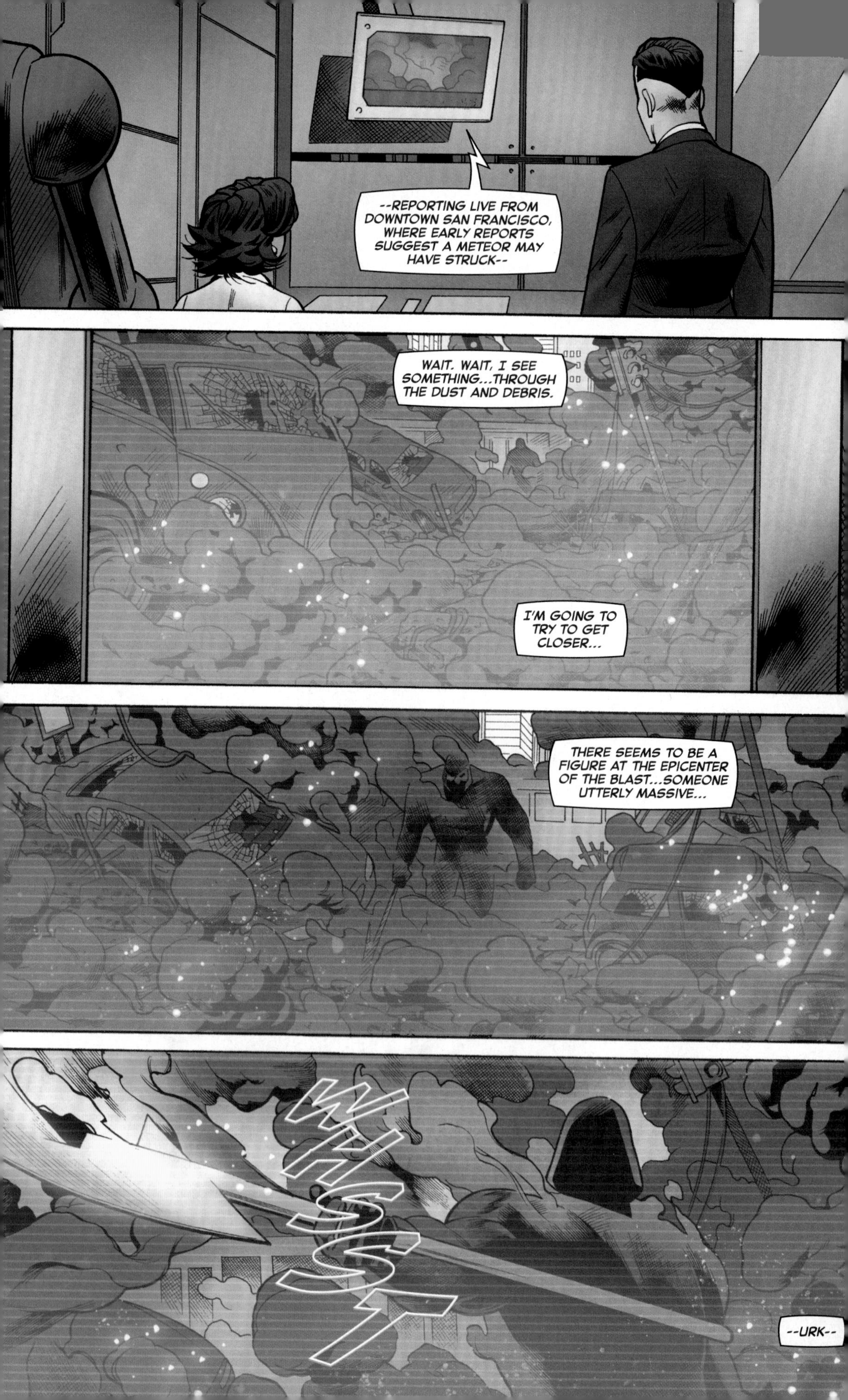
--REPORTING LIVE FROM DOWNTOWN SAN FRANCISCO, WHERE EARLY REPORTS SUGGEST A METEOR MAY HAVE STRUCK--
WAIT. WAIT, I SEE SOMETHING...THROUGH THE DUST AND DEBRIS.
I'M GOING TO TRY TO GET CLOSER...
THERE SEEMS TO BE A FIGURE AT THE EPICENTER OF THE BLAST...SOMEONE UTTERLY MASSIVE...
WHSSST
--URK--

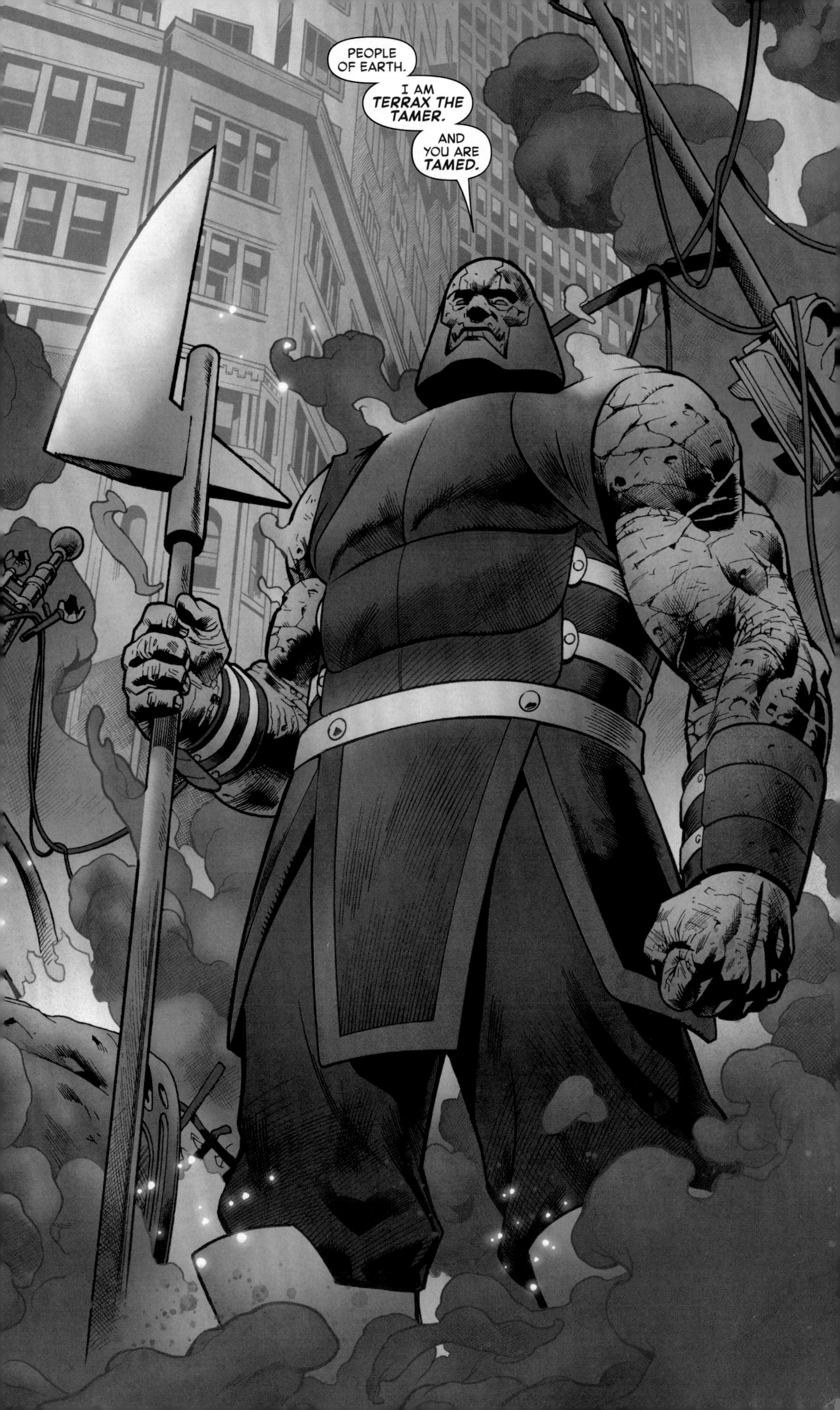
PEOPLE OF EARTH.
I AM **TERRAX THE TAMER.**
AND YOU ARE **TAMED.**

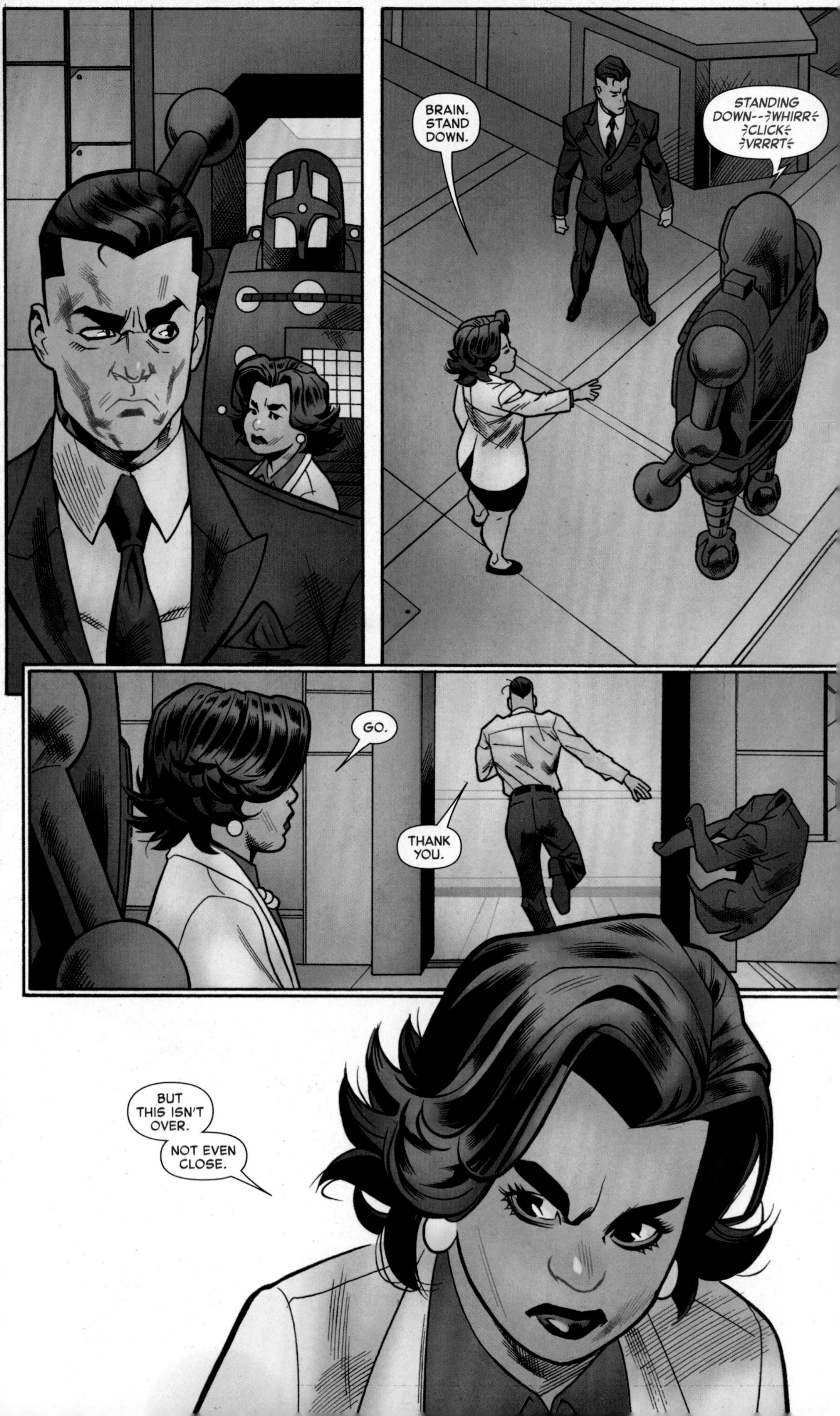
BRAIN. STAND DOWN.
STANDING DOWN-- ⸗WHIRR⸗ ⸗CLICK⸗ ⸗VRRRT⸗
GO.
THANK YOU.
BUT THIS ISN'T OVER.
NOT EVEN CLOSE.

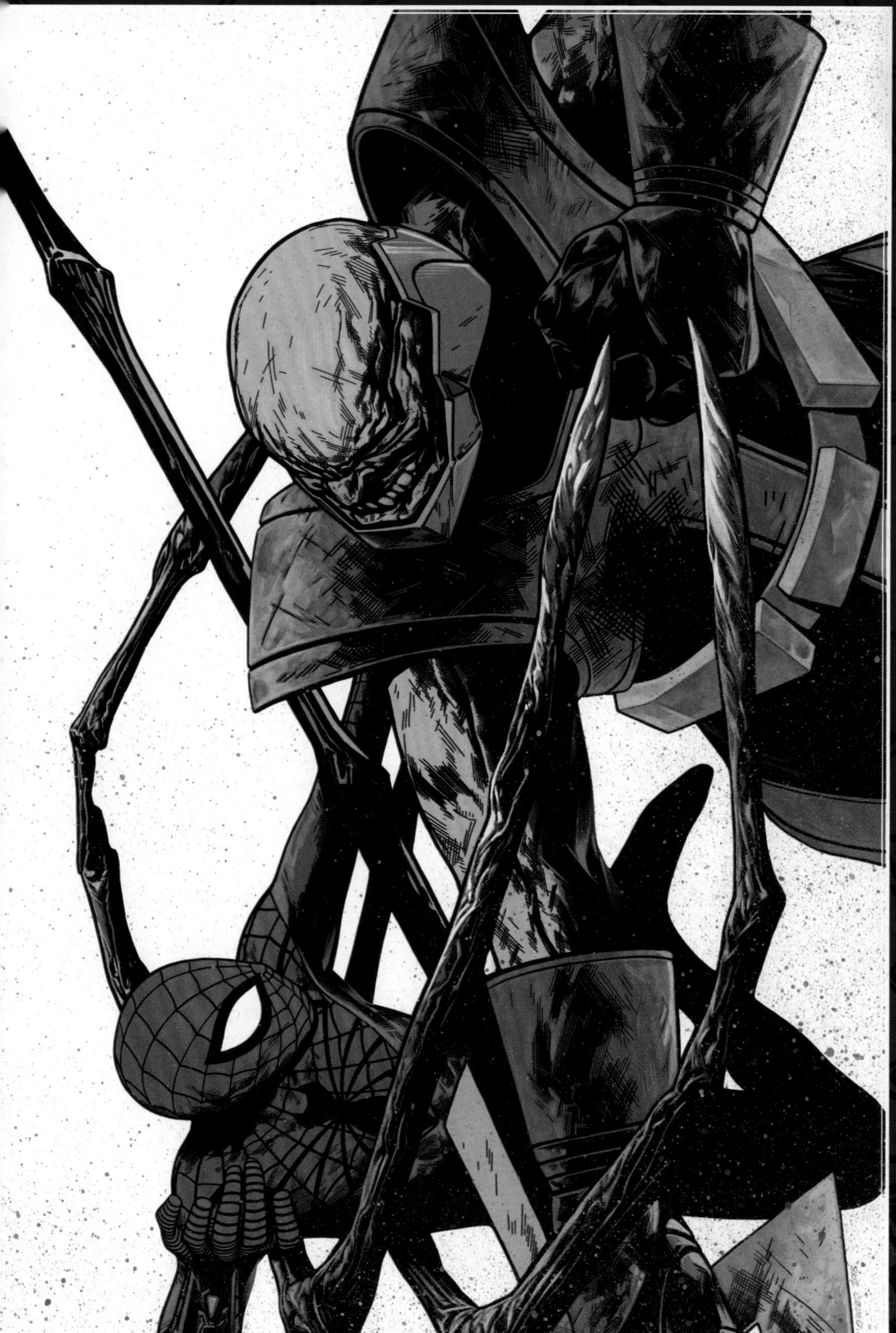

2

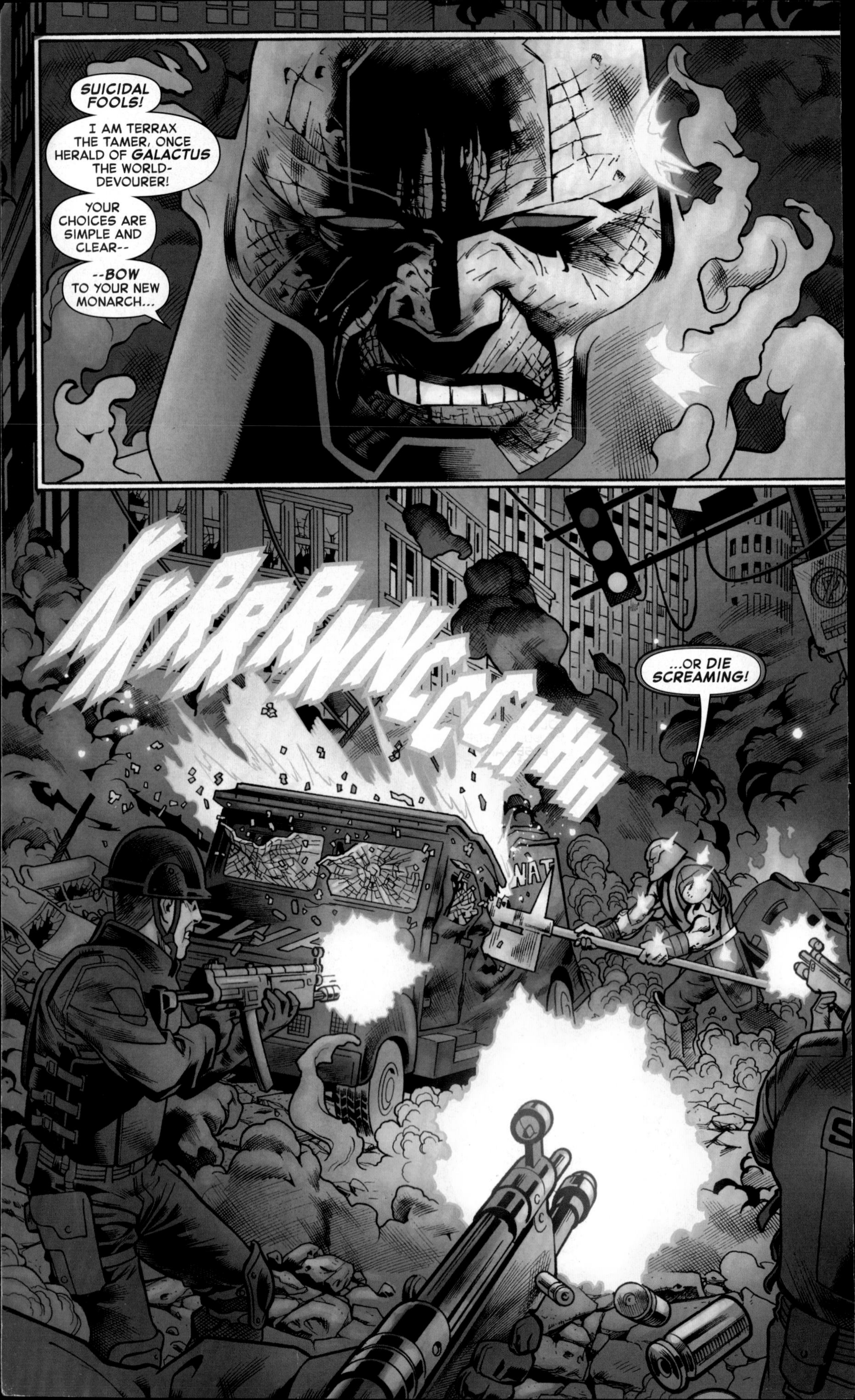
SUICIDAL FOOLS!
I AM TERRAX THE TAMER, ONCE HERALD OF GALACTUS THE WORLD-DEVOURER!
YOUR CHOICES ARE SIMPLE AND CLEAR--
--BOW TO YOUR NEW MONARCH...
KRRRRNNCCCHHH
...OR DIE SCREAMING!

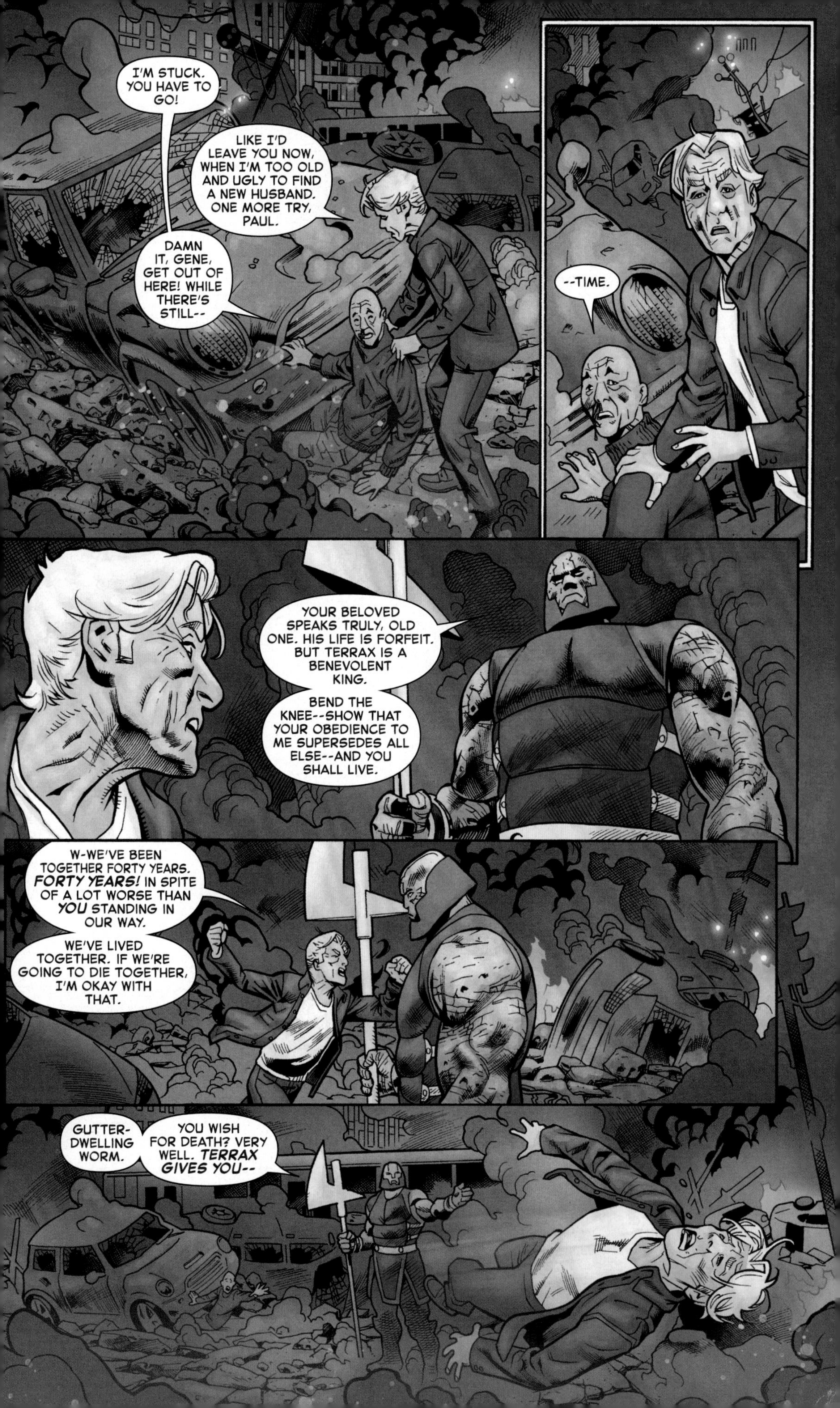
I'M STUCK. YOU HAVE TO GO!
LIKE I'D LEAVE YOU NOW, WHEN I'M TOO OLD AND UGLY TO FIND A NEW HUSBAND. ONE MORE TRY, PAUL.
DAMN IT, GENE, GET OUT OF HERE! WHILE THERE'S STILL--
--TIME.
YOUR BELOVED SPEAKS TRULY, OLD ONE. HIS LIFE IS FORFEIT. BUT TERRAX IS A BENEVOLENT KING.
BEND THE KNEE--SHOW THAT YOUR OBEDIENCE TO ME SUPERSEDES ALL ELSE--AND YOU SHALL LIVE.
W-WE'VE BEEN TOGETHER FORTY YEARS. ***FORTY YEARS!*** IN SPITE OF A LOT WORSE THAN ***YOU*** STANDING IN OUR WAY.
WE'VE LIVED TOGETHER. IF WE'RE GOING TO DIE TOGETHER, I'M OKAY WITH THAT.
GUTTER-DWELLING WORM.
YOU WISH FOR DEATH? VERY WELL. ***TERRAX GIVES YOU--***

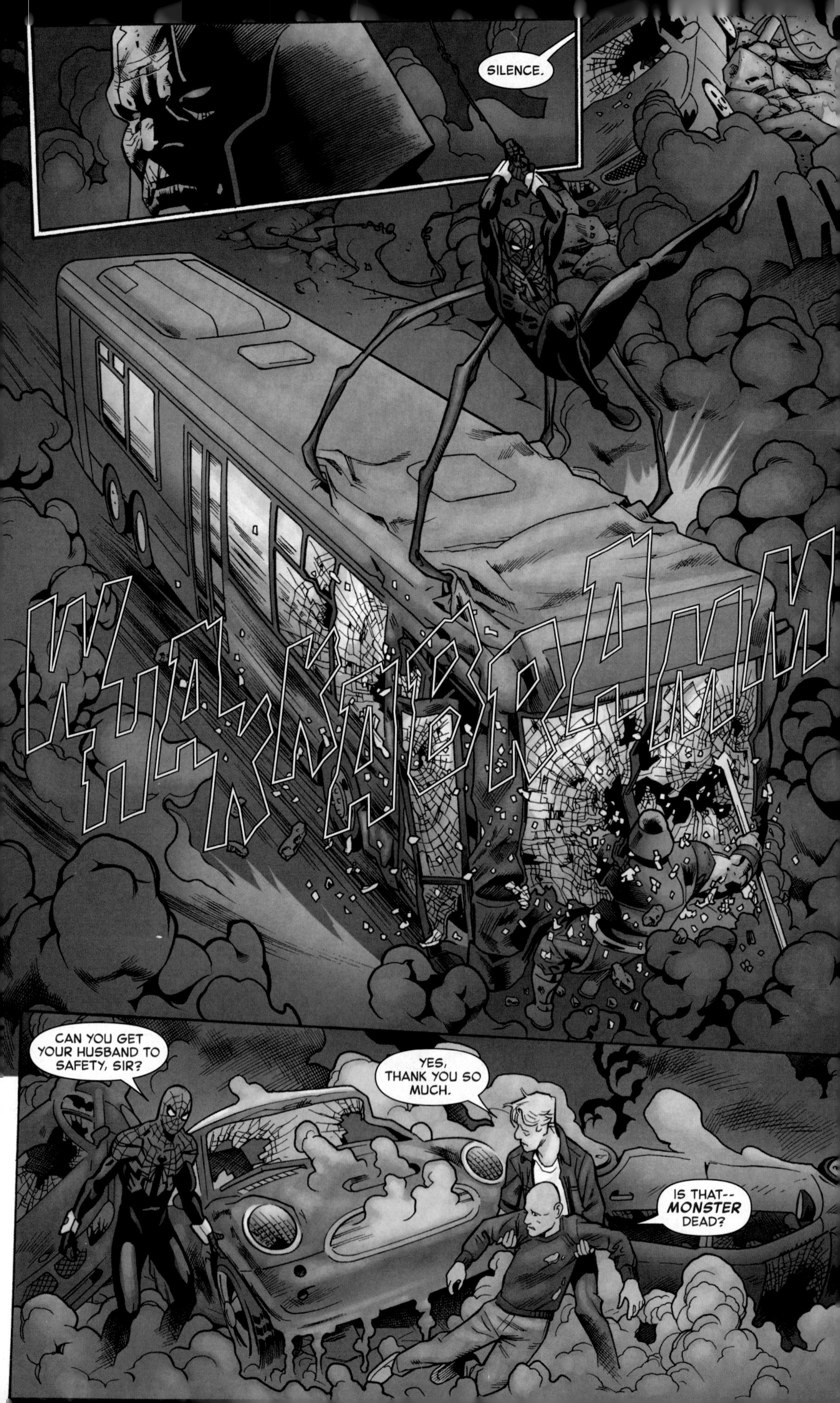
SILENCE.
KRAKABOOMM
CAN YOU GET YOUR HUSBAND TO SAFETY, SIR?
YES, THANK YOU SO MUCH.
IS THAT-- MONSTER DEAD?

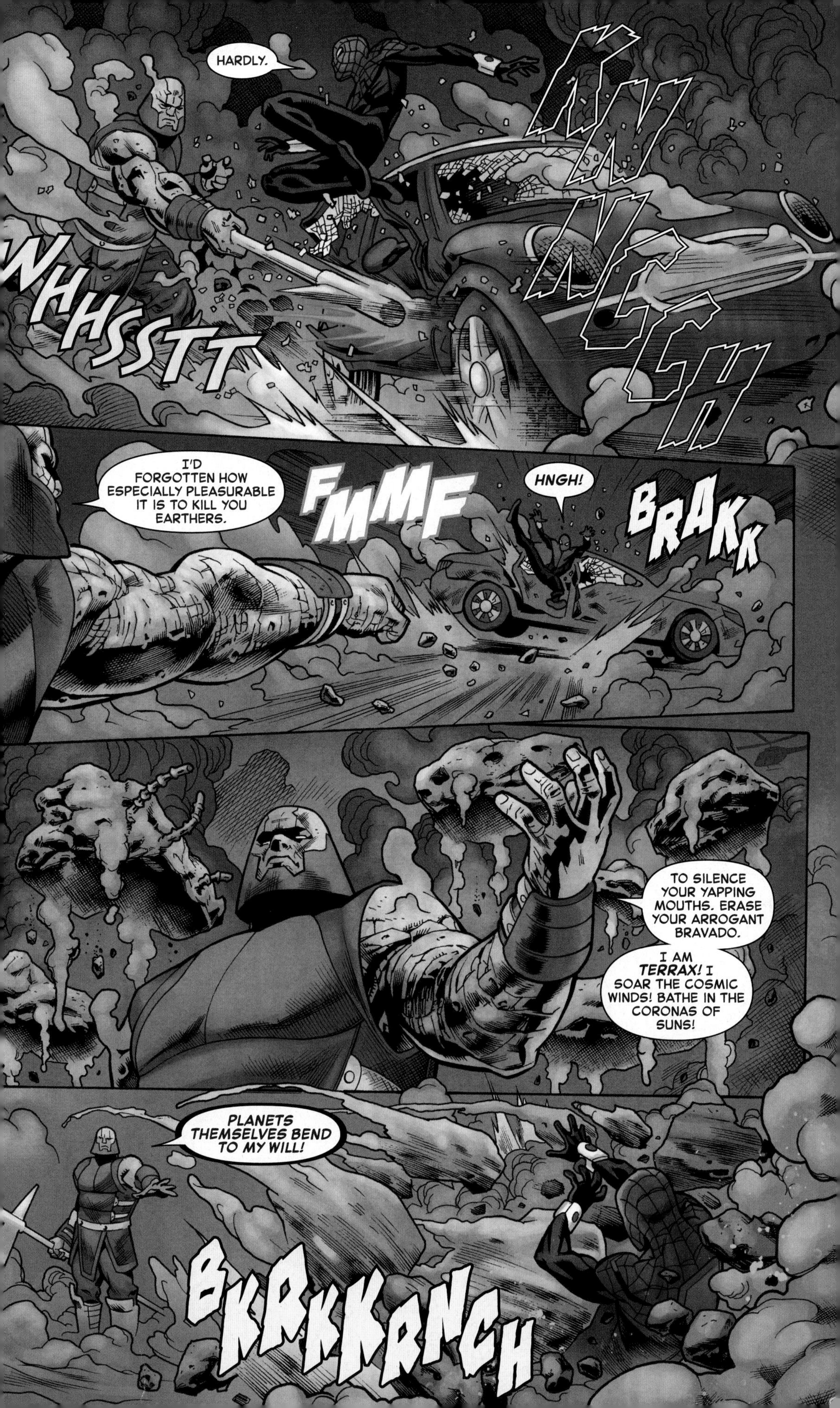
HARDLY.
KNNNGCH
WHHSSTT
I'D FORGOTTEN HOW ESPECIALLY PLEASURABLE IT IS TO KILL YOU EARTHERS.
FMMF
HNGH!
BRAKK
TO SILENCE YOUR YAPPING MOUTHS. ERASE YOUR ARROGANT BRAVADO.
I AM TERRAX! I SOAR THE COSMIC WINDS! BATHE IN THE CORONAS OF SUNS!
PLANETS THEMSELVES BEND TO MY WILL!
BKRKKRNCH

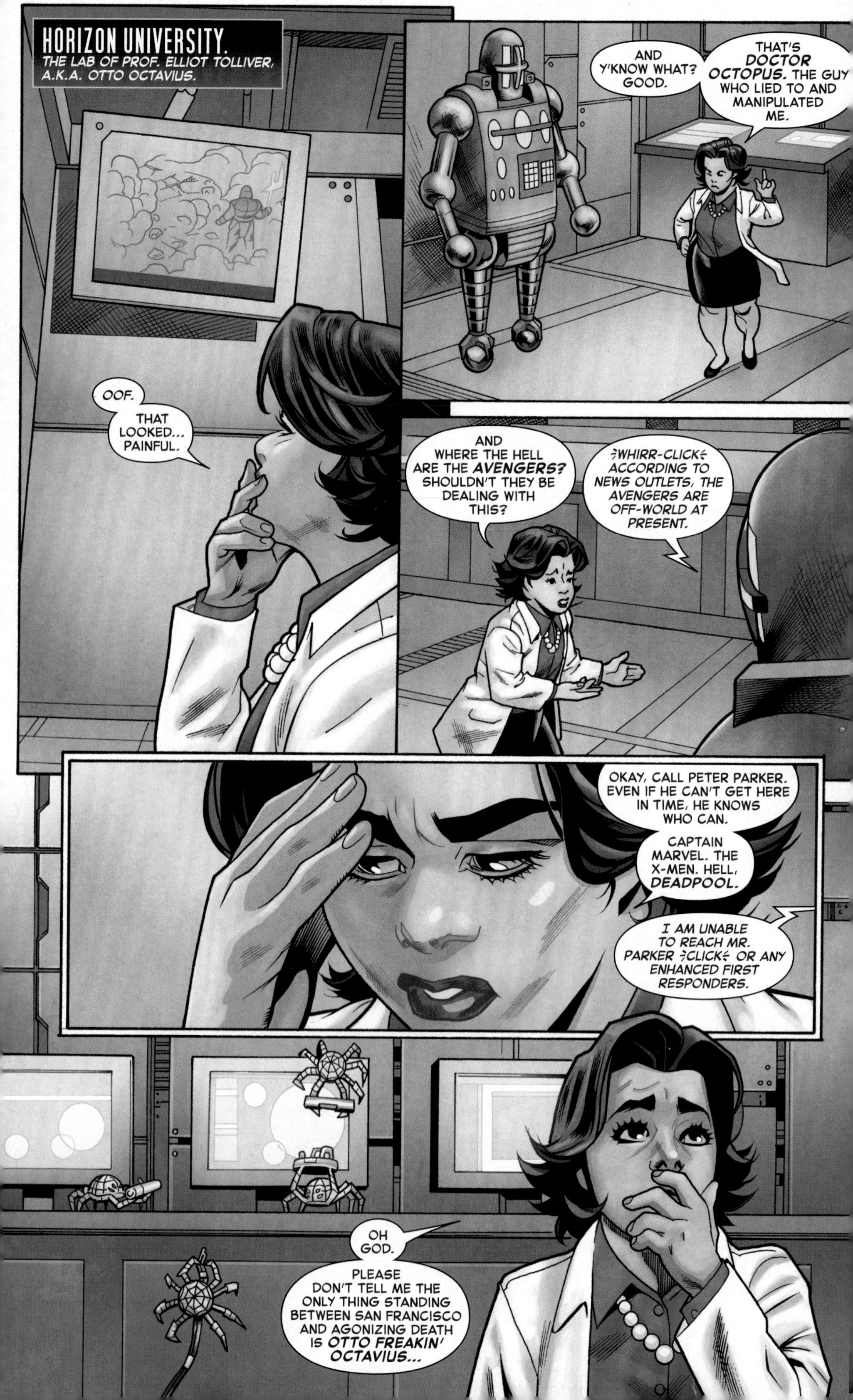
HORIZON UNIVERSITY.
THE LAB OF PROF. ELLIOT TOLLIVER, A.K.A. OTTO OCTAVIUS.
OOF.
THAT LOOKED... PAINFUL.
AND Y'KNOW WHAT? GOOD.
THAT'S DOCTOR OCTOPUS. THE GUY WHO LIED TO AND MANIPULATED ME.
AND WHERE THE HELL ARE THE AVENGERS? SHOULDN'T THEY BE DEALING WITH THIS?
WHIRR-CLICK ACCORDING TO NEWS OUTLETS, THE AVENGERS ARE OFF-WORLD AT PRESENT.
OKAY, CALL PETER PARKER. EVEN IF HE CAN'T GET HERE IN TIME, HE KNOWS WHO CAN.
CAPTAIN MARVEL. THE X-MEN. HELL, DEADPOOL.
I AM UNABLE TO REACH MR. PARKER CLICK OR ANY ENHANCED FIRST RESPONDERS.
OH GOD.
PLEASE DON'T TELL ME THE ONLY THING STANDING BETWEEN SAN FRANCISCO AND AGONIZING DEATH IS OTTO FREAKIN' OCTAVIUS...

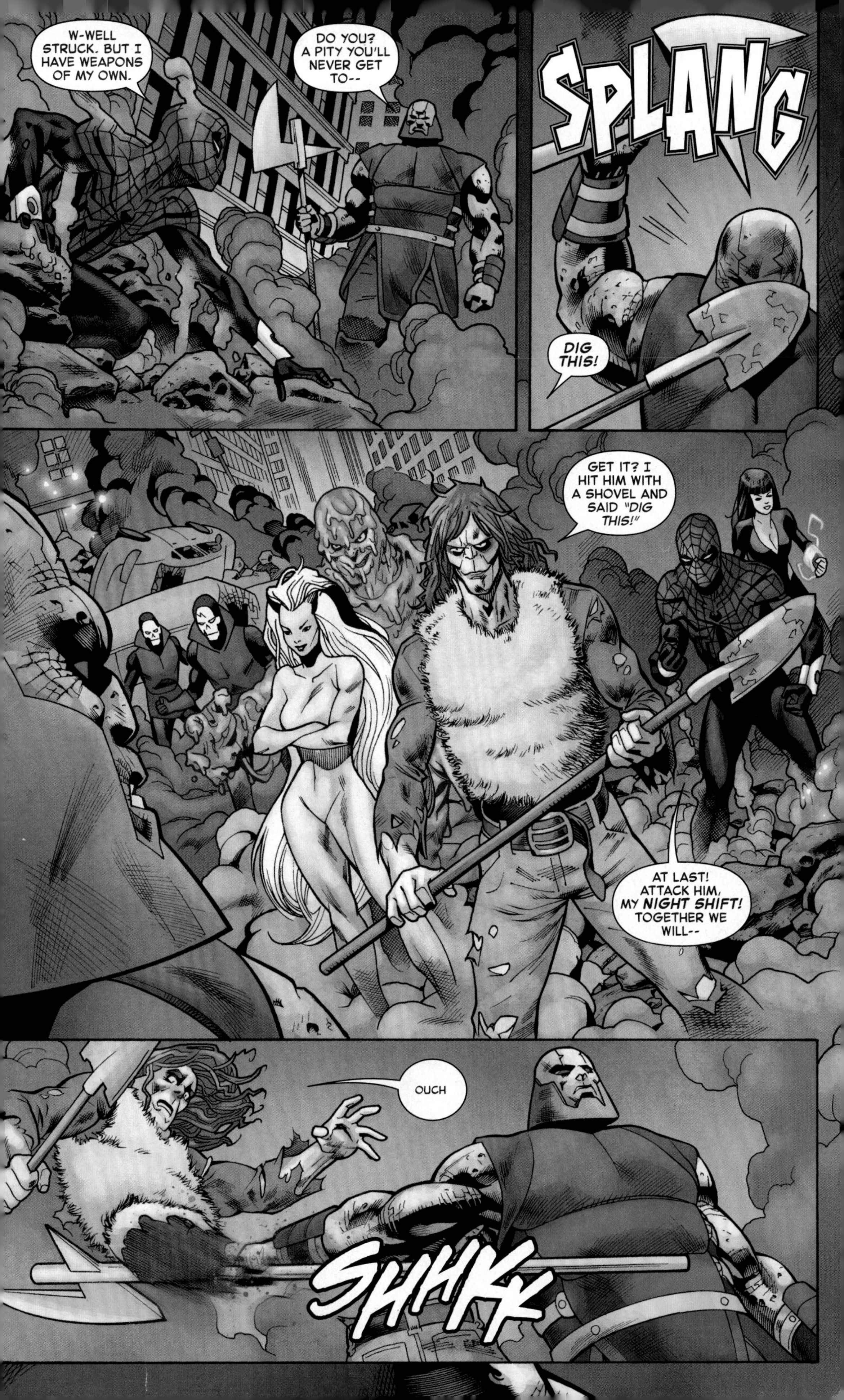
W-WELL STRUCK. BUT I HAVE WEAPONS OF MY OWN.
DO YOU? A PITY YOU'LL NEVER GET TO--
SPLANG
DIG THIS!
GET IT? I HIT HIM WITH A SHOVEL AND SAID "DIG THIS!"
AT LAST! ATTACK HIM, MY NIGHT SHIFT! TOGETHER WE WILL--
OUCH
SHHKK

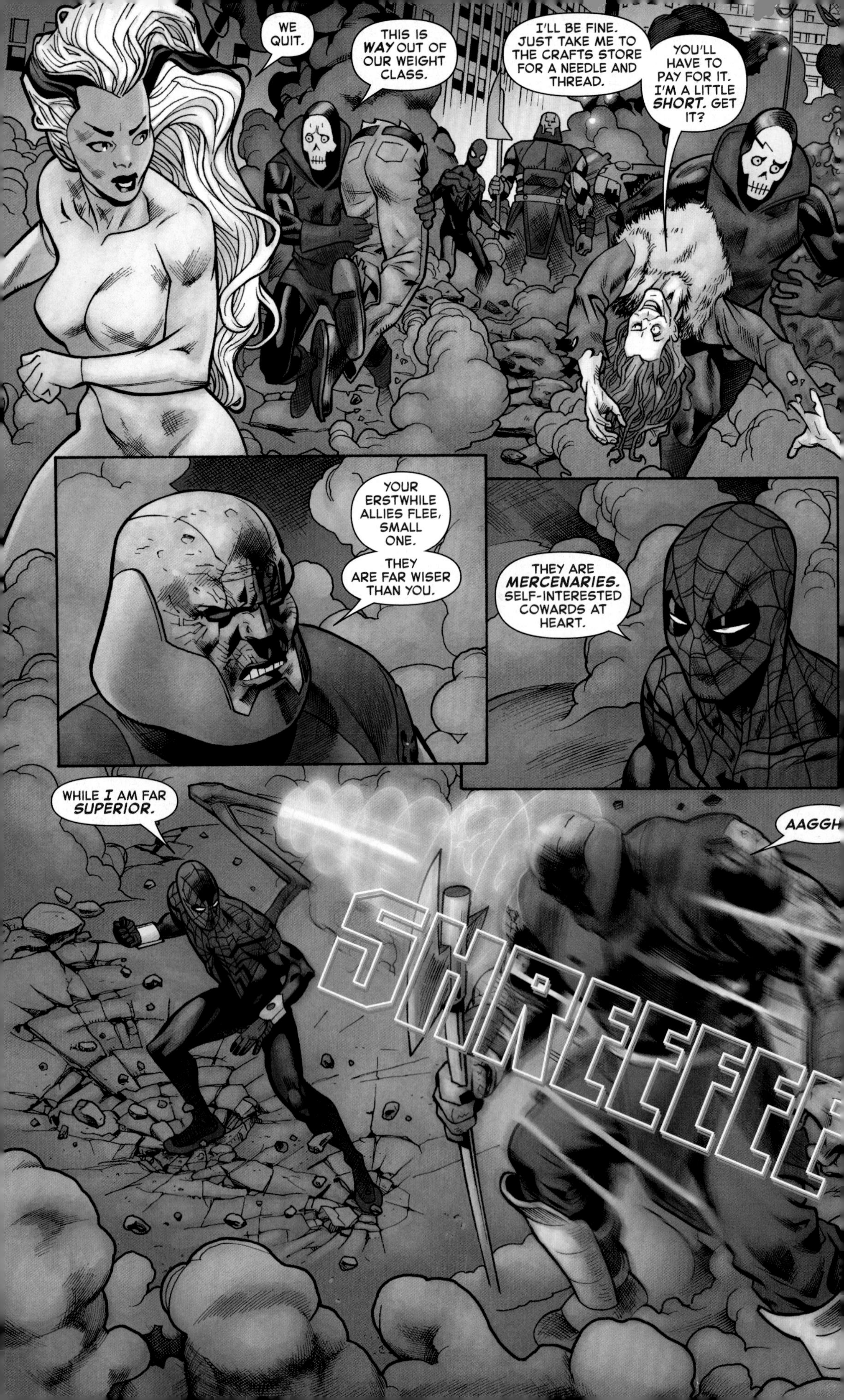
WE QUIT.
THIS IS WAY OUT OF OUR WEIGHT CLASS.
I'LL BE FINE. JUST TAKE ME TO THE CRAFTS STORE FOR A NEEDLE AND THREAD.
YOU'LL HAVE TO PAY FOR IT. I'M A LITTLE SHORT. GET IT?
YOUR ERSTWHILE ALLIES FLEE, SMALL ONE.
THEY ARE FAR WISER THAN YOU.
THEY ARE MERCENARIES. SELF-INTERESTED COWARDS AT HEART.
WHILE I AM FAR SUPERIOR.
AAGGH
SHREEEEE

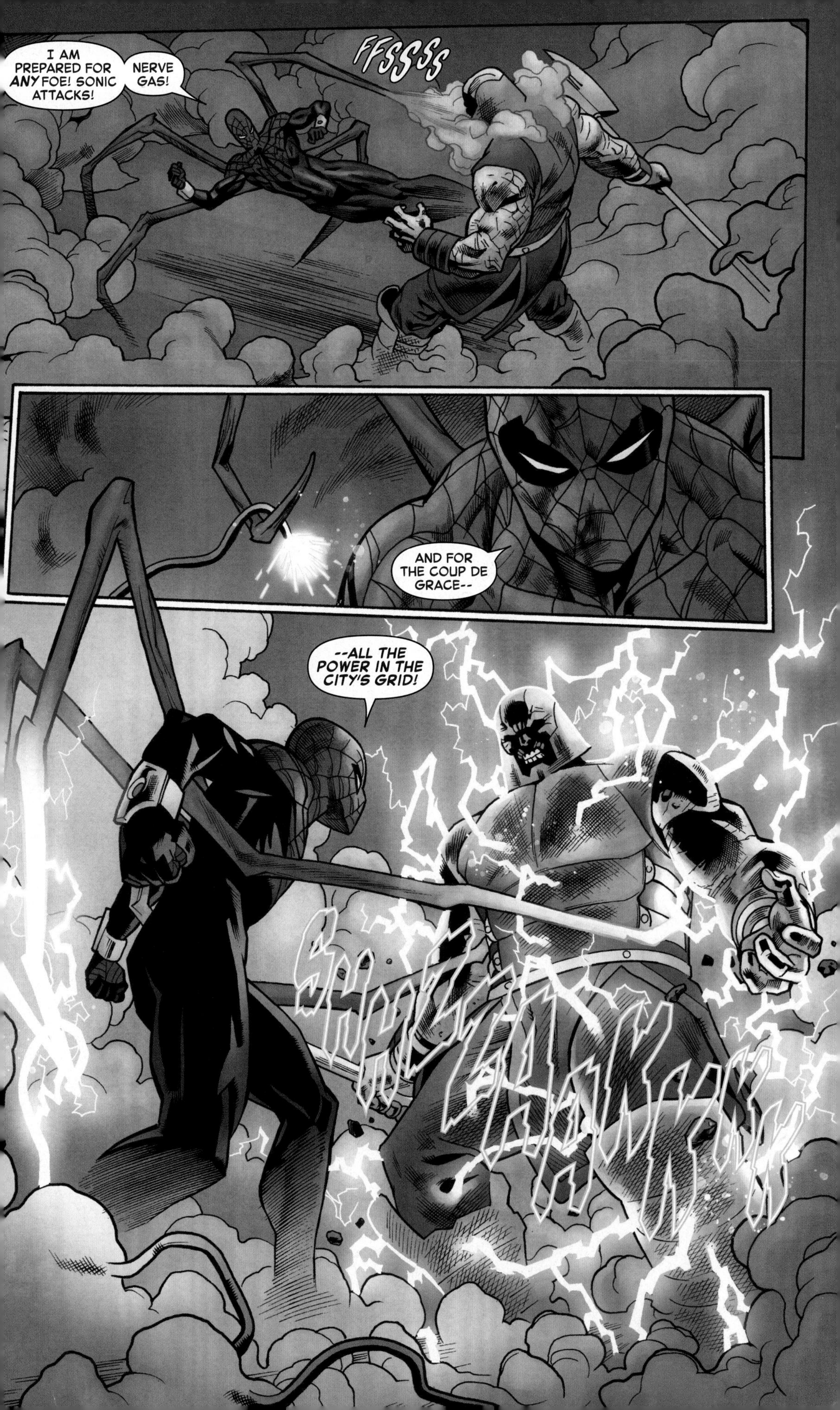
I AM PREPARED FOR ANY FOE! SONIC ATTACKS!
NERVE GAS!
FFSSSS
AND FOR THE COUP DE GRACE--
--ALL THE POWER IN THE CITY'S GRID!

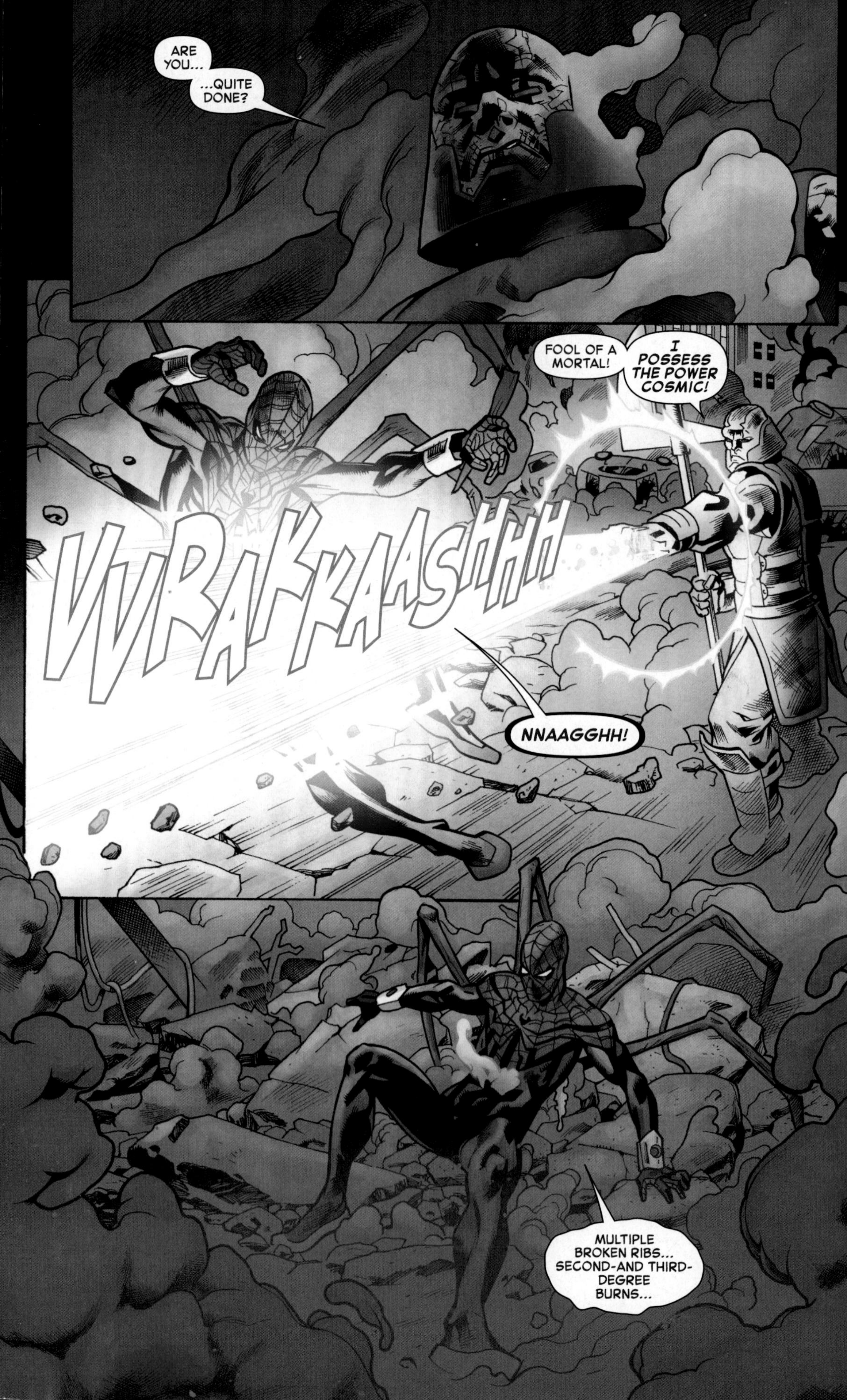
ARE YOU... ...QUITE DONE?
FOOL OF A MORTAL!
I POSSESS THE POWER COSMIC!
VVRAKKAASHHH
NNAAGGHH!
MULTIPLE BROKEN RIBS... SECOND-AND THIRD-DEGREE BURNS...

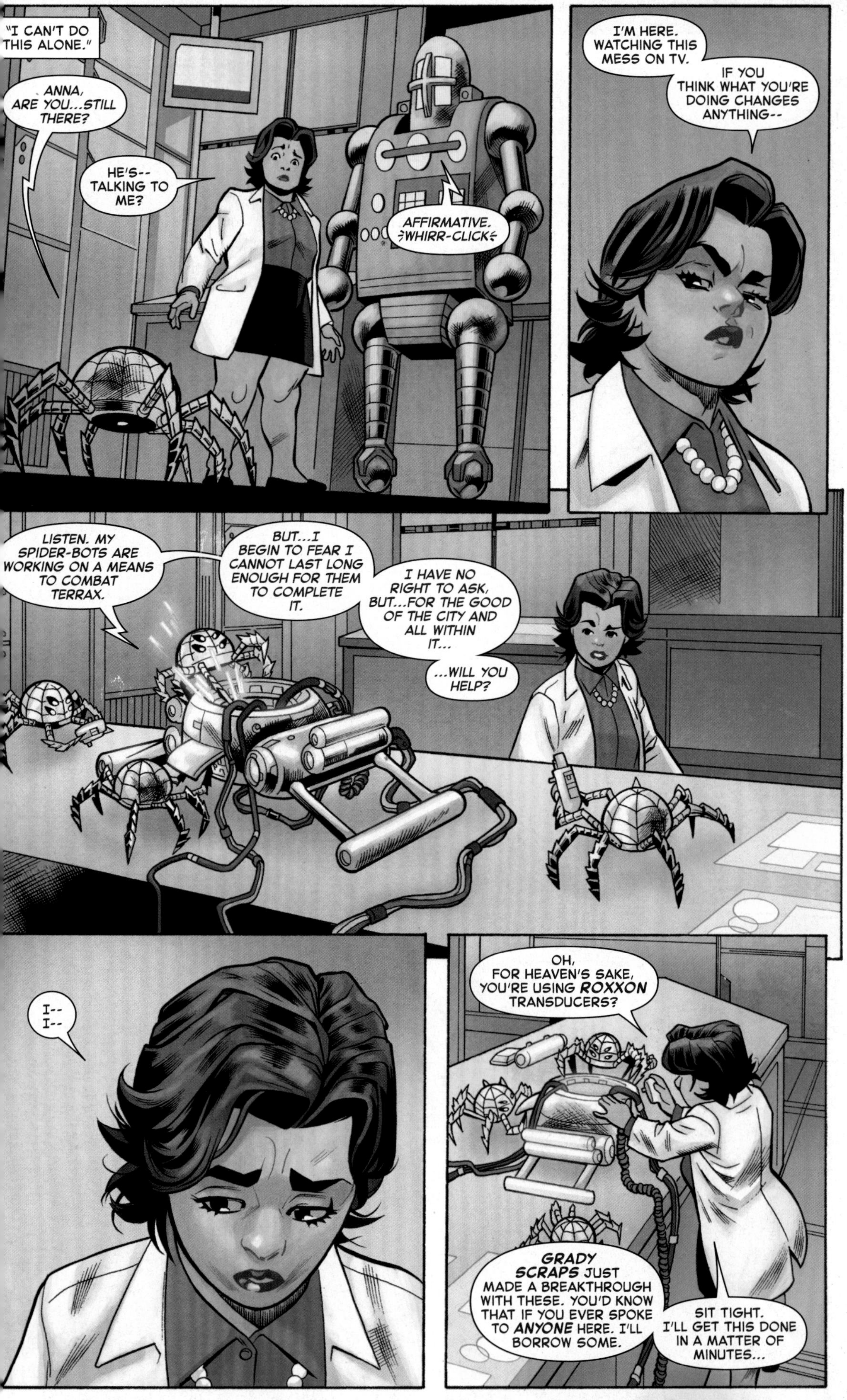
"I CAN'T DO THIS ALONE."
ANNA, ARE YOU...STILL THERE?
HE'S-- TALKING TO ME?
AFFIRMATIVE. ⋞WHIRR-CLICK⋞
I'M HERE. WATCHING THIS MESS ON TV.
IF YOU THINK WHAT YOU'RE DOING CHANGES ANYTHING--
LISTEN. MY SPIDER-BOTS ARE WORKING ON A MEANS TO COMBAT TERRAX.
BUT...I BEGIN TO FEAR I CANNOT LAST LONG ENOUGH FOR THEM TO COMPLETE IT.
I HAVE NO RIGHT TO ASK, BUT...FOR THE GOOD OF THE CITY AND ALL WITHIN IT...
...WILL YOU HELP?
I-- I--
OH, FOR HEAVEN'S SAKE, YOU'RE USING ROXXON TRANSDUCERS?
GRADY SCRAPS JUST MADE A BREAKTHROUGH WITH THESE. YOU'D KNOW THAT IF YOU EVER SPOKE TO ANYONE HERE. I'LL BORROW SOME.
SIT TIGHT. I'LL GET THIS DONE IN A MATTER OF MINUTES...

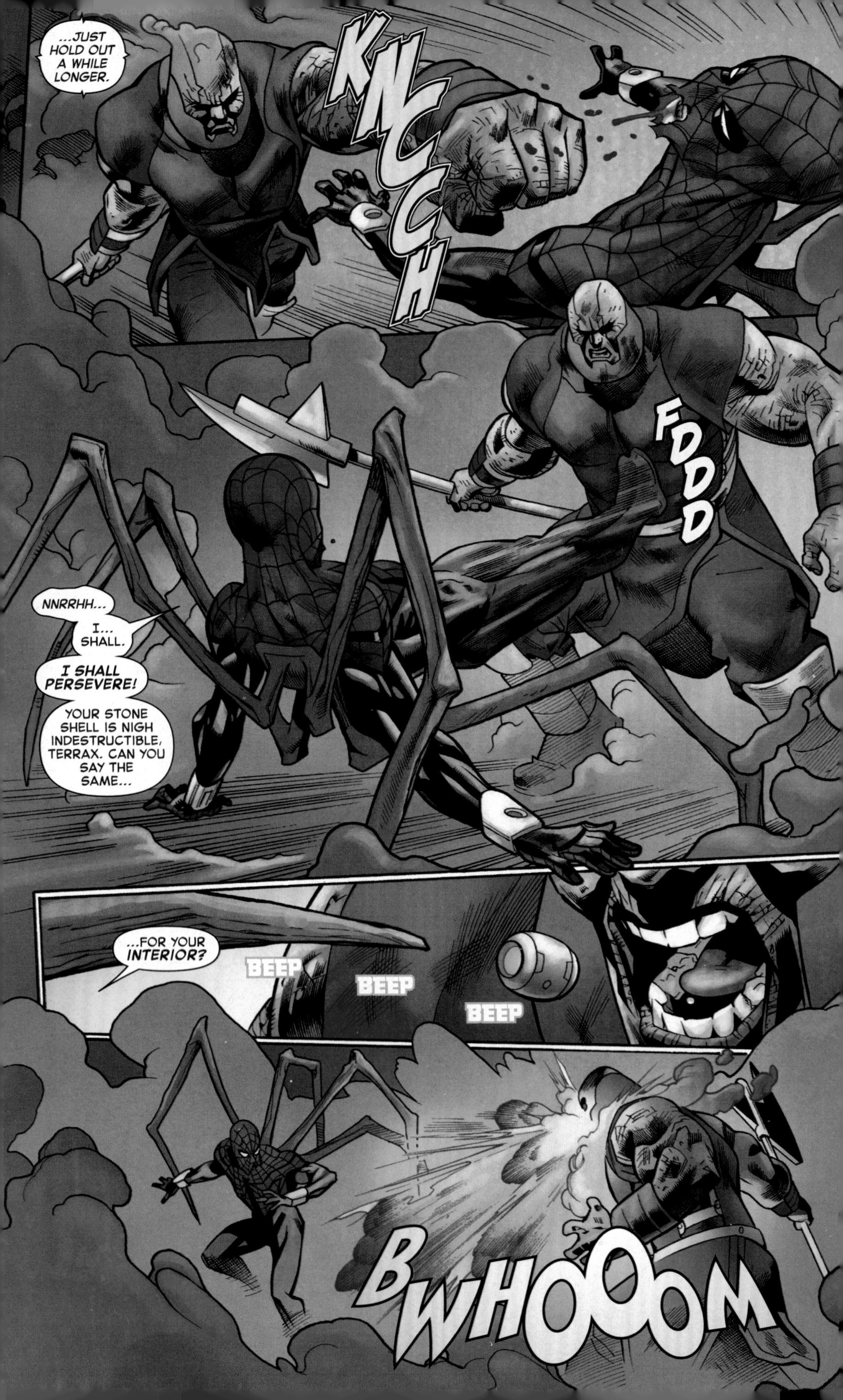

...JUST HOLD OUT A WHILE LONGER.
KNCH
FDDD
NNRRHH...
I... SHALL.
I SHALL PERSEVERE!
YOUR STONE SHELL IS NIGH INDESTRUCTIBLE, TERRAX. CAN YOU SAY THE SAME...
...FOR YOUR INTERIOR?
BEEP
BEEP
BEEP
BWHOOOOM

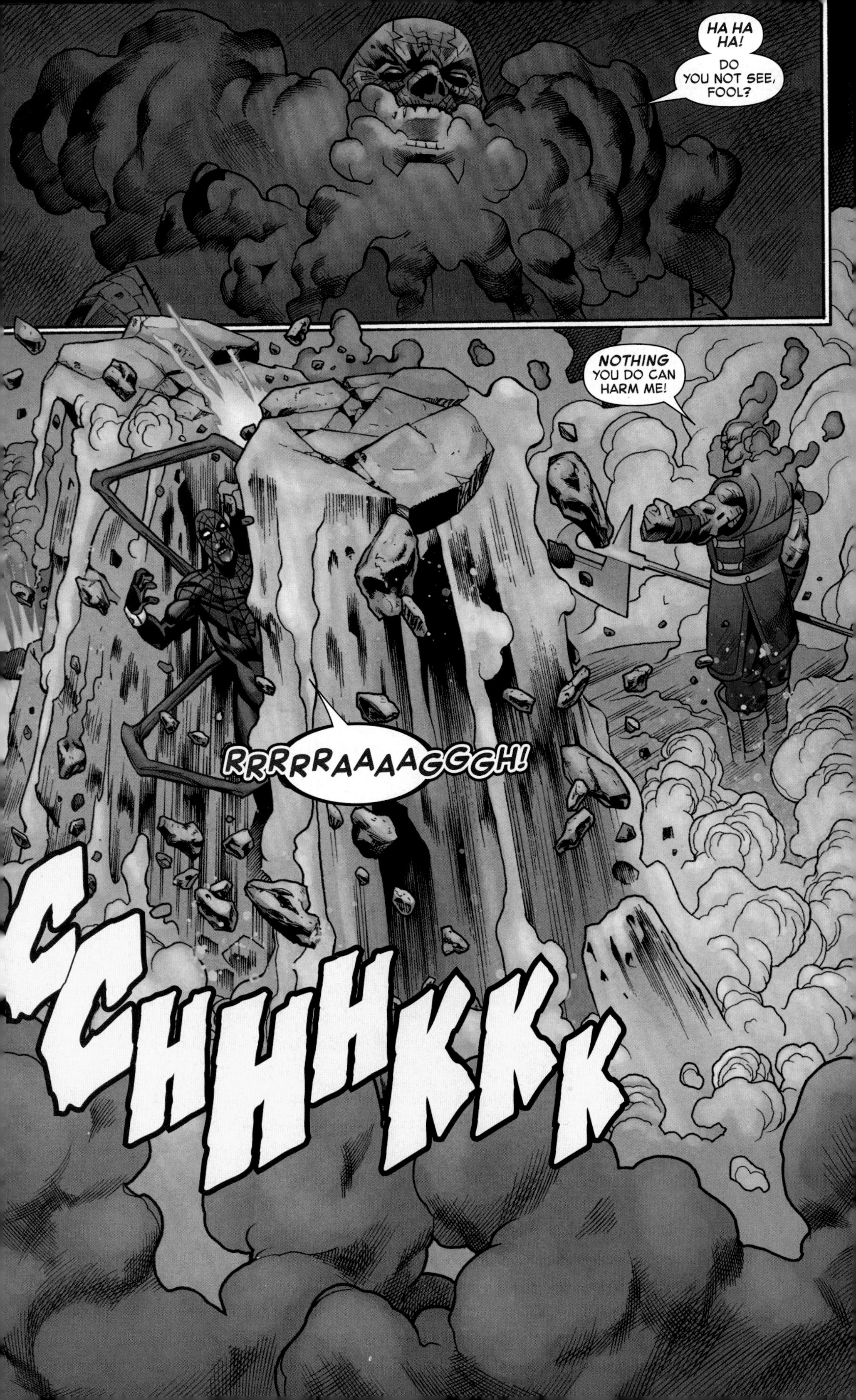
HA HA HA!
DO YOU NOT SEE, FOOL?
NOTHING YOU DO CAN HARM ME!
RRRRRAAAAGGGH!
CCHHHKKKK

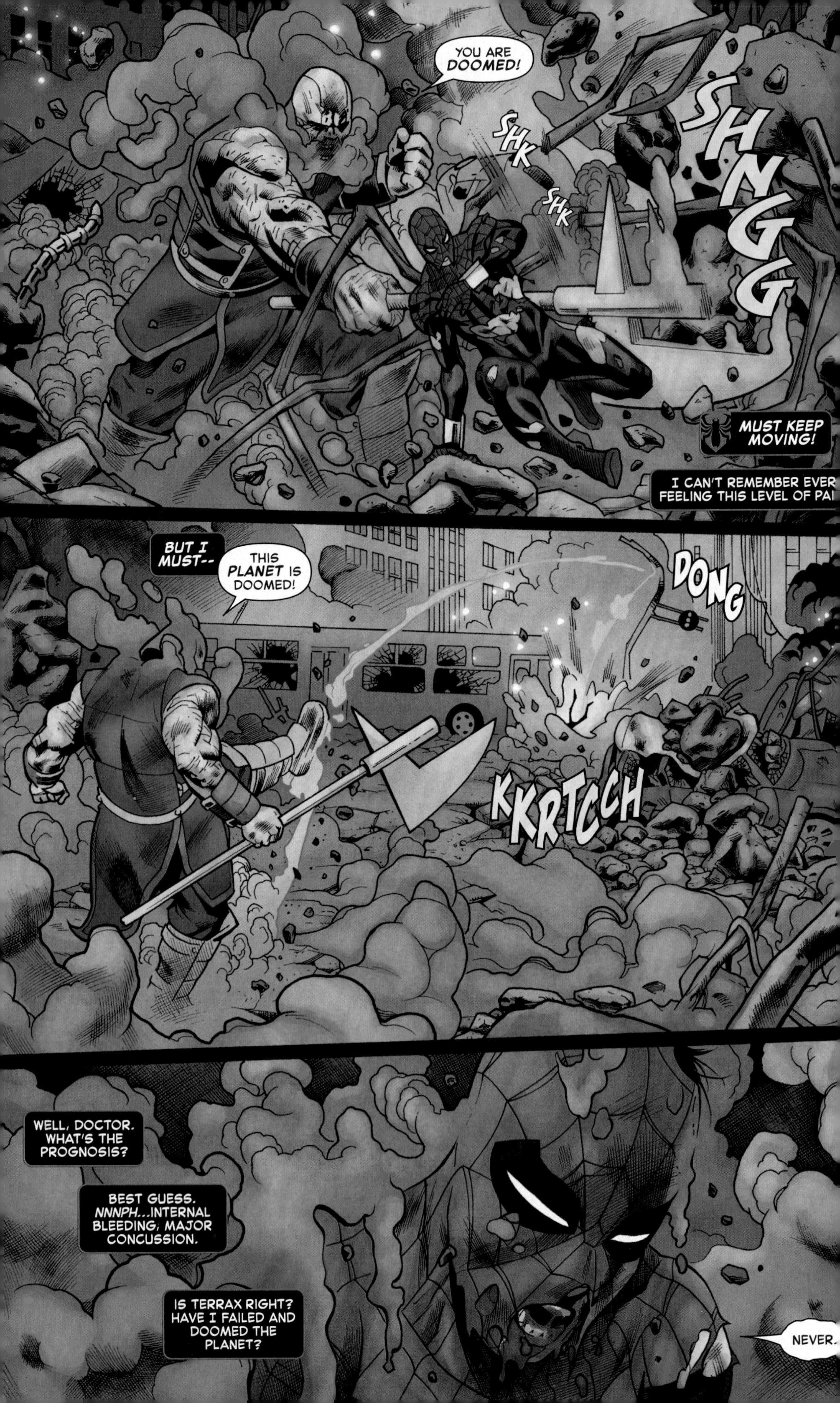
YOU ARE DOOMED!
SHK
SHK
SHNGG
MUST KEEP MOVING!
I CAN'T REMEMBER EVER FEELING THIS LEVEL OF PAI
BUT I MUST--
THIS PLANET IS DOOMED!
DONG
KKRTCCH
WELL, DOCTOR. WHAT'S THE PROGNOSIS?
BEST GUESS. NNNPH...INTERNAL BLEEDING, MAJOR CONCUSSION.
IS TERRAX RIGHT? HAVE I FAILED AND DOOMED THE PLANET?
NEVER.

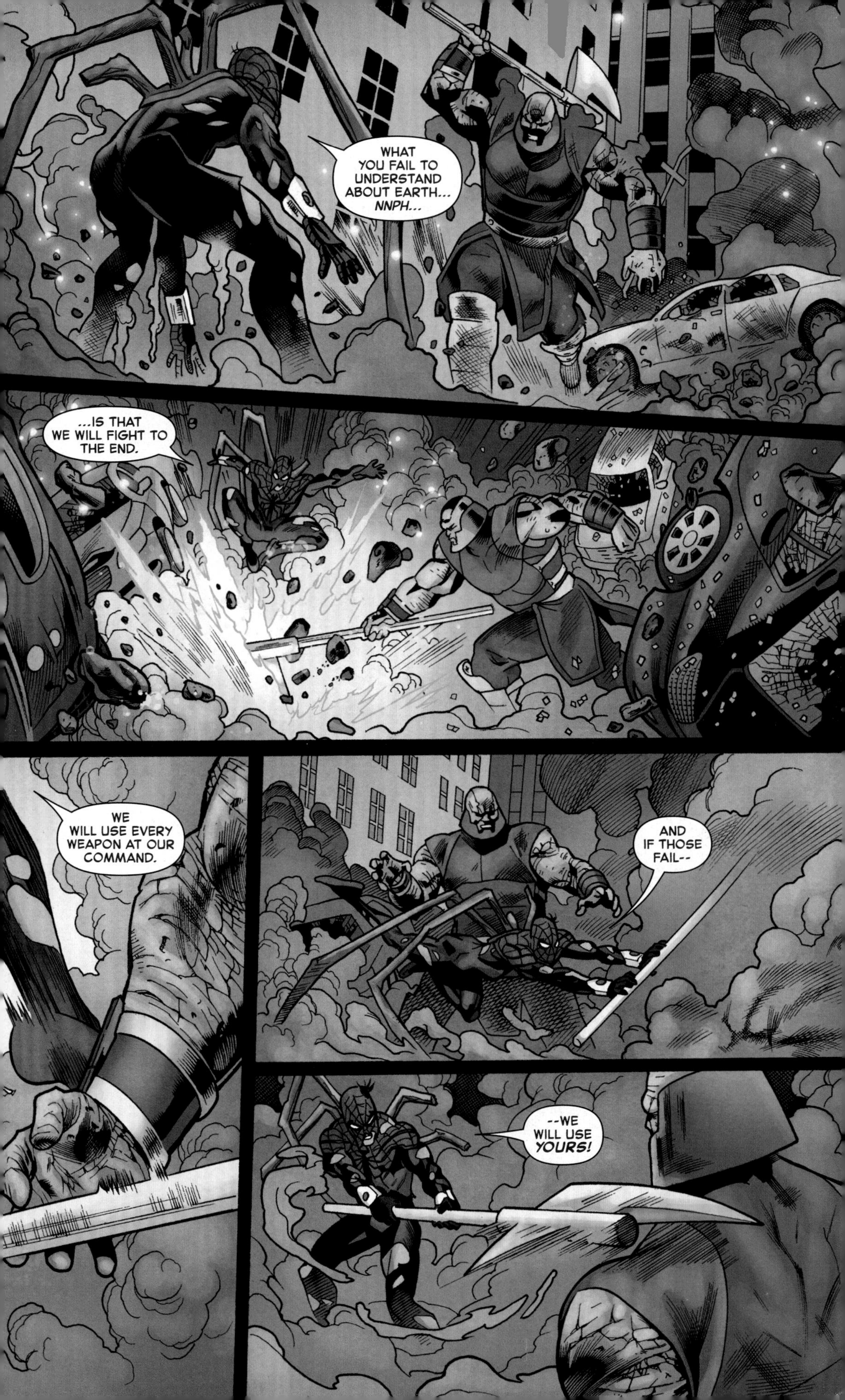
WHAT YOU FAIL TO UNDERSTAND ABOUT EARTH... *NNPH...*
...IS THAT WE WILL FIGHT TO THE END.
WE WILL USE EVERY WEAPON AT OUR COMMAND.
AND IF THOSE FAIL--
--WE WILL USE *YOURS!*

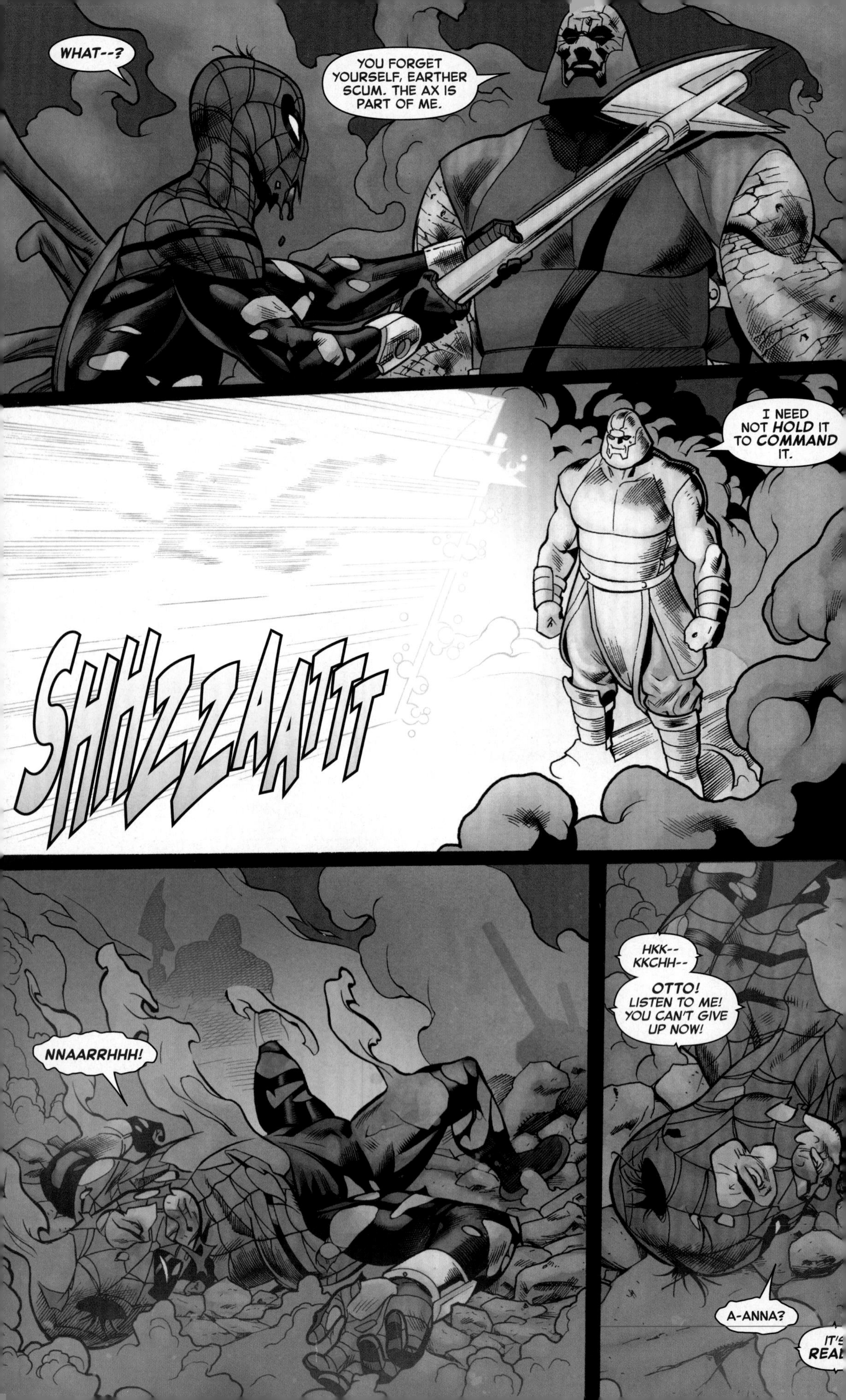
WHAT--?
YOU FORGET YOURSELF, EARTHER SCUM. THE AX IS PART OF ME.
SHHZZAAITTT
I NEED NOT HOLD IT TO COMMAND IT.
NNAARRHHH!
HKK-- KKCHH--
OTTO! LISTEN TO ME! YOU CAN'T GIVE UP NOW!
A-ANNA?

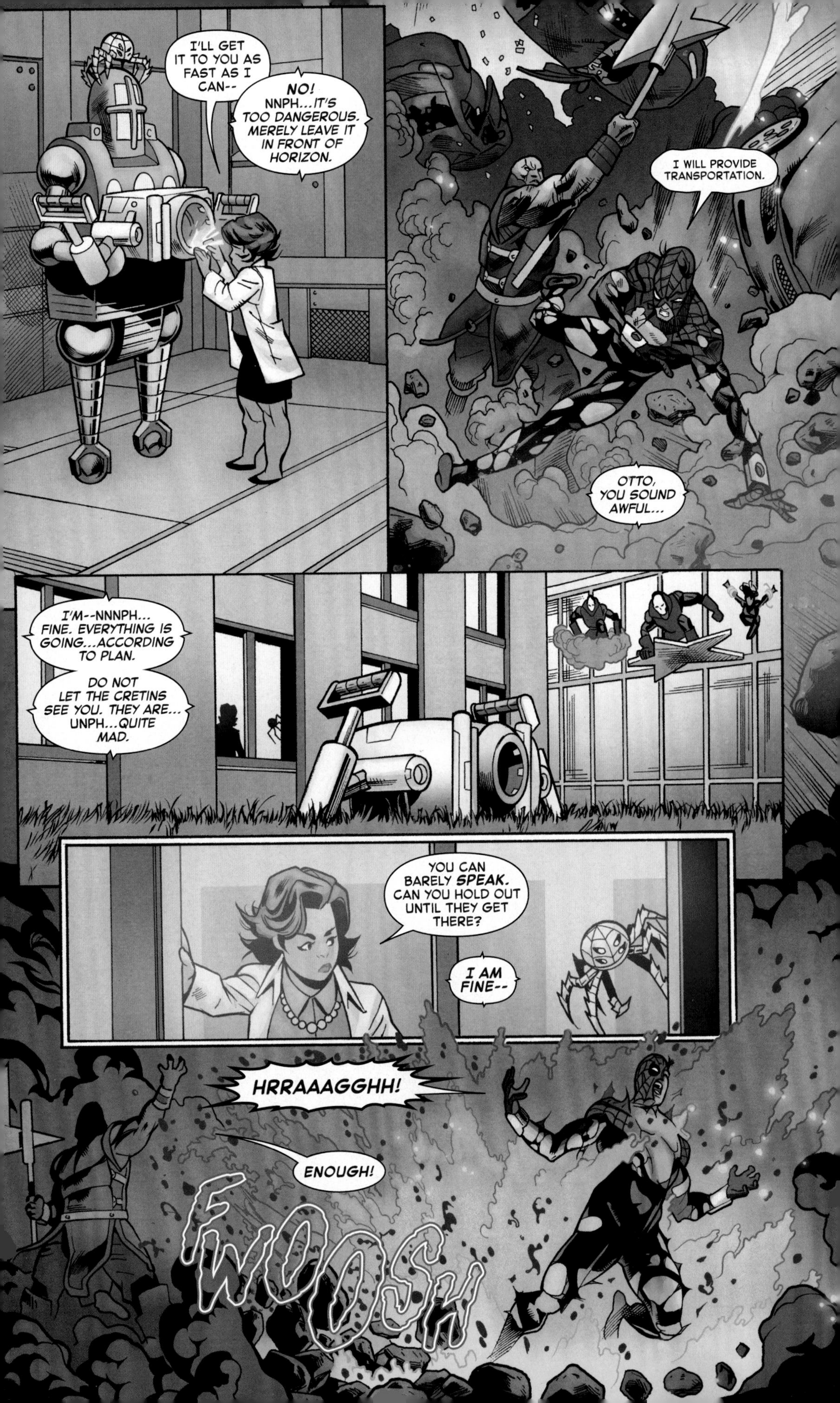
I'LL GET IT TO YOU AS FAST AS I CAN--
NO! NNPH...IT'S TOO DANGEROUS. MERELY LEAVE IT IN FRONT OF HORIZON.
I WILL PROVIDE TRANSPORTATION.
OTTO, YOU SOUND AWFUL...
I'M--NNNPH... FINE. EVERYTHING IS GOING...ACCORDING TO PLAN.
DO NOT LET THE CRETINS SEE YOU. THEY ARE... UNPH...QUITE MAD.
YOU CAN BARELY SPEAK. CAN YOU HOLD OUT UNTIL THEY GET THERE?
I AM FINE--
HRRAAAGGHH!
ENOUGH!
FWOOSH

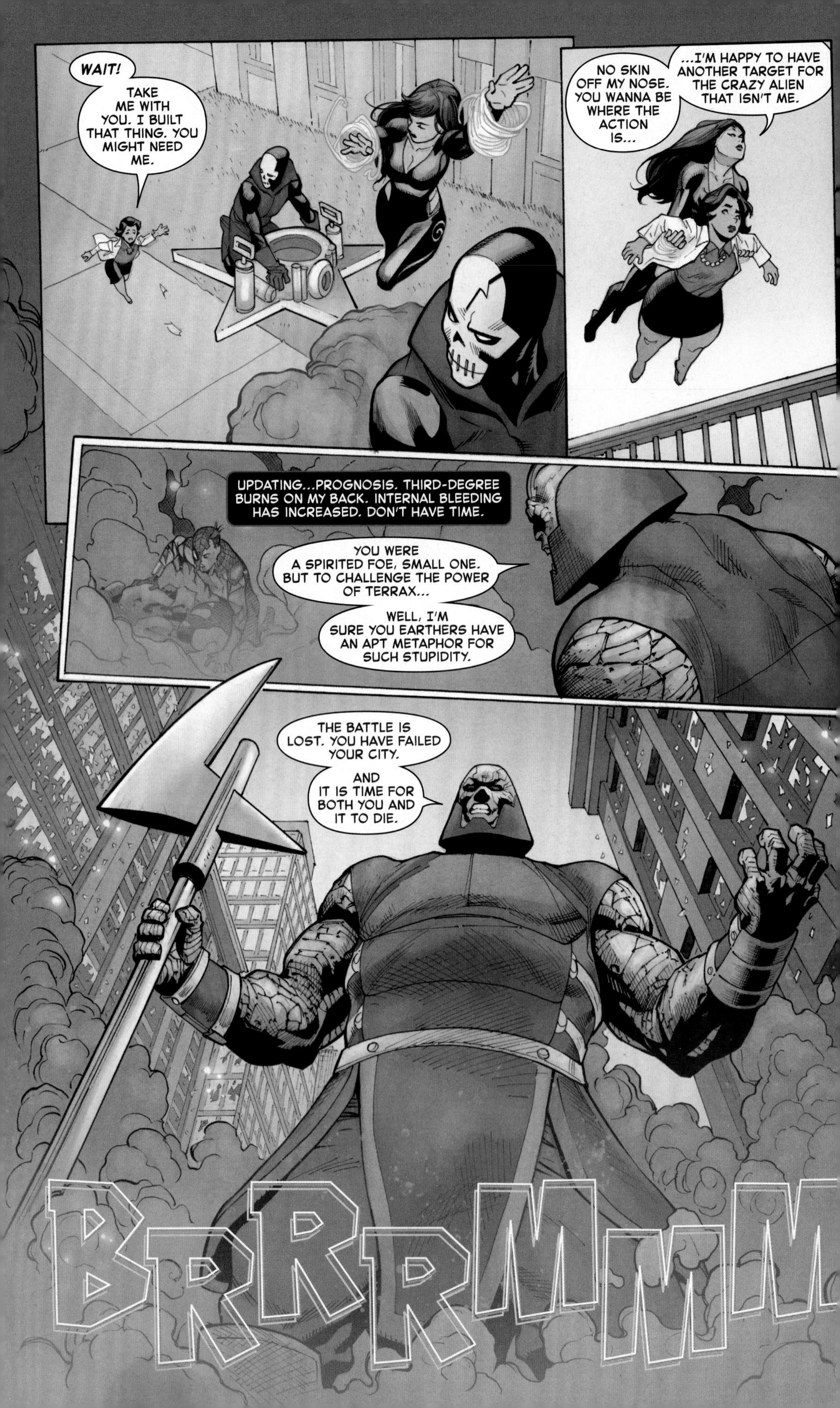
WAIT!
TAKE ME WITH YOU. I BUILT THAT THING. YOU MIGHT NEED ME.
NO SKIN OFF MY NOSE. YOU WANNA BE WHERE THE ACTION IS...
...I'M HAPPY TO HAVE ANOTHER TARGET FOR THE CRAZY ALIEN THAT ISN'T ME.
UPDATING...PROGNOSIS. THIRD-DEGREE BURNS ON MY BACK. INTERNAL BLEEDING HAS INCREASED. DON'T HAVE TIME.
YOU WERE A SPIRITED FOE, SMALL ONE. BUT TO CHALLENGE THE POWER OF TERRAX...
WELL, I'M SURE YOU EARTHERS HAVE AN APT METAPHOR FOR SUCH STUPIDITY.
THE BATTLE IS LOST. YOU HAVE FAILED YOUR CITY.
AND IT IS TIME FOR BOTH YOU AND IT TO DIE.
BRRMMM

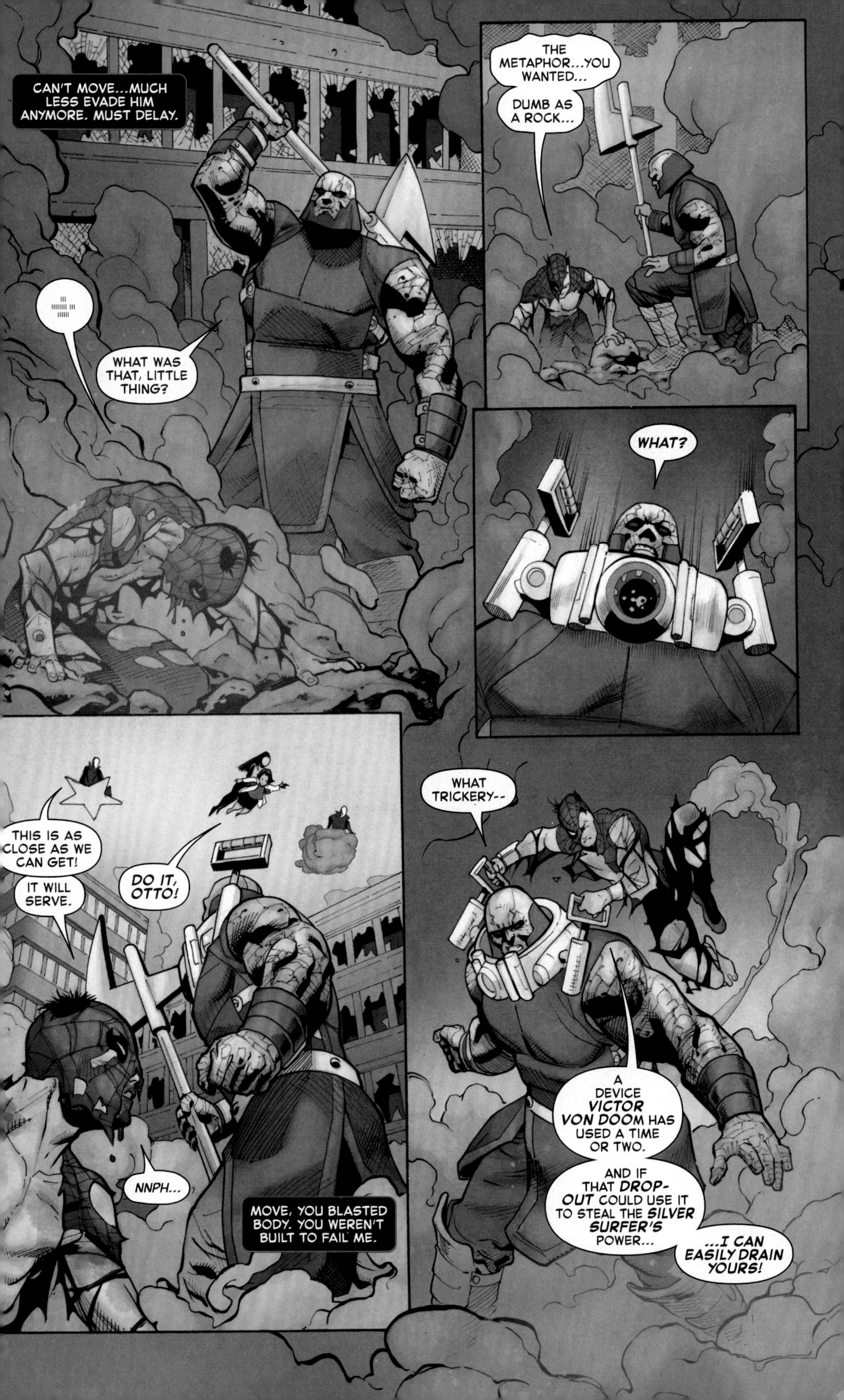
CAN'T MOVE...MUCH LESS EVADE HIM ANYMORE. MUST DELAY.
WHAT WAS THAT, LITTLE THING?
THE METAPHOR...YOU WANTED...
DUMB AS A ROCK...
WHAT?
THIS IS AS CLOSE AS WE CAN GET!
IT WILL SERVE.
DO IT, OTTO!
NNPH...
MOVE, YOU BLASTED BODY. YOU WEREN'T BUILT TO FAIL ME.
WHAT TRICKERY--
A DEVICE VICTOR VON DOOM HAS USED A TIME OR TWO.
AND IF THAT DROP-OUT COULD USE IT TO STEAL THE SILVER SURFER'S POWER...
...I CAN EASILY DRAIN YOURS!

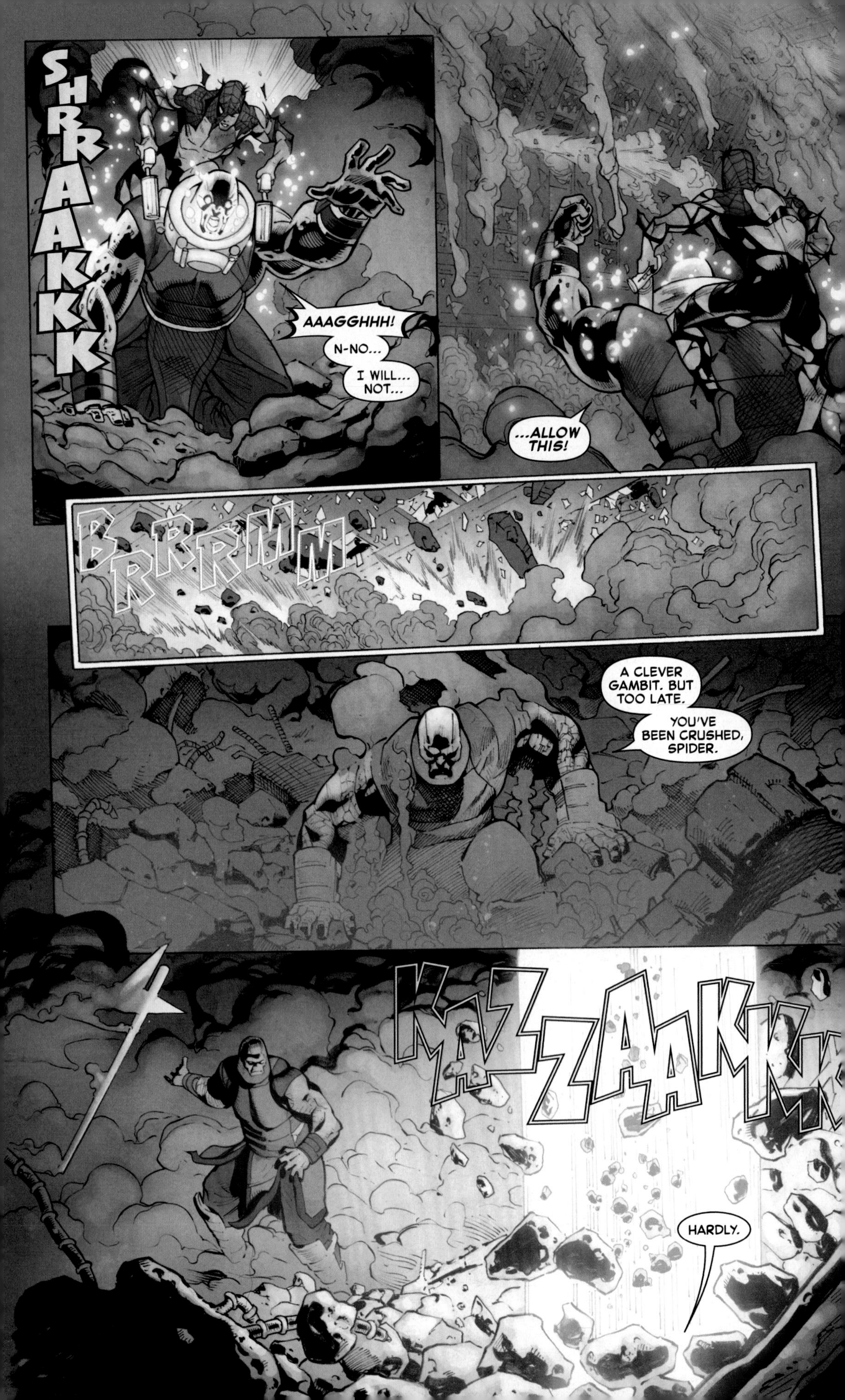
SHRRAAKKK
AAAGGHHH!
N-NO...
I WILL... NOT...
...ALLOW THIS!
BRRRMM
A CLEVER GAMBIT. BUT TOO LATE.
YOU'VE BEEN CRUSHED, SPIDER.
KAZAAKK
HARDLY.

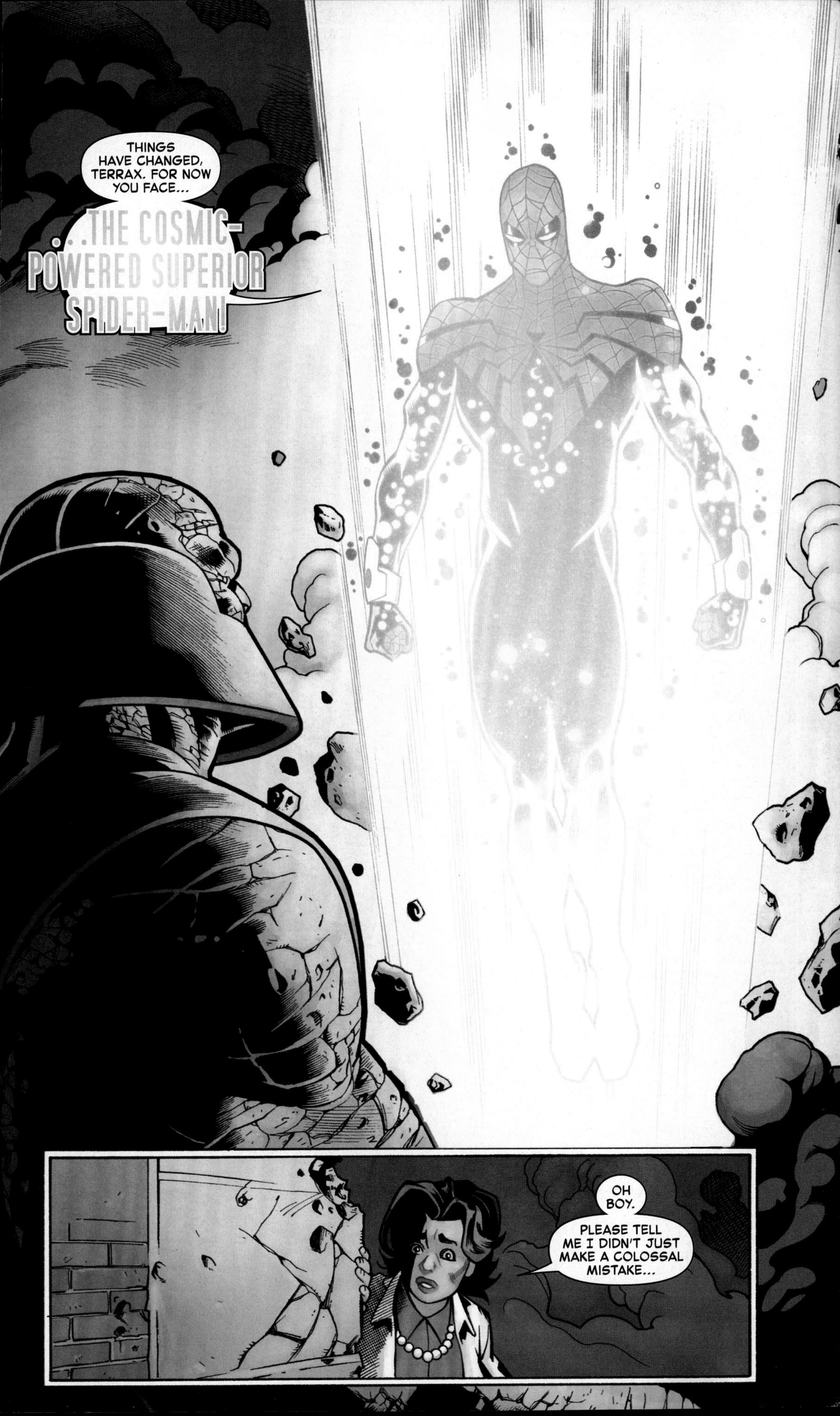
THINGS HAVE CHANGED, TERRAX. FOR NOW YOU FACE...
...THE COSMIC-POWERED SUPERIOR SPIDER-MAN!
OH BOY.
PLEASE TELL ME I DIDN'T JUST MAKE A COLOSSAL MISTAKE...

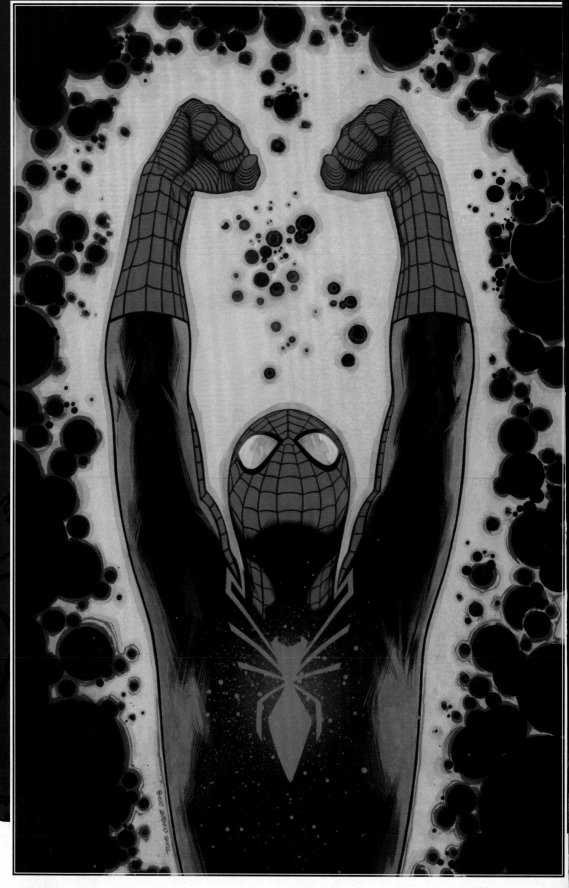

3

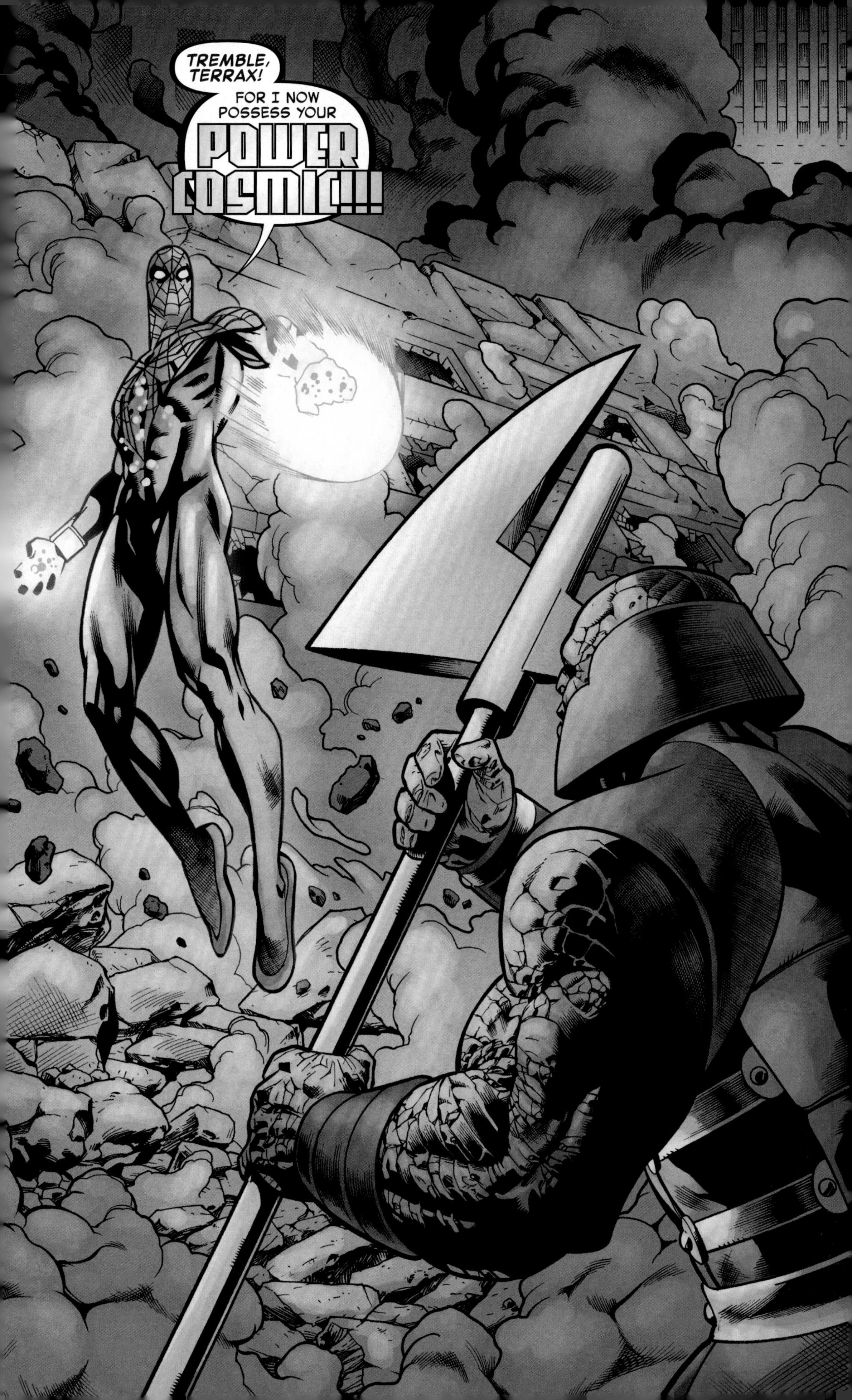
TREMBLE, TERRAX!
FOR I NOW POSSESS YOUR
POWER COSMIC!!!

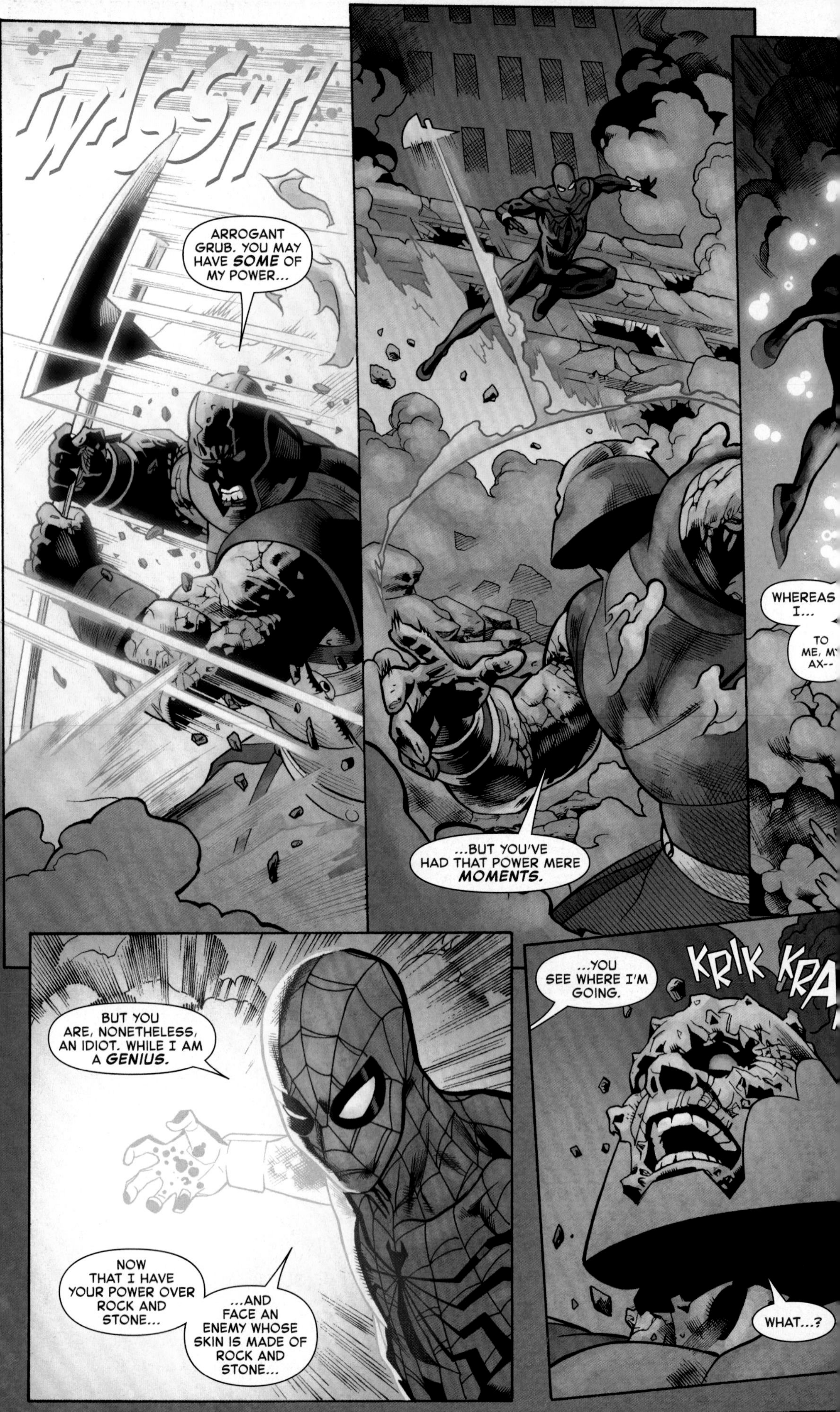

FWASSHH
ARROGANT GRUB. YOU MAY HAVE SOME OF MY POWER...
...BUT YOU'VE HAD THAT POWER MERE MOMENTS.
WHEREAS I...
TO ME, MY AX--
BUT YOU ARE, NONETHELESS, AN IDIOT. WHILE I AM A GENIUS.
NOW THAT I HAVE YOUR POWER OVER ROCK AND STONE...
...AND FACE AN ENEMY WHOSE SKIN IS MADE OF ROCK AND STONE...
...YOU SEE WHERE I'M GOING.
KRIK KRA
WHAT...?

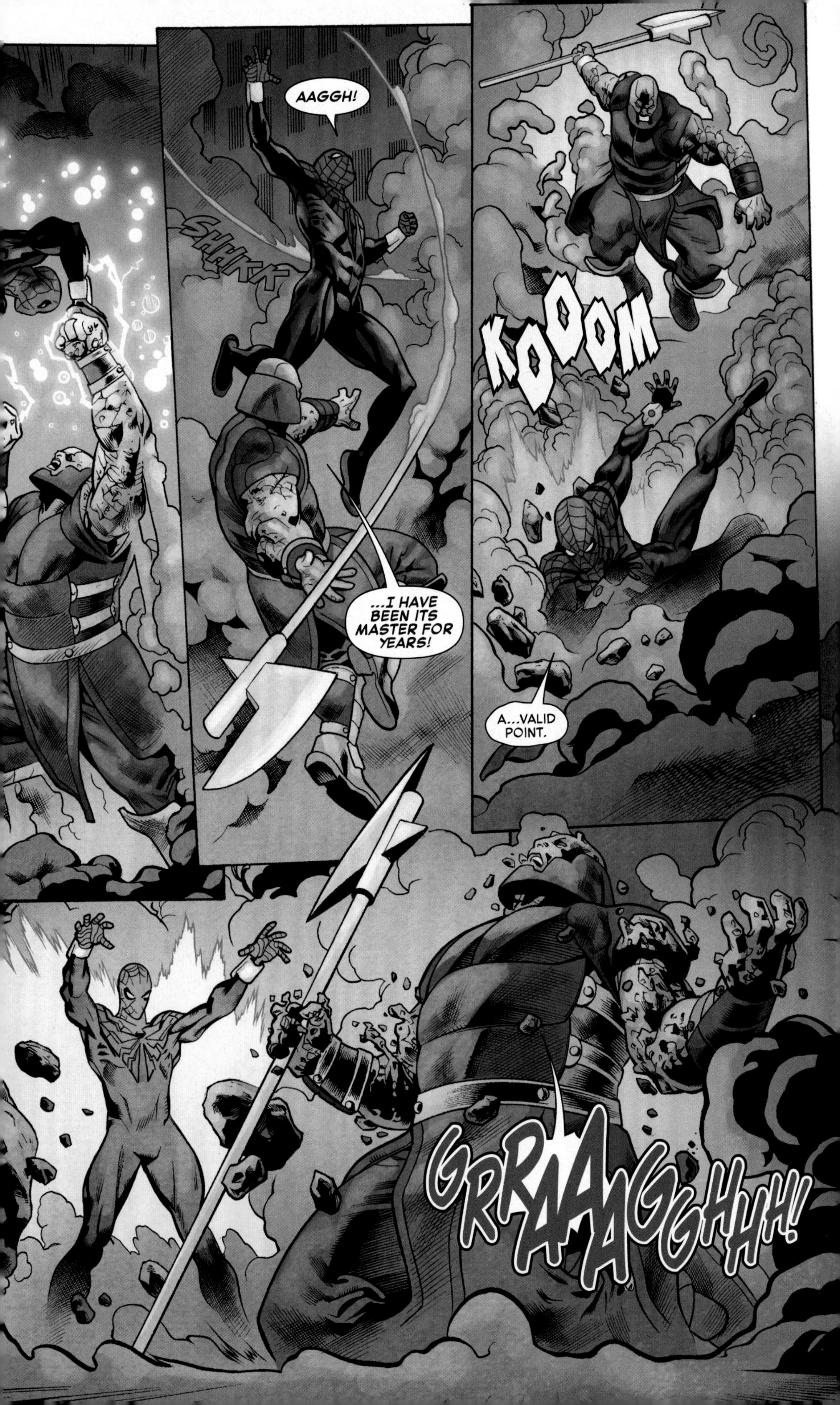
AAGGH!
SHHKK
...I HAVE BEEN ITS MASTER FOR YEARS!
KOOOM
A...VALID POINT.
GRRAAAAGHHH!

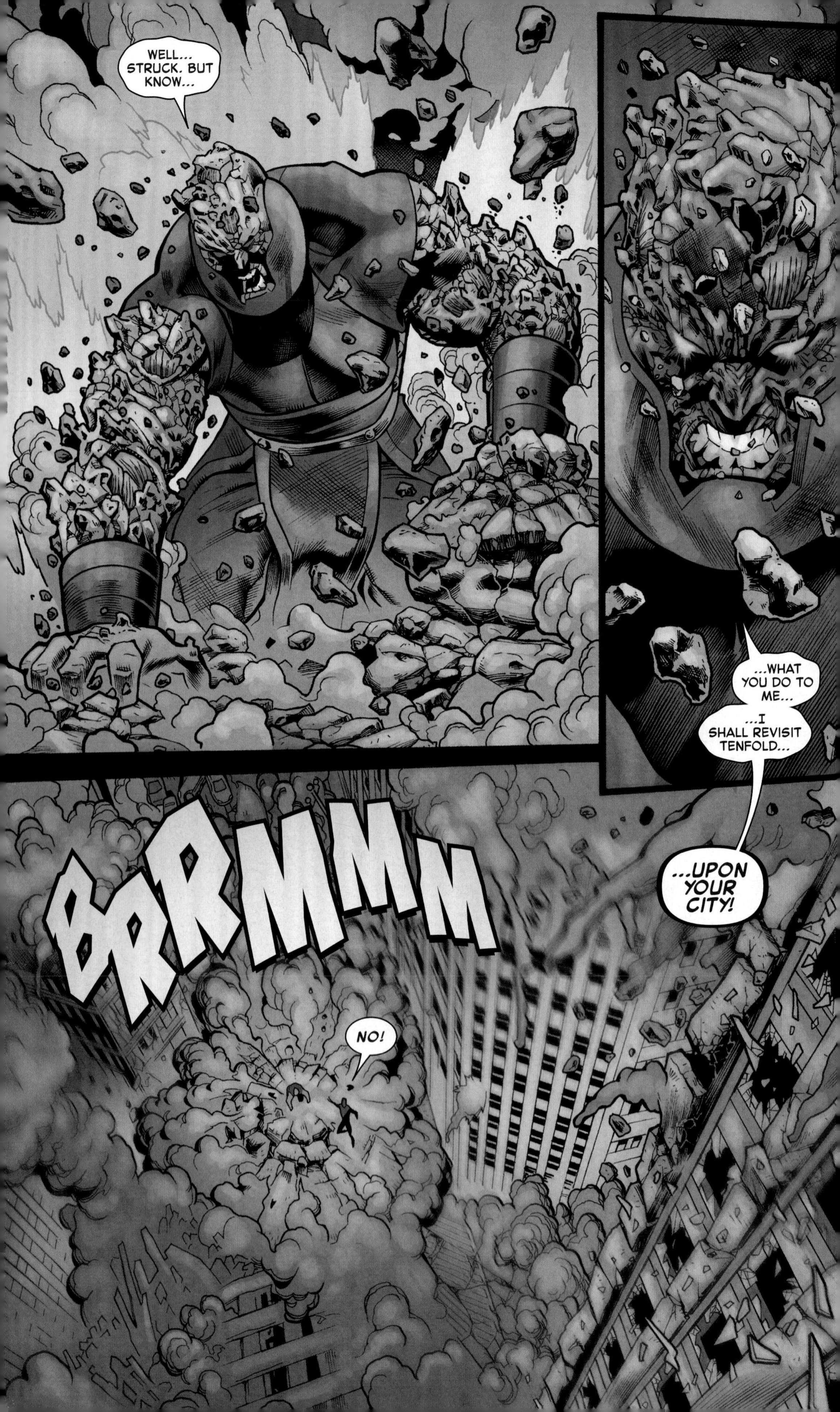
WELL... STRUCK. BUT KNOW...
...WHAT YOU DO TO ME...
...I SHALL REVISIT TENFOLD...
...UPON YOUR CITY!
BRRMMMM
NO!

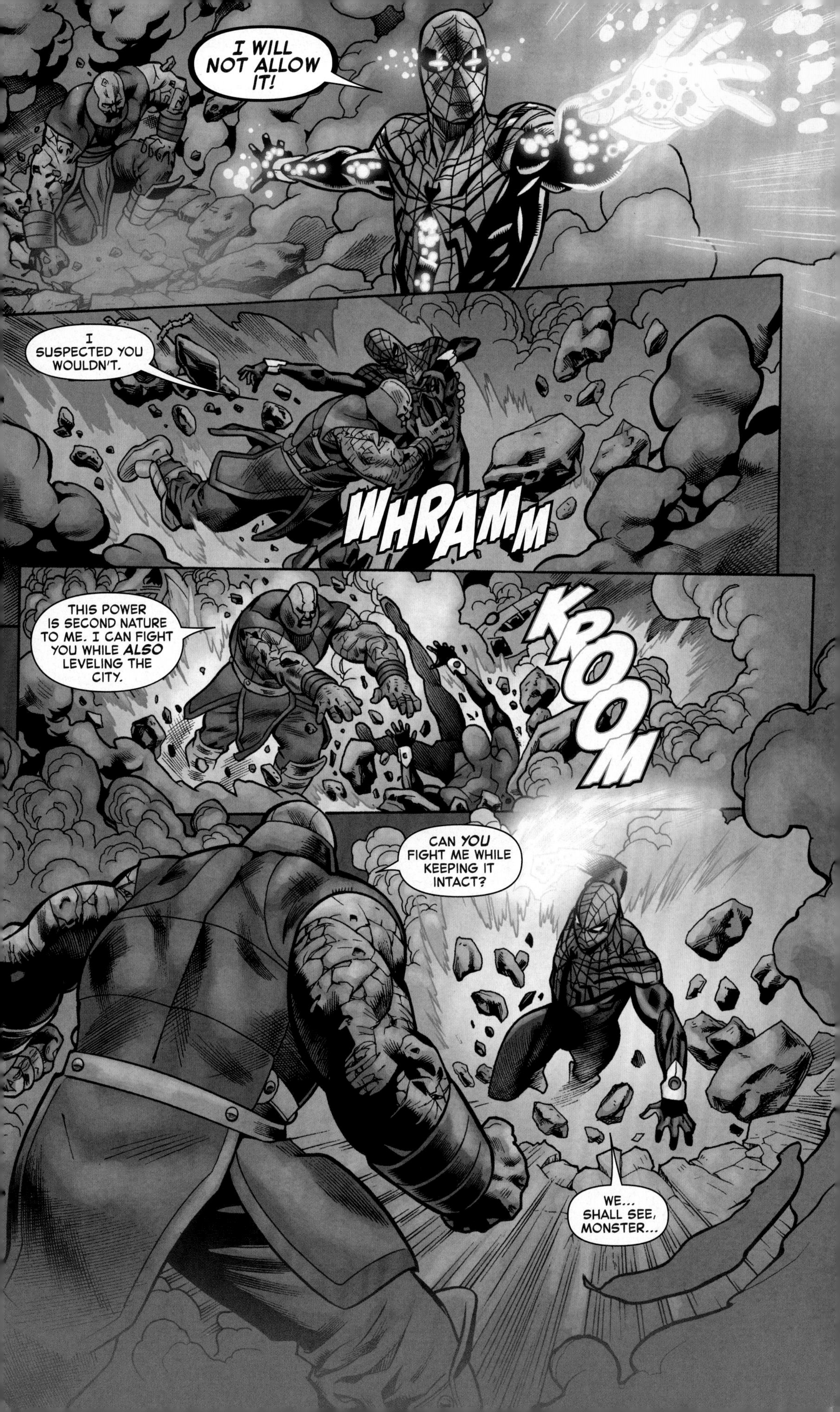
I WILL NOT ALLOW IT!
I SUSPECTED YOU WOULDN'T.
WHRAMM
THIS POWER IS SECOND NATURE TO ME. I CAN FIGHT YOU WHILE *ALSO* LEVELING THE CITY.
KROOM
CAN *YOU* FIGHT ME WHILE KEEPING IT INTACT?
WE... SHALL SEE, MONSTER...

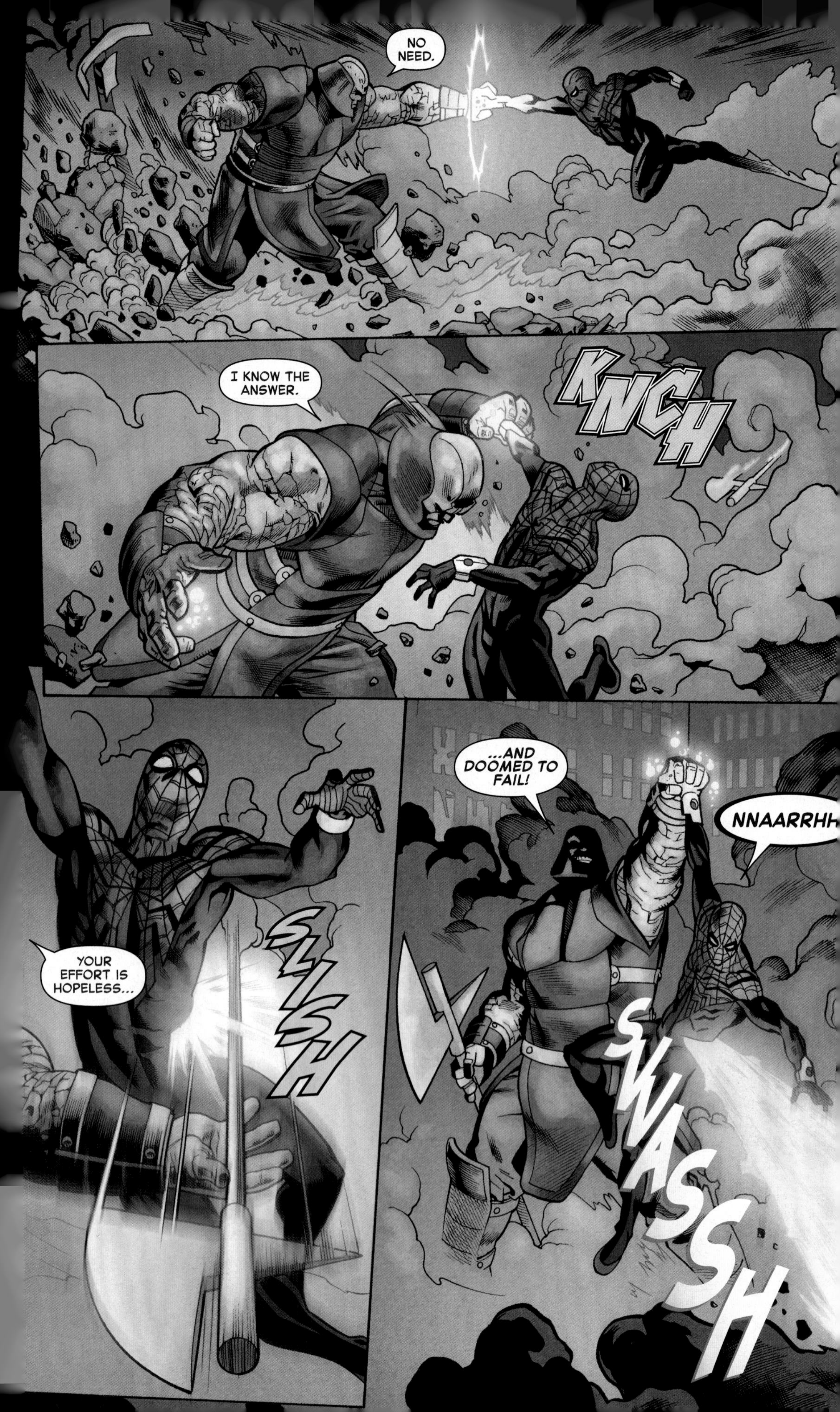
NO NEED.
I KNOW THE ANSWER.
KNCH
YOUR EFFORT IS HOPELESS...
SLISH
...AND DOOMED TO FAIL!
NNAARRHH
SWASSH

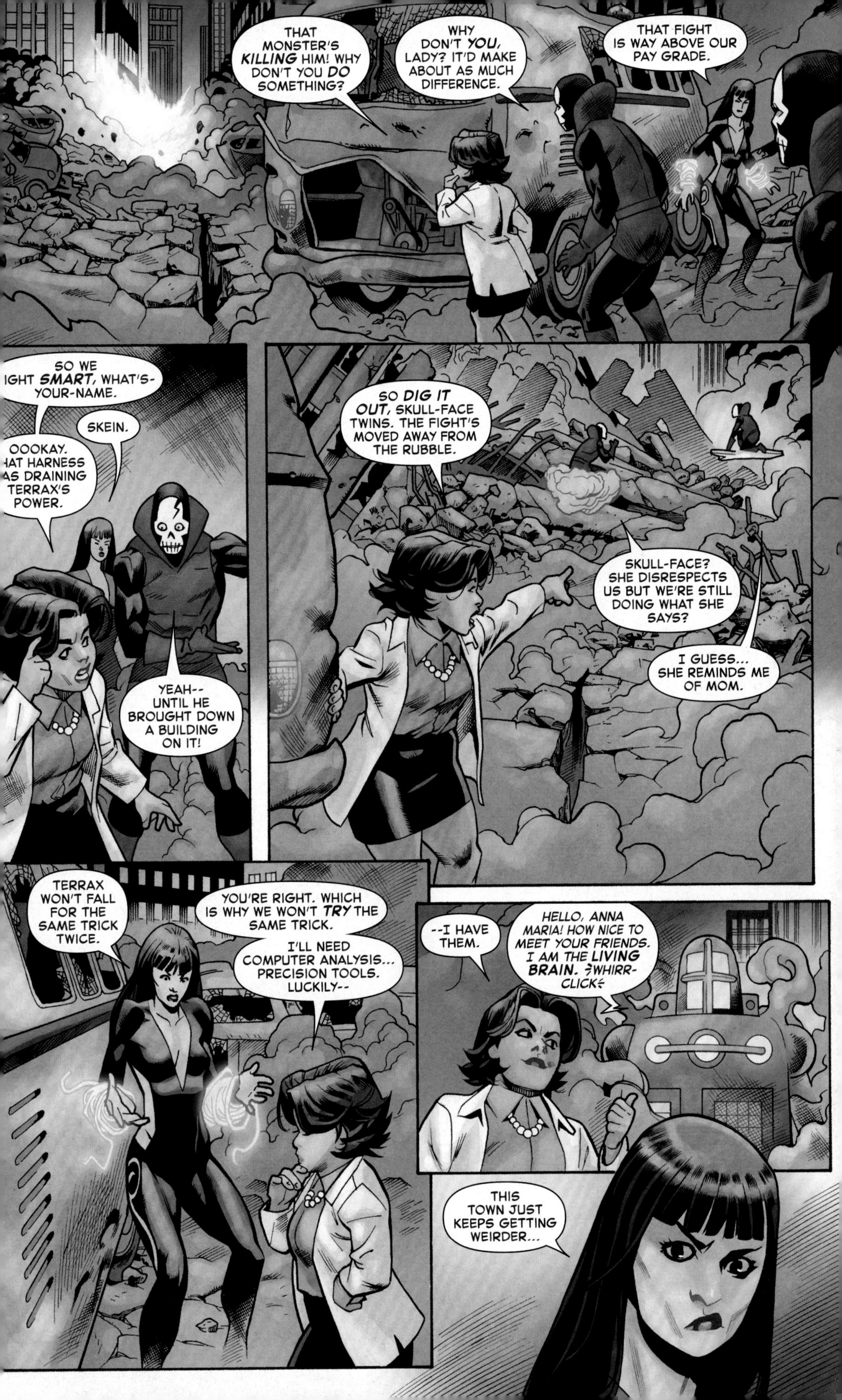

THAT MONSTER'S KILLING HIM! WHY DON'T YOU DO SOMETHING?
WHY DON'T YOU, LADY? IT'D MAKE ABOUT AS MUCH DIFFERENCE.
THAT FIGHT IS WAY ABOVE OUR PAY GRADE.
SO WE IGHT SMART, WHAT'S-YOUR-NAME.
SKEIN.
OOOKAY. HAT HARNESS AS DRAINING TERRAX'S POWER.
YEAH-- UNTIL HE BROUGHT DOWN A BUILDING ON IT!
SO DIG IT OUT, SKULL-FACE TWINS. THE FIGHT'S MOVED AWAY FROM THE RUBBLE.
SKULL-FACE? SHE DISRESPECTS US BUT WE'RE STILL DOING WHAT SHE SAYS?
I GUESS... SHE REMINDS ME OF MOM.
TERRAX WON'T FALL FOR THE SAME TRICK TWICE.
YOU'RE RIGHT. WHICH IS WHY WE WON'T TRY THE SAME TRICK.
I'LL NEED COMPUTER ANALYSIS... PRECISION TOOLS. LUCKILY--
--I HAVE THEM.
HELLO, ANNA MARIA! HOW NICE TO MEET YOUR FRIENDS. I AM THE LIVING BRAIN. ⋛WHIRR-CLICK⋚
THIS TOWN JUST KEEPS GETTING WEIRDER...

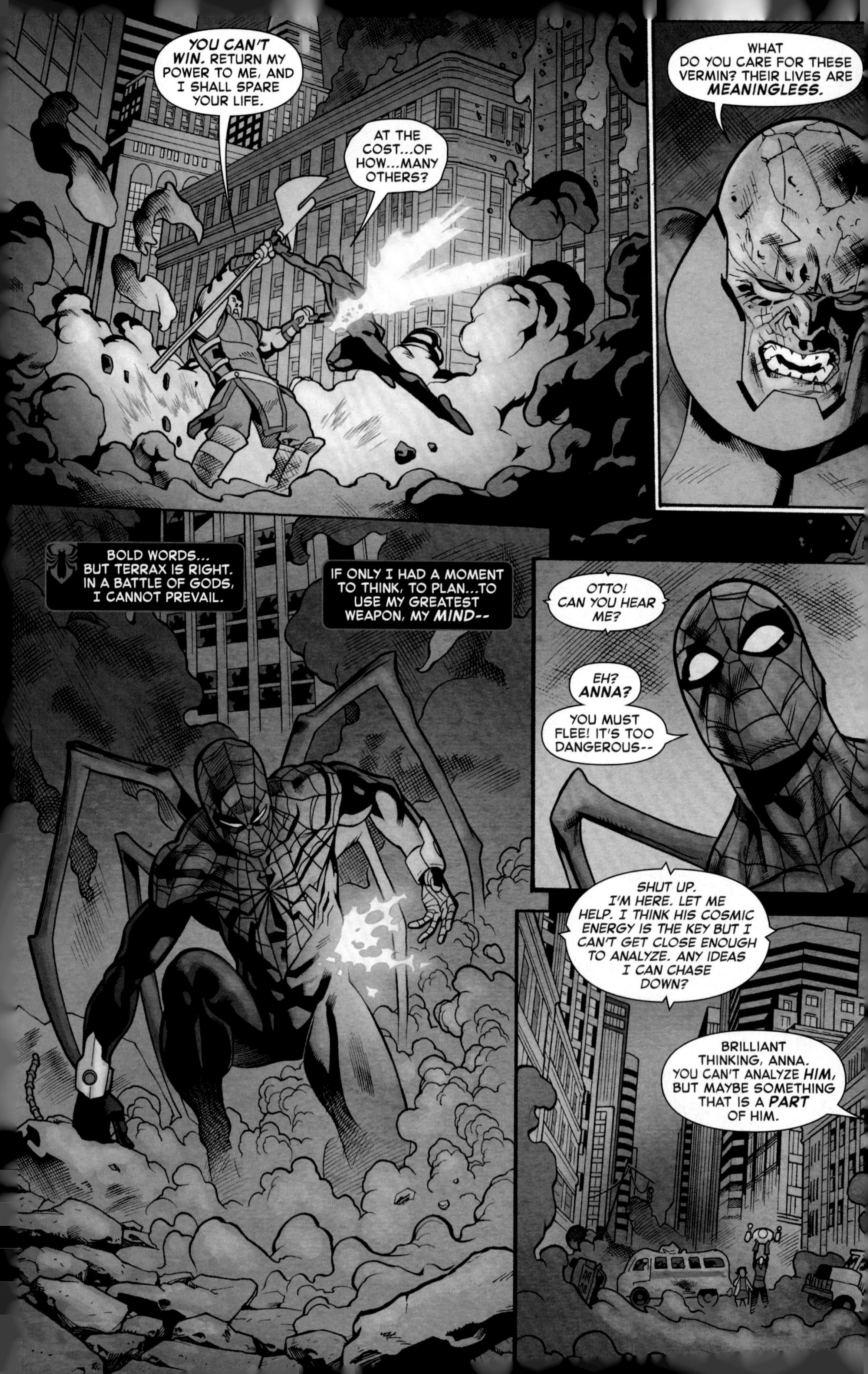
YOU CAN'T WIN. RETURN MY POWER TO ME, AND I SHALL SPARE YOUR LIFE.
AT THE COST...OF HOW...MANY OTHERS?
WHAT DO YOU CARE FOR THESE VERMIN? THEIR LIVES ARE MEANINGLESS.
BOLD WORDS... BUT TERRAX IS RIGHT. IN A BATTLE OF GODS, I CANNOT PREVAIL.
IF ONLY I HAD A MOMENT TO THINK, TO PLAN...TO USE MY GREATEST WEAPON, MY MIND--
OTTO! CAN YOU HEAR ME?
EH? ANNA?
YOU MUST FLEE! IT'S TOO DANGEROUS--
SHUT UP. I'M HERE. LET ME HELP. I THINK HIS COSMIC ENERGY IS THE KEY BUT I CAN'T GET CLOSE ENOUGH TO ANALYZE. ANY IDEAS I CAN CHASE DOWN?
BRILLIANT THINKING, ANNA. YOU CAN'T ANALYZE HIM, BUT MAYBE SOMETHING THAT IS A PART OF HIM.

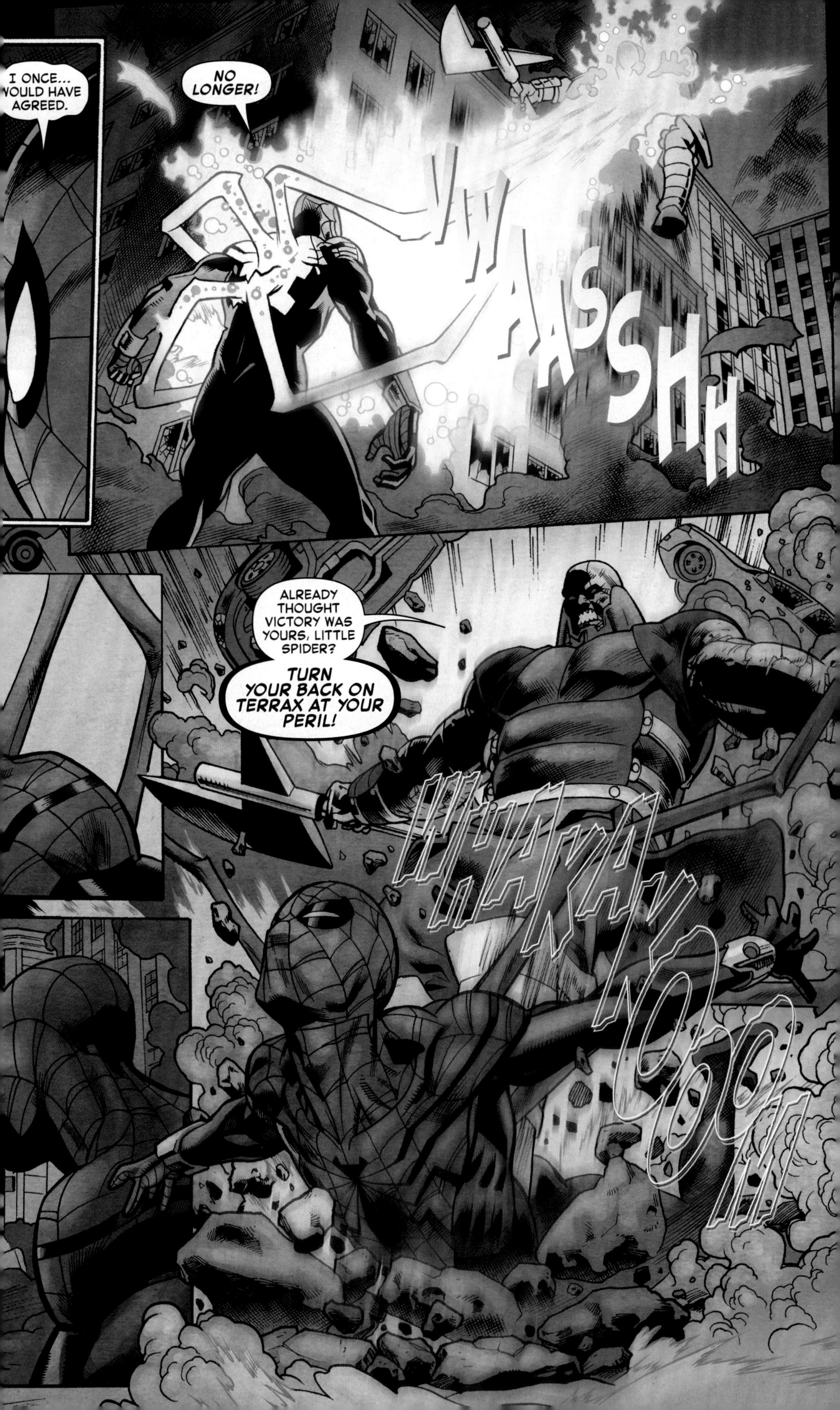
I ONCE... WOULD HAVE AGREED.
NO LONGER!
VWAASSHH
ALREADY THOUGHT VICTORY WAS YOURS, LITTLE SPIDER?
TURN YOUR BACK ON TERRAX AT YOUR PERIL!
KKHRAKOOM

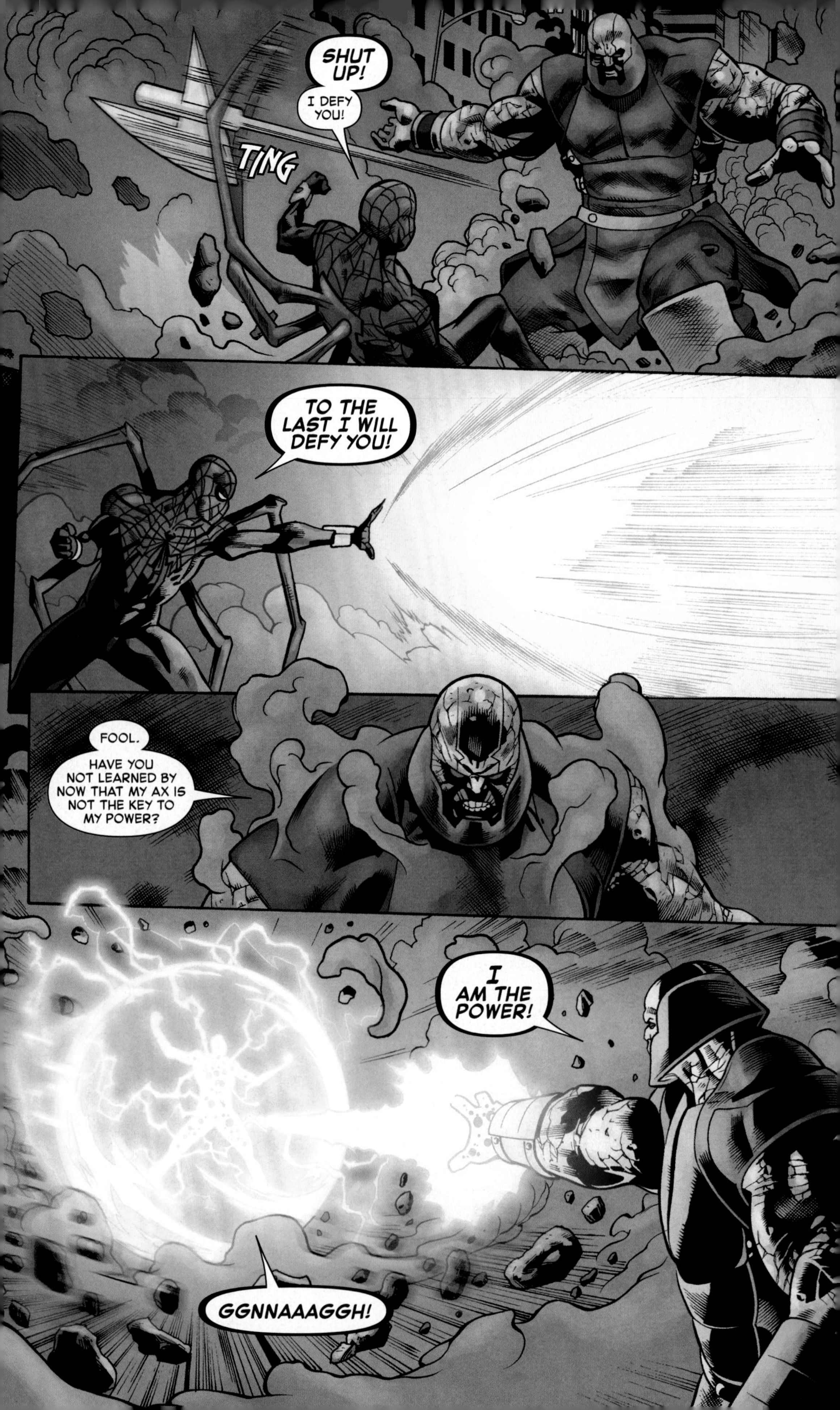

SHUT UP!
I DEFY YOU!
TING
TO THE LAST I WILL DEFY YOU!
FOOL.
HAVE YOU NOT LEARNED BY NOW THAT MY AX IS NOT THE KEY TO MY POWER?
I AM THE POWER!
GGNNAAAGGH!

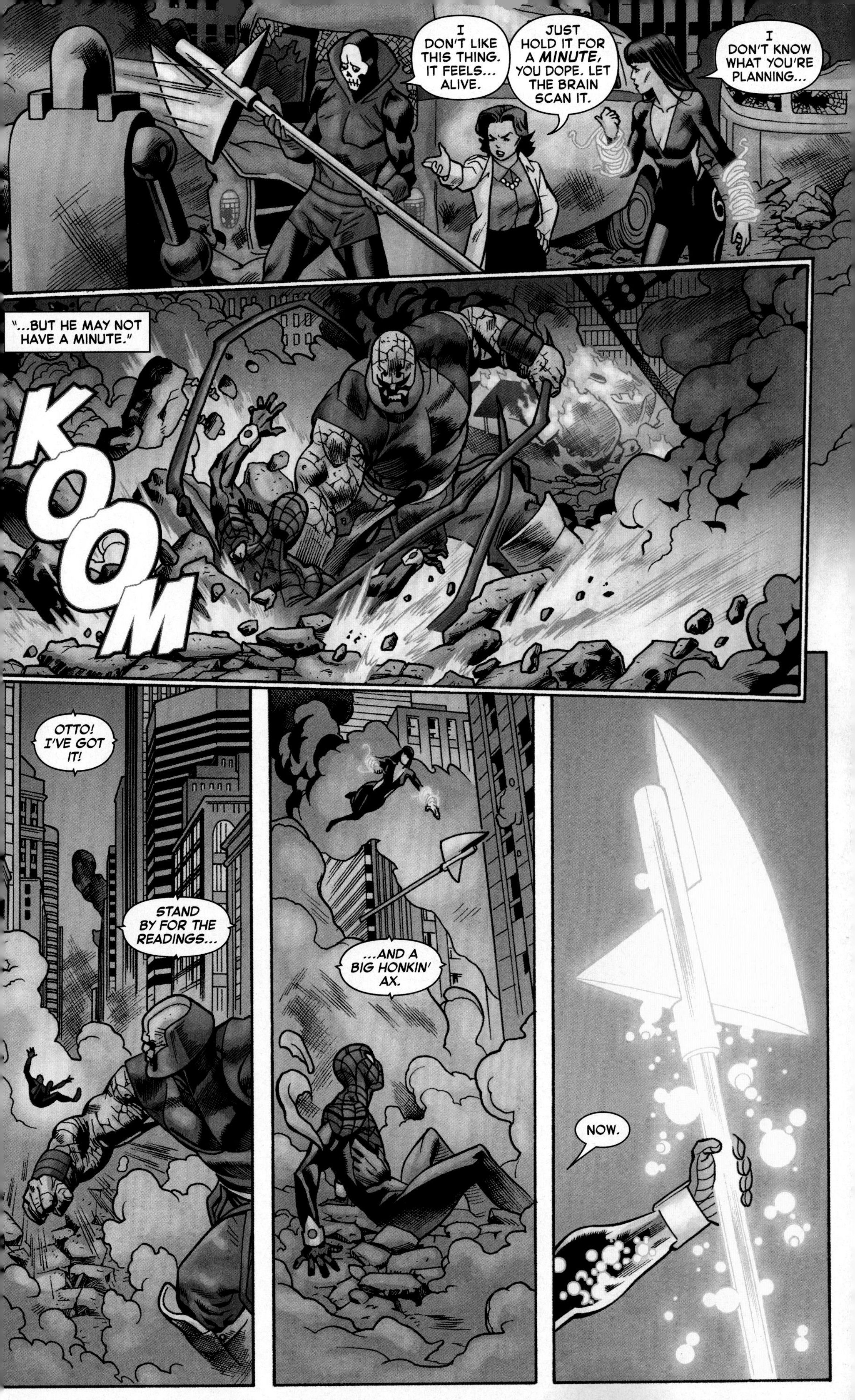
I DON'T LIKE THIS THING. IT FEELS... ALIVE.
JUST HOLD IT FOR A *MINUTE*, YOU DOPE. LET THE BRAIN SCAN IT.
I DON'T KNOW WHAT YOU'RE PLANNING...
"...BUT HE MAY NOT HAVE A MINUTE."
KOOM
OTTO! I'VE GOT IT!
STAND BY FOR THE READINGS...
...AND A BIG HONKIN' AX.
NOW.

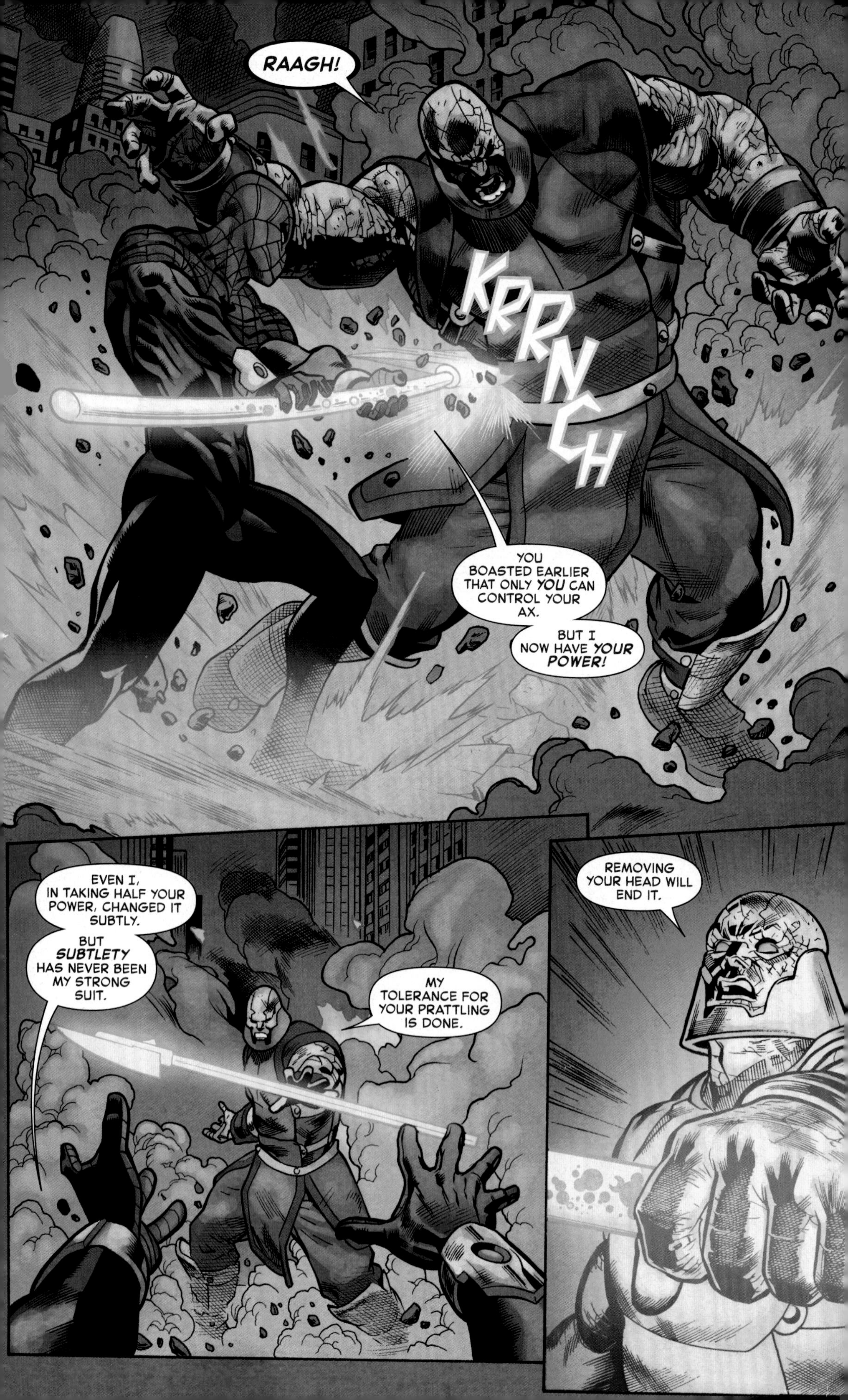
RAAGH!
KRRNCH
YOU BOASTED EARLIER THAT ONLY YOU CAN CONTROL YOUR AX.
BUT I NOW HAVE YOUR POWER!
EVEN I, IN TAKING HALF YOUR POWER, CHANGED IT SUBTLY.
BUT SUBTLETY HAS NEVER BEEN MY STRONG SUIT.
MY TOLERANCE FOR YOUR PRATTLING IS DONE.
REMOVING YOUR HEAD WILL END IT.

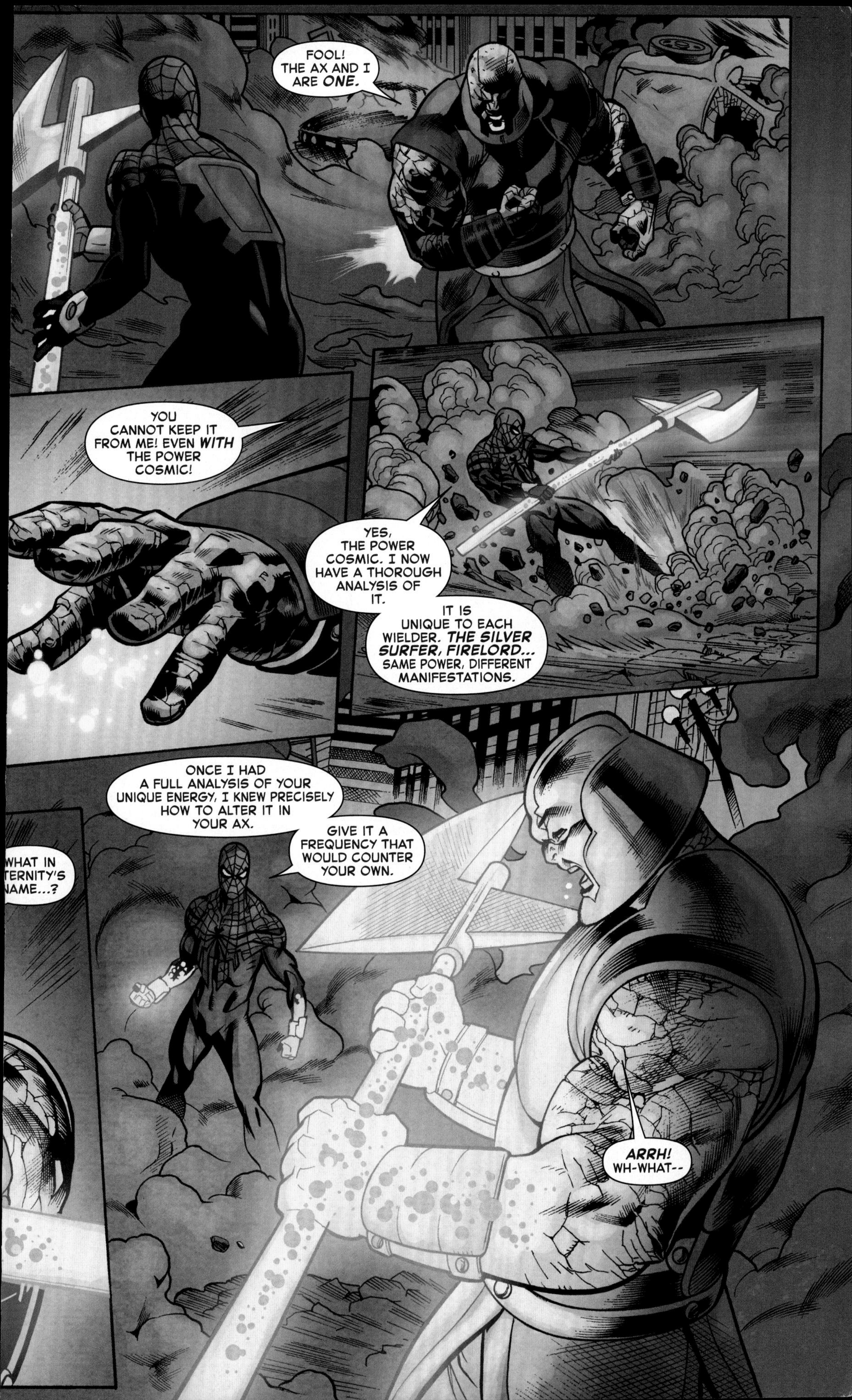
FOOL! THE AX AND I ARE *ONE.*
YOU CANNOT KEEP IT FROM ME! EVEN *WITH* THE POWER COSMIC!
YES, THE POWER COSMIC. I NOW HAVE A THOROUGH ANALYSIS OF IT.
IT IS UNIQUE TO EACH WIELDER. *THE SILVER SURFER, FIRELORD...* SAME POWER, DIFFERENT MANIFESTATIONS.
ONCE I HAD A FULL ANALYSIS OF YOUR UNIQUE ENERGY, I KNEW PRECISELY HOW TO ALTER IT IN YOUR AX.
GIVE IT A FREQUENCY THAT WOULD COUNTER YOUR OWN.
WHAT IN
TERNITY'S
NAME...?
ARRH! WH-WHAT--

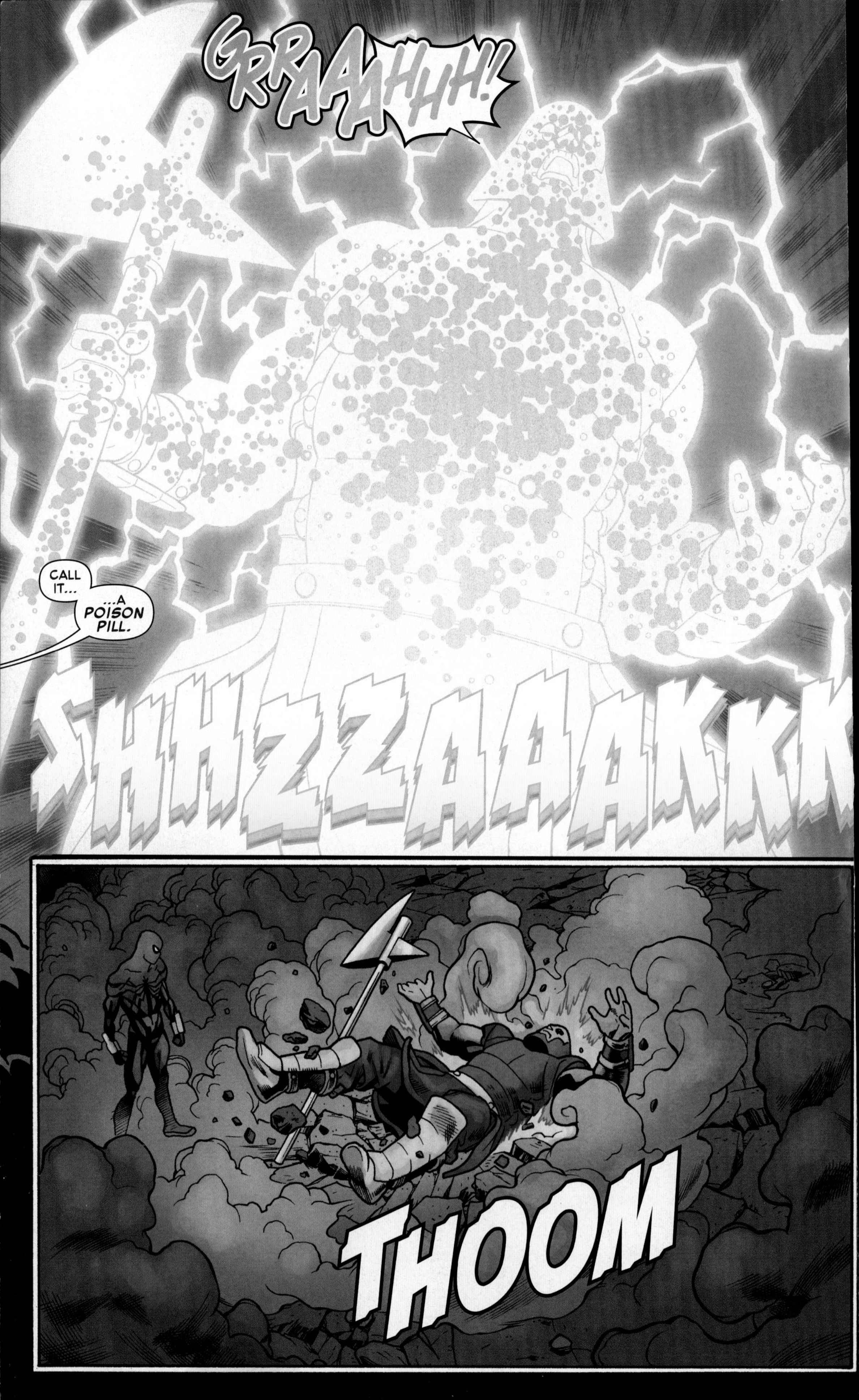
GRAAAHHH!
CALL IT...
...A POISON PILL.
SHZZAAAKK
THOOM

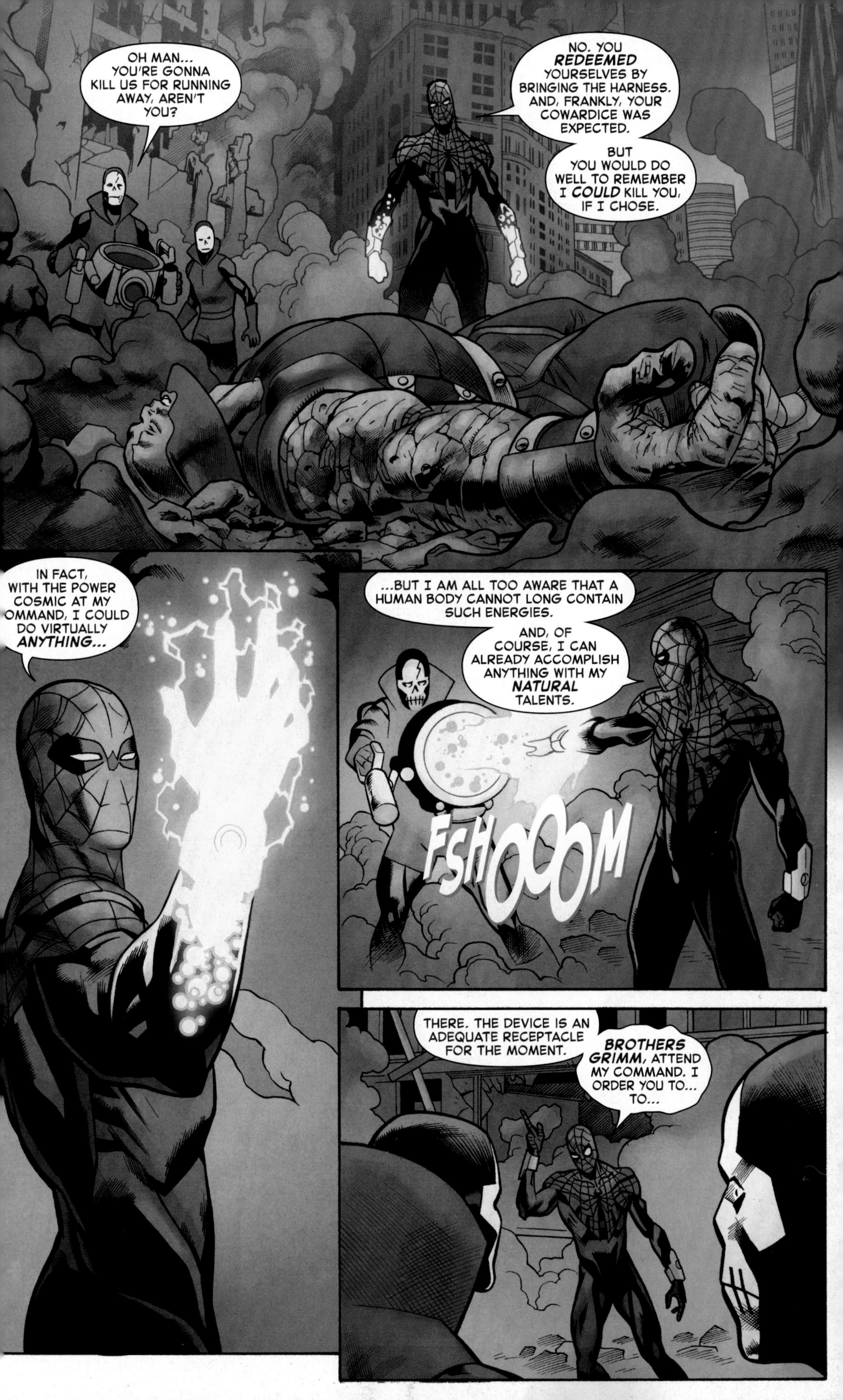

OH MAN... YOU'RE GONNA KILL US FOR RUNNING AWAY, AREN'T YOU?
NO. YOU REDEEMED YOURSELVES BY BRINGING THE HARNESS. AND, FRANKLY, YOUR COWARDICE WAS EXPECTED.
BUT YOU WOULD DO WELL TO REMEMBER I COULD KILL YOU, IF I CHOSE.
IN FACT, WITH THE POWER COSMIC AT MY OMMAND, I COULD DO VIRTUALLY ANYTHING...
...BUT I AM ALL TOO AWARE THAT A HUMAN BODY CANNOT LONG CONTAIN SUCH ENERGIES.
AND, OF COURSE, I CAN ALREADY ACCOMPLISH ANYTHING WITH MY NATURAL TALENTS.
FSHOOOOM
THERE. THE DEVICE IS AN ADEQUATE RECEPTACLE FOR THE MOMENT.
BROTHERS GRIMM, ATTEND MY COMMAND. I ORDER YOU TO... TO...

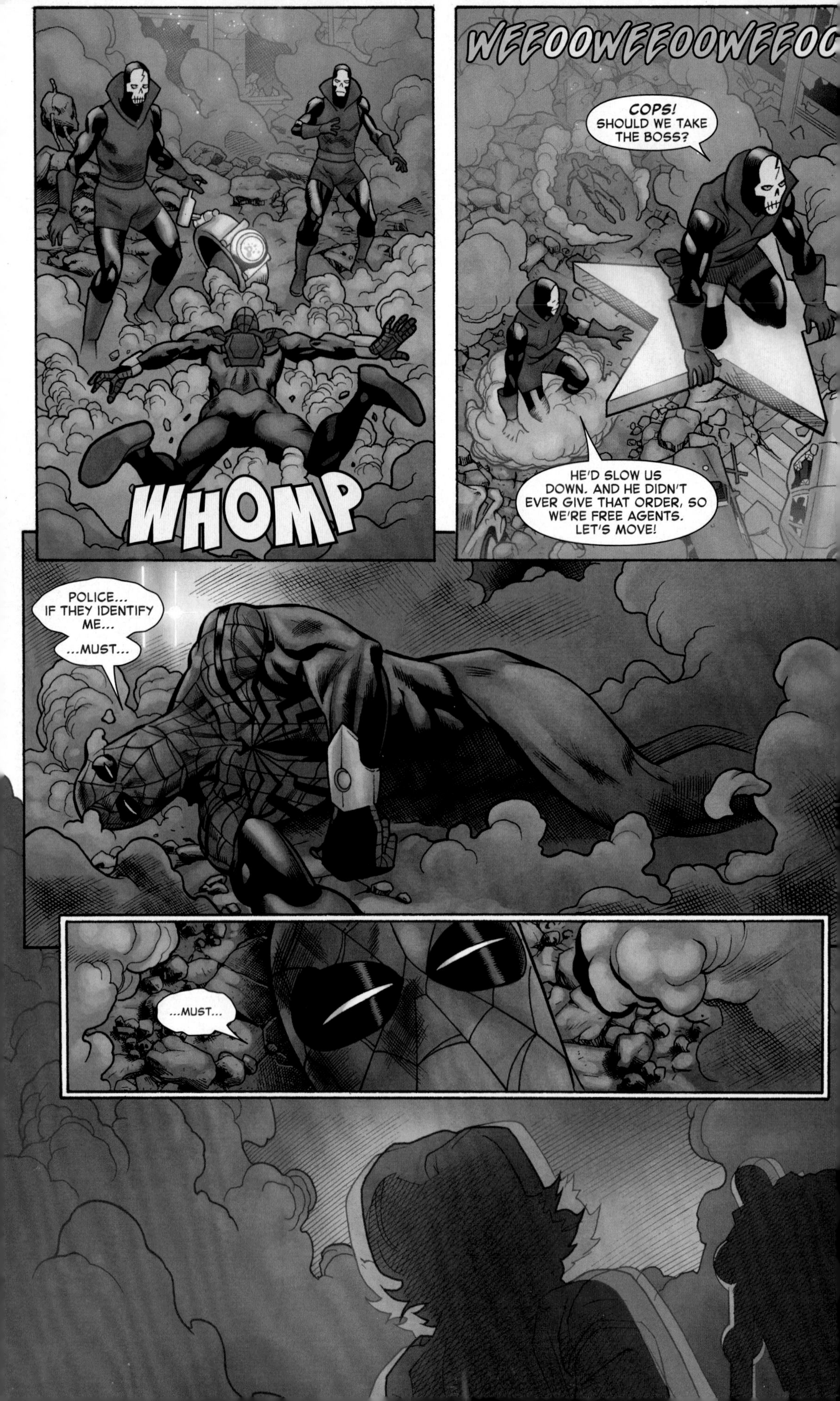
WHOMP
WEEOOWEEOOWEEOO
COPS! SHOULD WE TAKE THE BOSS?
HE'D SLOW US DOWN. AND HE DIDN'T EVER GIVE THAT ORDER, SO WE'RE FREE AGENTS. LET'S MOVE!
POLICE... IF THEY IDENTIFY ME...
...MUST...
...MUST...

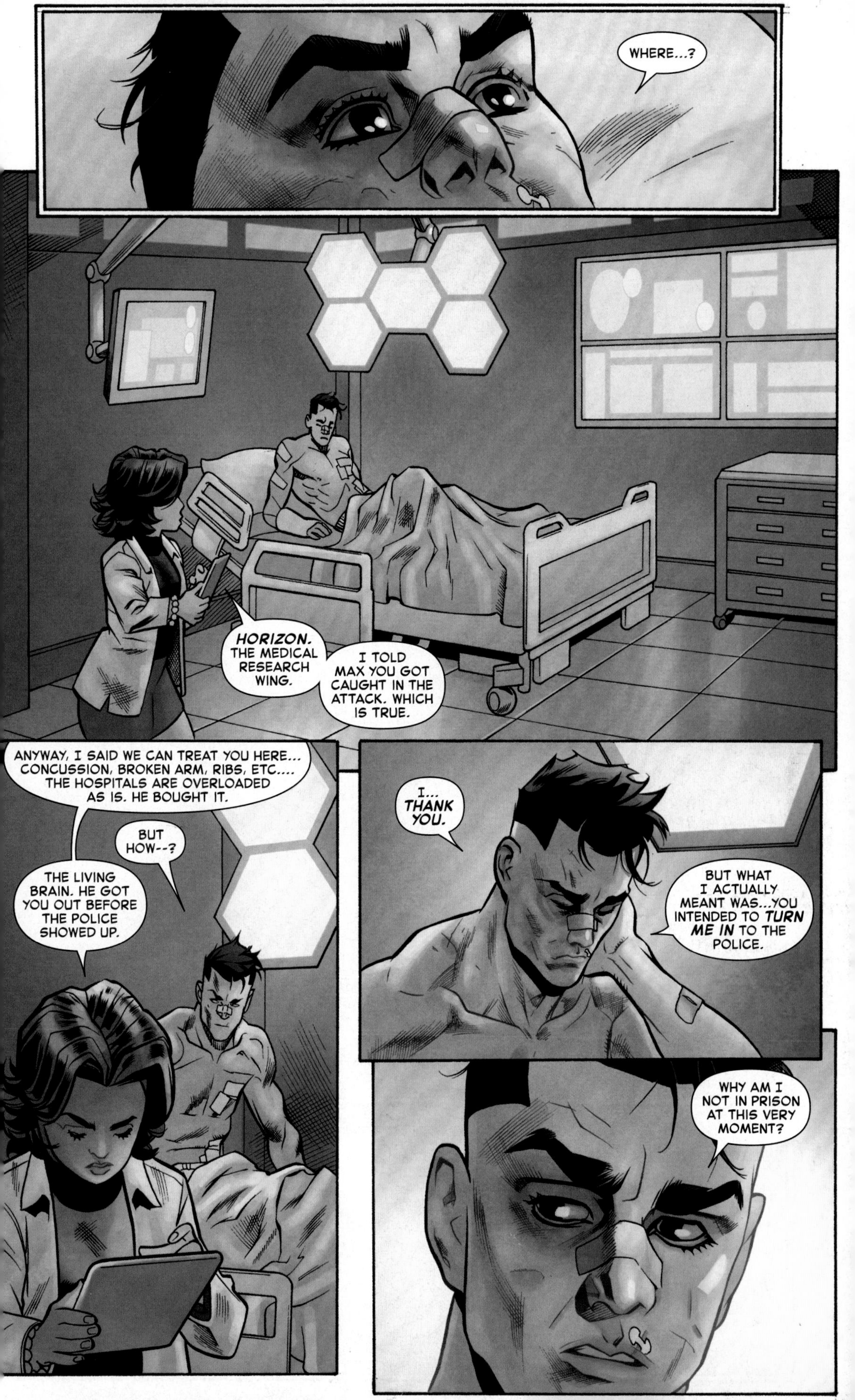
WHERE...?
HORIZON. THE MEDICAL RESEARCH WING.
I TOLD MAX YOU GOT CAUGHT IN THE ATTACK. WHICH IS TRUE.
ANYWAY, I SAID WE CAN TREAT YOU HERE... CONCUSSION, BROKEN ARM, RIBS, ETC.... THE HOSPITALS ARE OVERLOADED AS IS. HE BOUGHT IT.
BUT HOW--?
THE LIVING BRAIN. HE GOT YOU OUT BEFORE THE POLICE SHOWED UP.
I... THANK YOU.
BUT WHAT I ACTUALLY MEANT WAS...YOU INTENDED TO TURN ME IN TO THE POLICE.
WHY AM I NOT IN PRISON AT THIS VERY MOMENT?

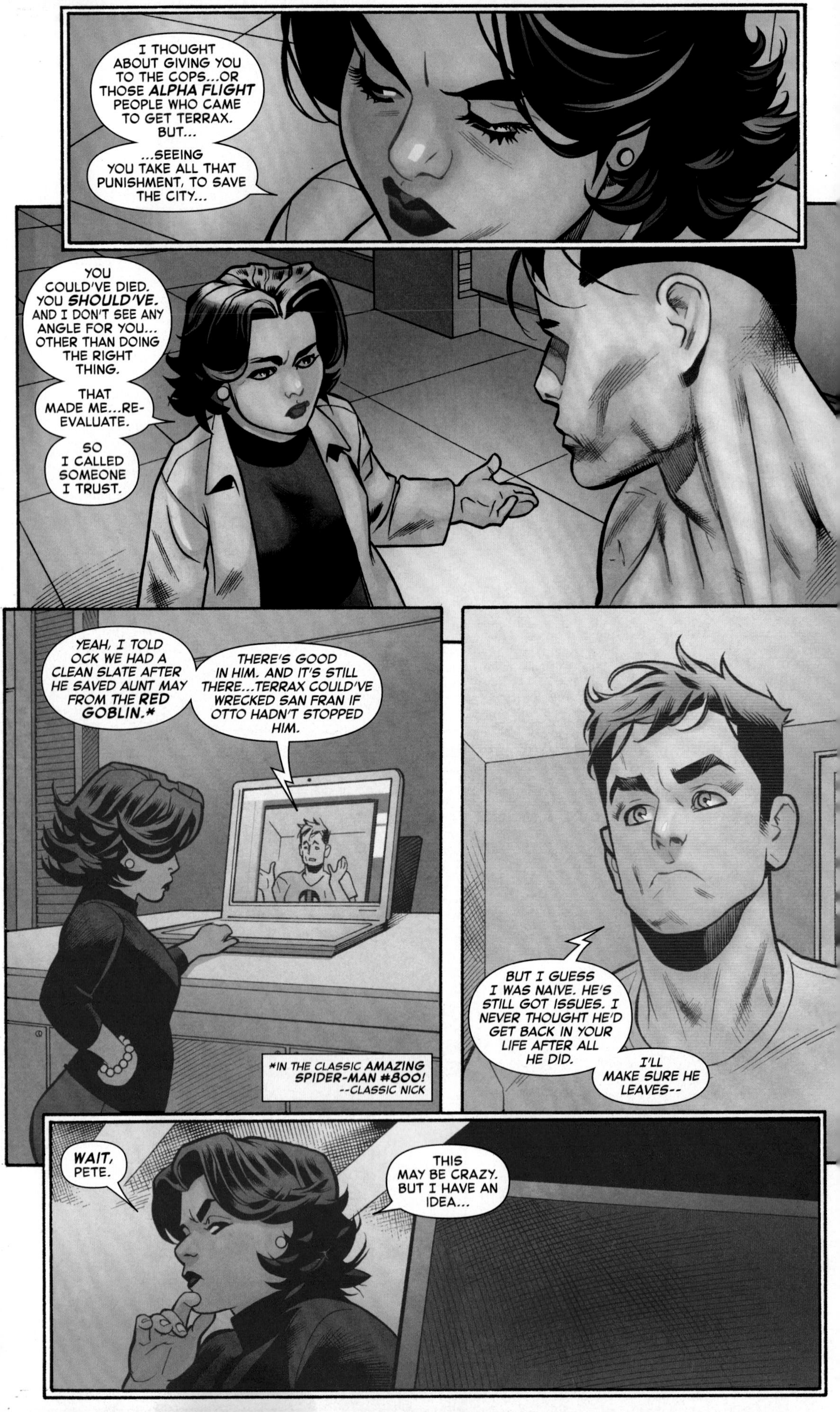

I THOUGHT ABOUT GIVING YOU TO THE COPS...OR THOSE ALPHA FLIGHT PEOPLE WHO CAME TO GET TERRAX. BUT...
...SEEING YOU TAKE ALL THAT PUNISHMENT, TO SAVE THE CITY...
YOU COULD'VE DIED. YOU SHOULD'VE. AND I DON'T SEE ANY ANGLE FOR YOU... OTHER THAN DOING THE RIGHT THING.
THAT MADE ME...RE-EVALUATE.
SO I CALLED SOMEONE I TRUST.
YEAH, I TOLD OCK WE HAD A CLEAN SLATE AFTER HE SAVED AUNT MAY FROM THE RED GOBLIN.*
THERE'S GOOD IN HIM. AND IT'S STILL THERE...TERRAX COULD'VE WRECKED SAN FRAN IF OTTO HADN'T STOPPED HIM.
*IN THE CLASSIC AMAZING SPIDER-MAN #800! --CLASSIC NICK
BUT I GUESS I WAS NAIVE. HE'S STILL GOT ISSUES. I NEVER THOUGHT HE'D GET BACK IN YOUR LIFE AFTER ALL HE DID.
I'LL MAKE SURE HE LEAVES--
WAIT, PETE.
THIS MAY BE CRAZY. BUT I HAVE AN IDEA...

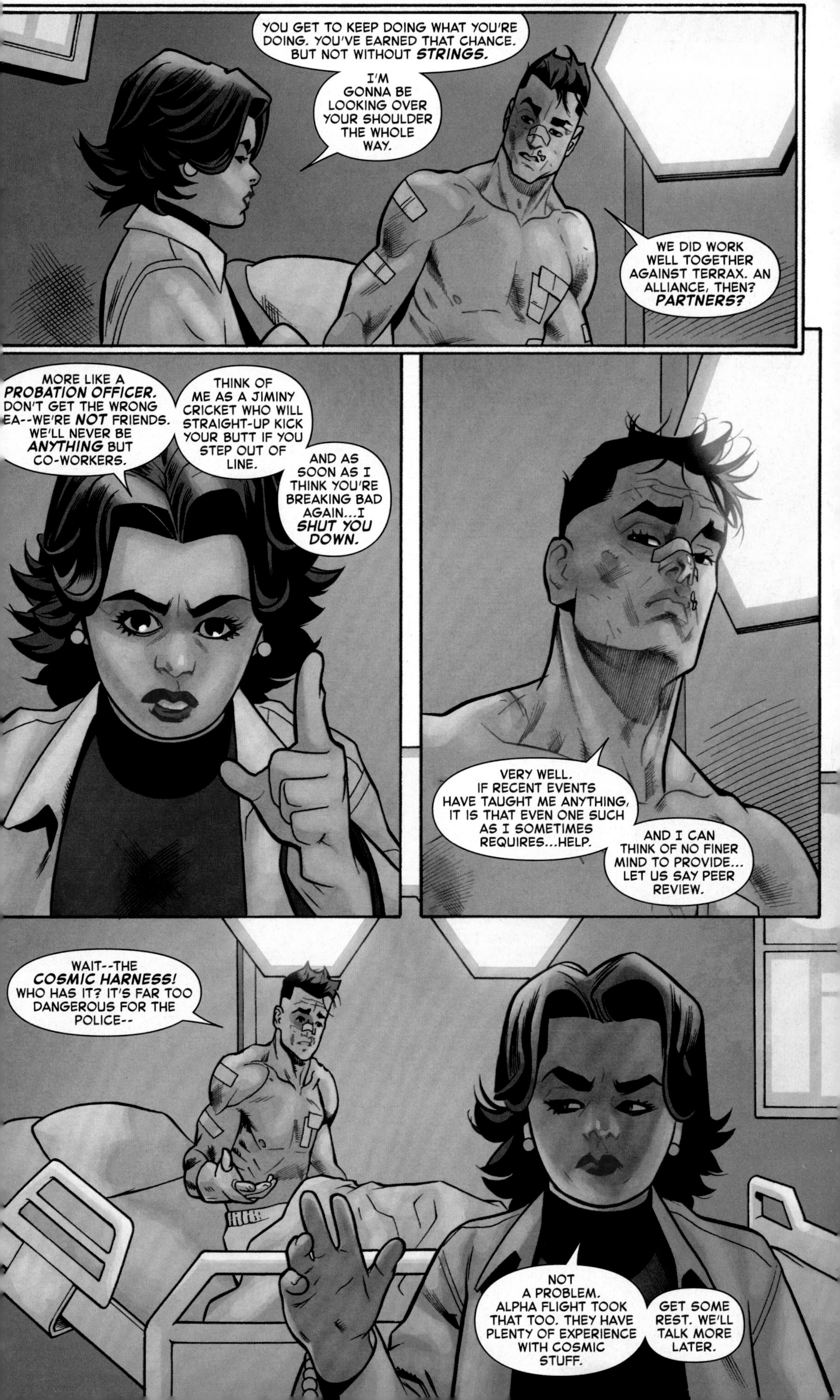
YOU GET TO KEEP DOING WHAT YOU'RE DOING. YOU'VE EARNED THAT CHANCE. BUT NOT WITHOUT STRINGS.
I'M GONNA BE LOOKING OVER YOUR SHOULDER THE WHOLE WAY.
WE DID WORK WELL TOGETHER AGAINST TERRAX. AN ALLIANCE, THEN? PARTNERS?
MORE LIKE A PROBATION OFFICER. DON'T GET THE WRONG EA--WE'RE NOT FRIENDS. WE'LL NEVER BE ANYTHING BUT CO-WORKERS.
THINK OF ME AS A JIMINY CRICKET WHO WILL STRAIGHT-UP KICK YOUR BUTT IF YOU STEP OUT OF LINE.
AND AS SOON AS I THINK YOU'RE BREAKING BAD AGAIN...I SHUT YOU DOWN.
VERY WELL. IF RECENT EVENTS HAVE TAUGHT ME ANYTHING, IT IS THAT EVEN ONE SUCH AS I SOMETIMES REQUIRES...HELP.
AND I CAN THINK OF NO FINER MIND TO PROVIDE... LET US SAY PEER REVIEW.
WAIT--THE COSMIC HARNESS! WHO HAS IT? IT'S FAR TOO DANGEROUS FOR THE POLICE--
NOT A PROBLEM. ALPHA FLIGHT TOOK THAT TOO. THEY HAVE PLENTY OF EXPERIENCE WITH COSMIC STUFF.
GET SOME REST. WE'LL TALK MORE LATER.

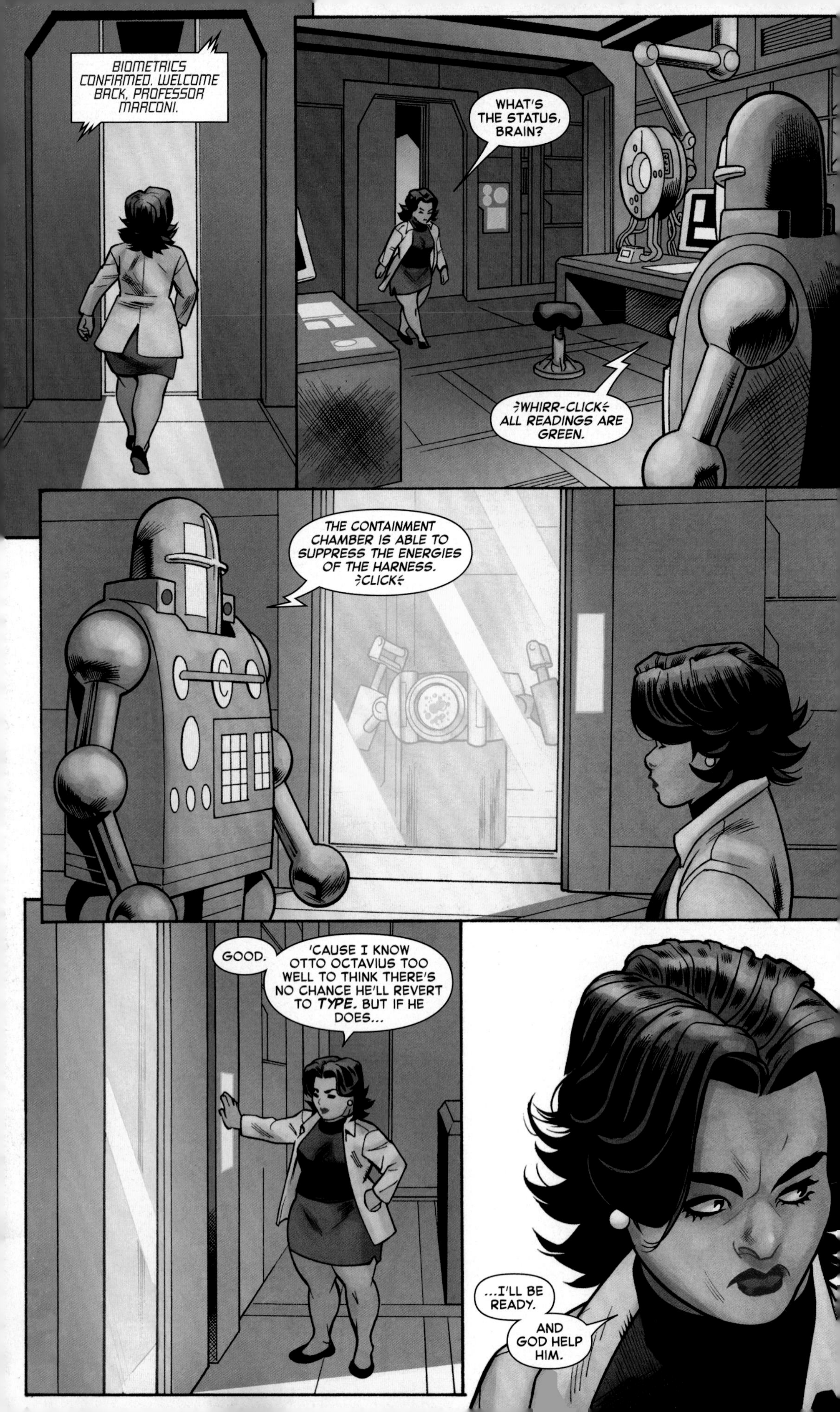
BIOMETRICS CONFIRMED. WELCOME BACK, PROFESSOR MARCONI.
WHAT'S THE STATUS, BRAIN?
≑WHIRR-CLICK≑ ALL READINGS ARE GREEN.
THE CONTAINMENT CHAMBER IS ABLE TO SUPPRESS THE ENERGIES OF THE HARNESS. ≑CLICK≑
GOOD.
'CAUSE I KNOW OTTO OCTAVIUS TOO WELL TO THINK THERE'S NO CHANCE HE'LL REVERT TO *TYPE.* BUT IF HE DOES...
...I'LL BE READY.
AND GOD HELP HIM.

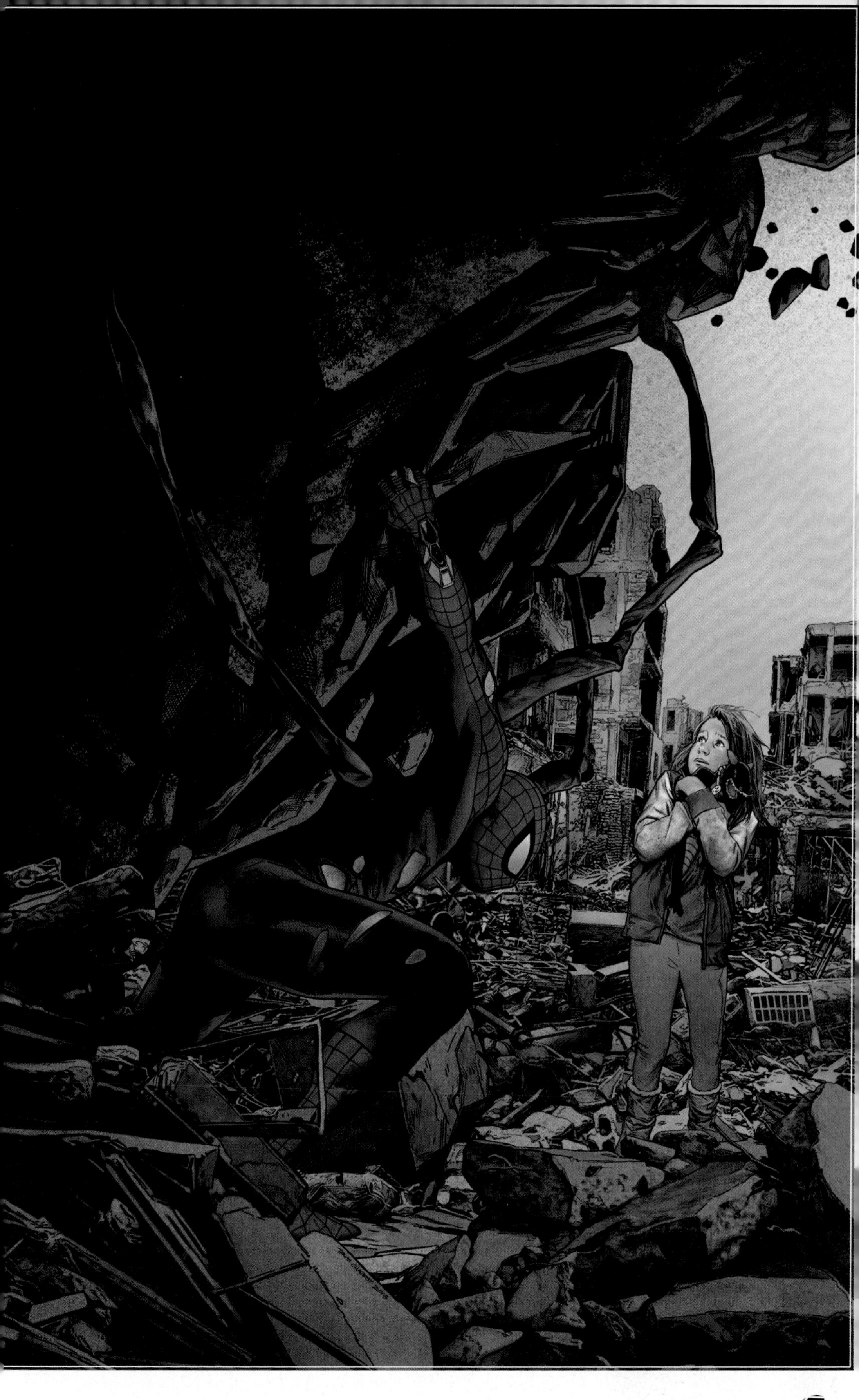

4

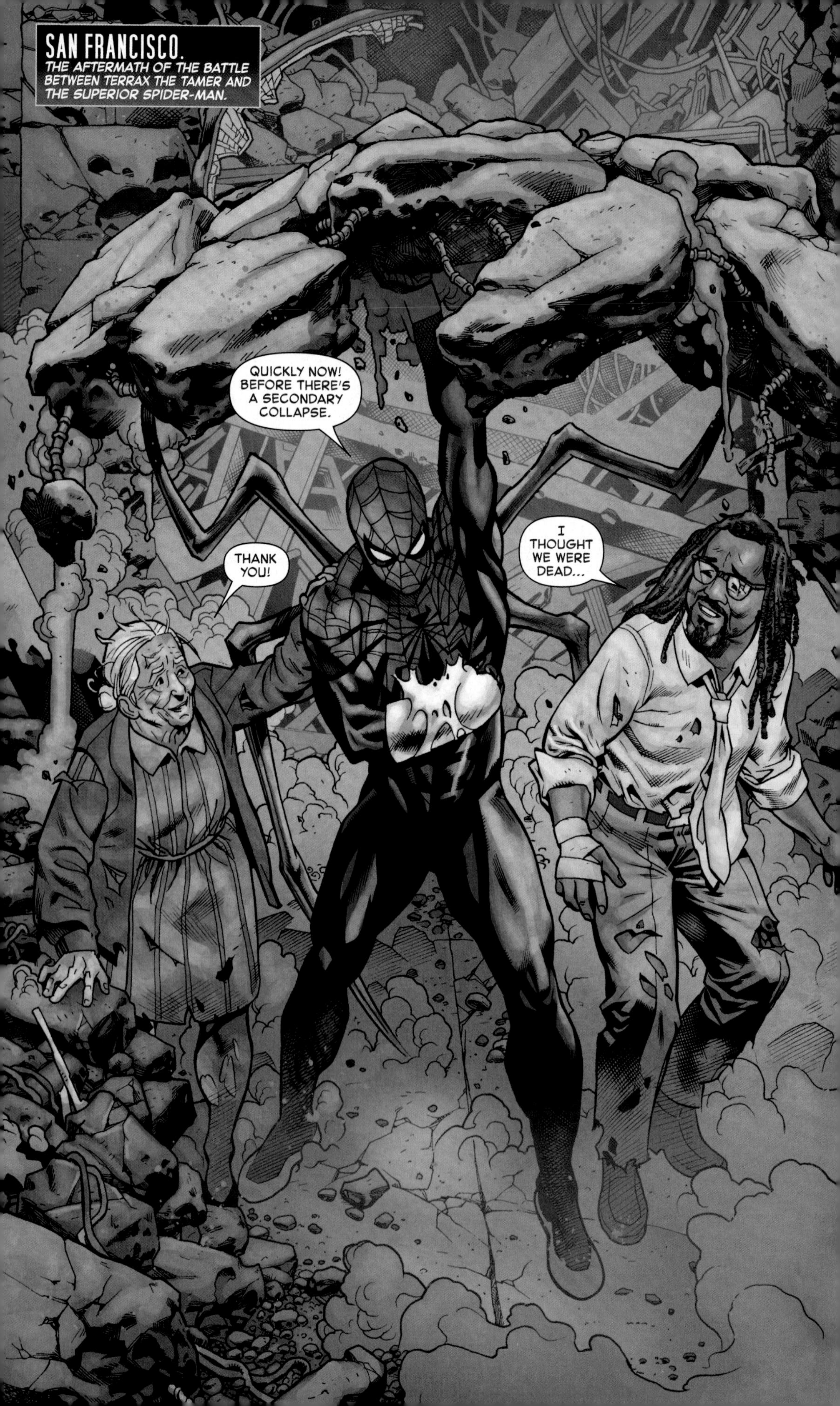
SAN FRANCISCO.
THE AFTERMATH OF THE BATTLE BETWEEN TERRAX THE TAMER AND THE SUPERIOR SPIDER-MAN.
QUICKLY NOW! BEFORE THERE'S A SECONDARY COLLAPSE.
THANK YOU!
I THOUGHT WE WERE DEAD...

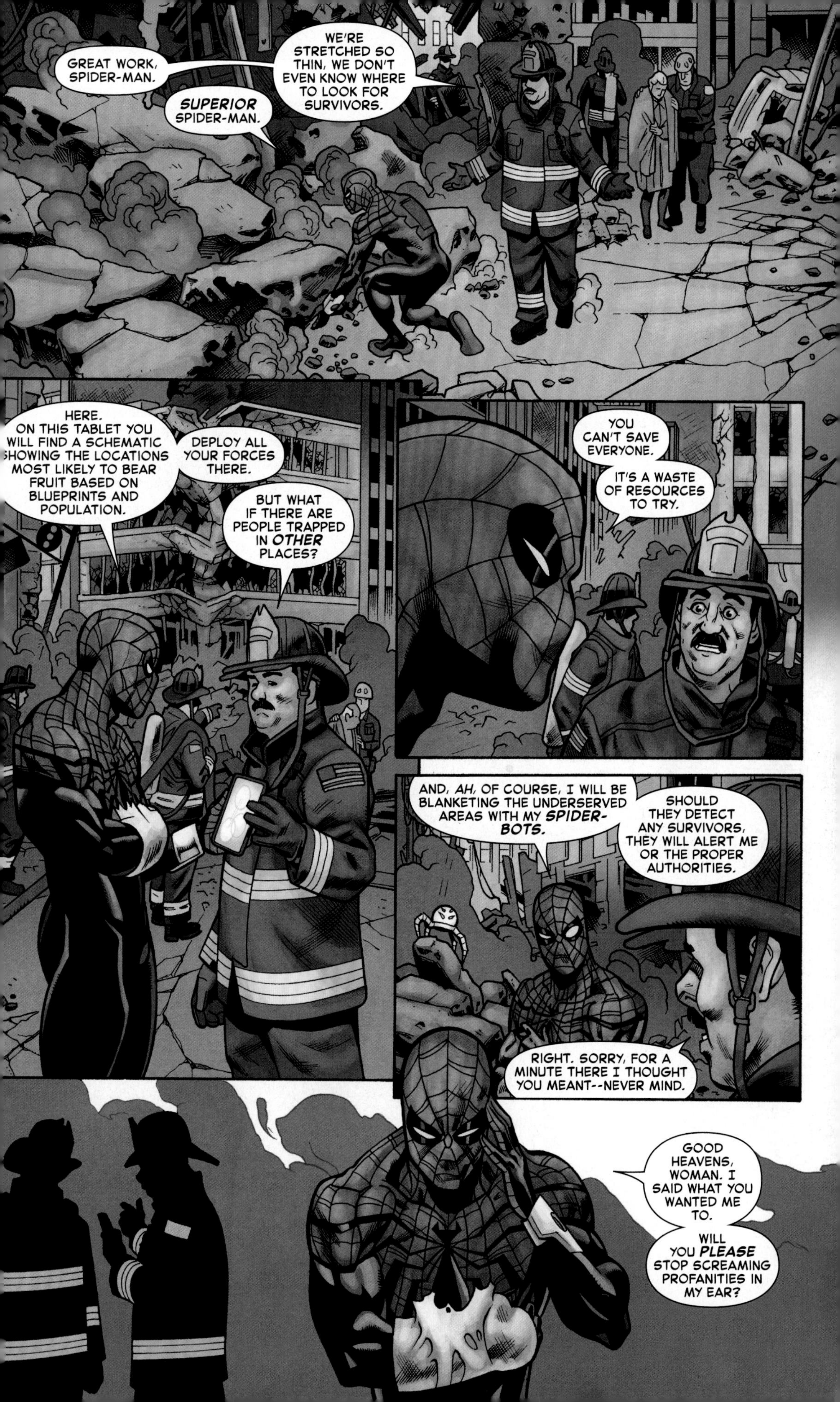
GREAT WORK, SPIDER-MAN.
WE'RE STRETCHED SO THIN, WE DON'T EVEN KNOW WHERE TO LOOK FOR SURVIVORS.
SUPERIOR SPIDER-MAN.
HERE. ON THIS TABLET YOU WILL FIND A SCHEMATIC SHOWING THE LOCATIONS MOST LIKELY TO BEAR FRUIT BASED ON BLUEPRINTS AND POPULATION.
DEPLOY ALL YOUR FORCES THERE.
BUT WHAT IF THERE ARE PEOPLE TRAPPED IN OTHER PLACES?
YOU CAN'T SAVE EVERYONE.
IT'S A WASTE OF RESOURCES TO TRY.
AND, AH, OF COURSE, I WILL BE BLANKETING THE UNDERSERVED AREAS WITH MY SPIDER-BOTS.
SHOULD THEY DETECT ANY SURVIVORS, THEY WILL ALERT ME OR THE PROPER AUTHORITIES.
RIGHT. SORRY, FOR A MINUTE THERE I THOUGHT YOU MEANT--NEVER MIND.
GOOD HEAVENS, WOMAN. I SAID WHAT YOU WANTED ME TO.
WILL YOU PLEASE STOP SCREAMING PROFANITIES IN MY EAR?

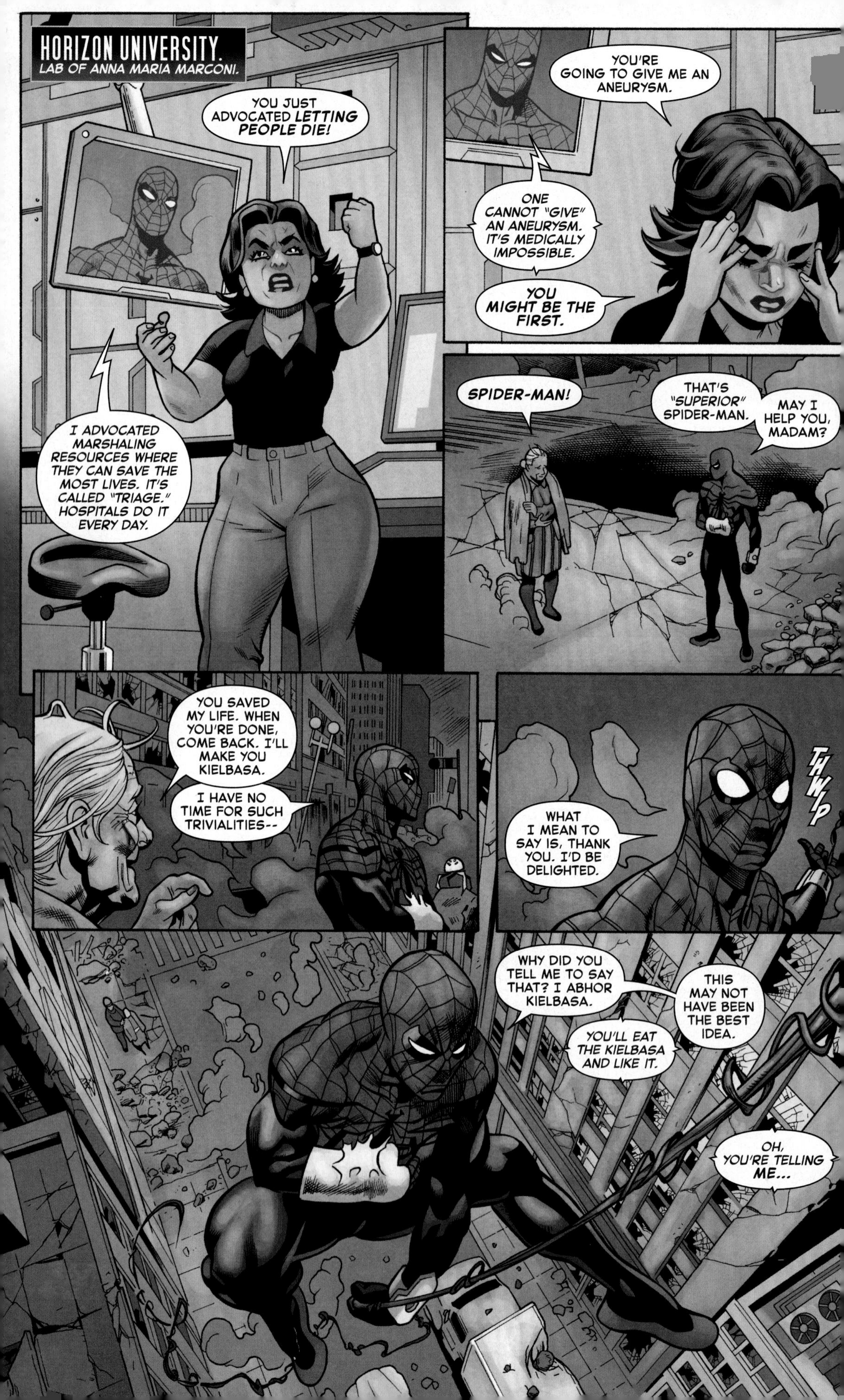
HORIZON UNIVERSITY.
LAB OF ANNA MARIA MARCONI.
YOU JUST ADVOCATED LETTING PEOPLE DIE!
I ADVOCATED MARSHALING RESOURCES WHERE THEY CAN SAVE THE MOST LIVES. IT'S CALLED "TRIAGE." HOSPITALS DO IT EVERY DAY.
YOU'RE GOING TO GIVE ME AN ANEURYSM.
ONE CANNOT "GIVE" AN ANEURYSM. IT'S MEDICALLY IMPOSSIBLE.
YOU MIGHT BE THE FIRST.
SPIDER-MAN!
THAT'S "SUPERIOR" SPIDER-MAN.
MAY I HELP YOU, MADAM?
YOU SAVED MY LIFE. WHEN YOU'RE DONE, COME BACK. I'LL MAKE YOU KIELBASA.
I HAVE NO TIME FOR SUCH TRIVIALITIES--
WHAT I MEAN TO SAY IS, THANK YOU. I'D BE DELIGHTED.
THWIP
WHY DID YOU TELL ME TO SAY THAT? I ABHOR KIELBASA.
THIS MAY NOT HAVE BEEN THE BEST IDEA.
YOU'LL EAT THE KIELBASA AND LIKE IT.
OH, YOU'RE TELLING ME...

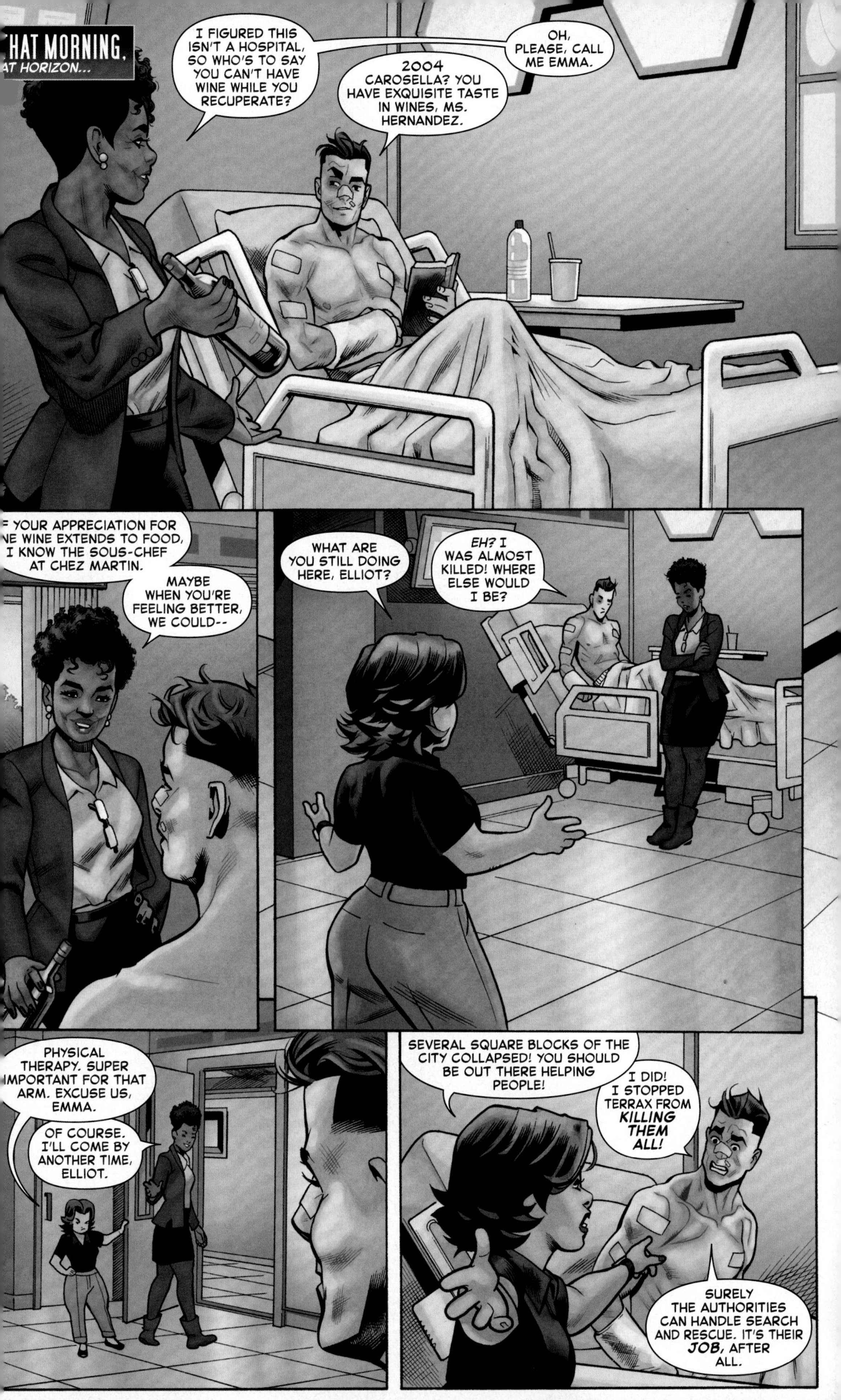

HAT MORNING, AT HORIZON...
I FIGURED THIS ISN'T A HOSPITAL, SO WHO'S TO SAY YOU CAN'T HAVE WINE WHILE YOU RECUPERATE?
2004 CAROSELLA? YOU HAVE EXQUISITE TASTE IN WINES, MS. HERNANDEZ.
OH, PLEASE, CALL ME EMMA.
F YOUR APPRECIATION FOR NE WINE EXTENDS TO FOOD, I KNOW THE SOUS-CHEF AT CHEZ MARTIN.
MAYBE WHEN YOU'RE FEELING BETTER, WE COULD--
WHAT ARE YOU STILL DOING HERE, ELLIOT?
EH? I WAS ALMOST KILLED! WHERE ELSE WOULD I BE?
PHYSICAL THERAPY. SUPER MPORTANT FOR THAT ARM. EXCUSE US, EMMA.
OF COURSE. I'LL COME BY ANOTHER TIME, ELLIOT.
SEVERAL SQUARE BLOCKS OF THE CITY COLLAPSED! YOU SHOULD BE OUT THERE HELPING PEOPLE!
I DID! I STOPPED TERRAX FROM KILLING THEM ALL!
SURELY THE AUTHORITIES CAN HANDLE SEARCH AND RESCUE. IT'S THEIR JOB, AFTER ALL.

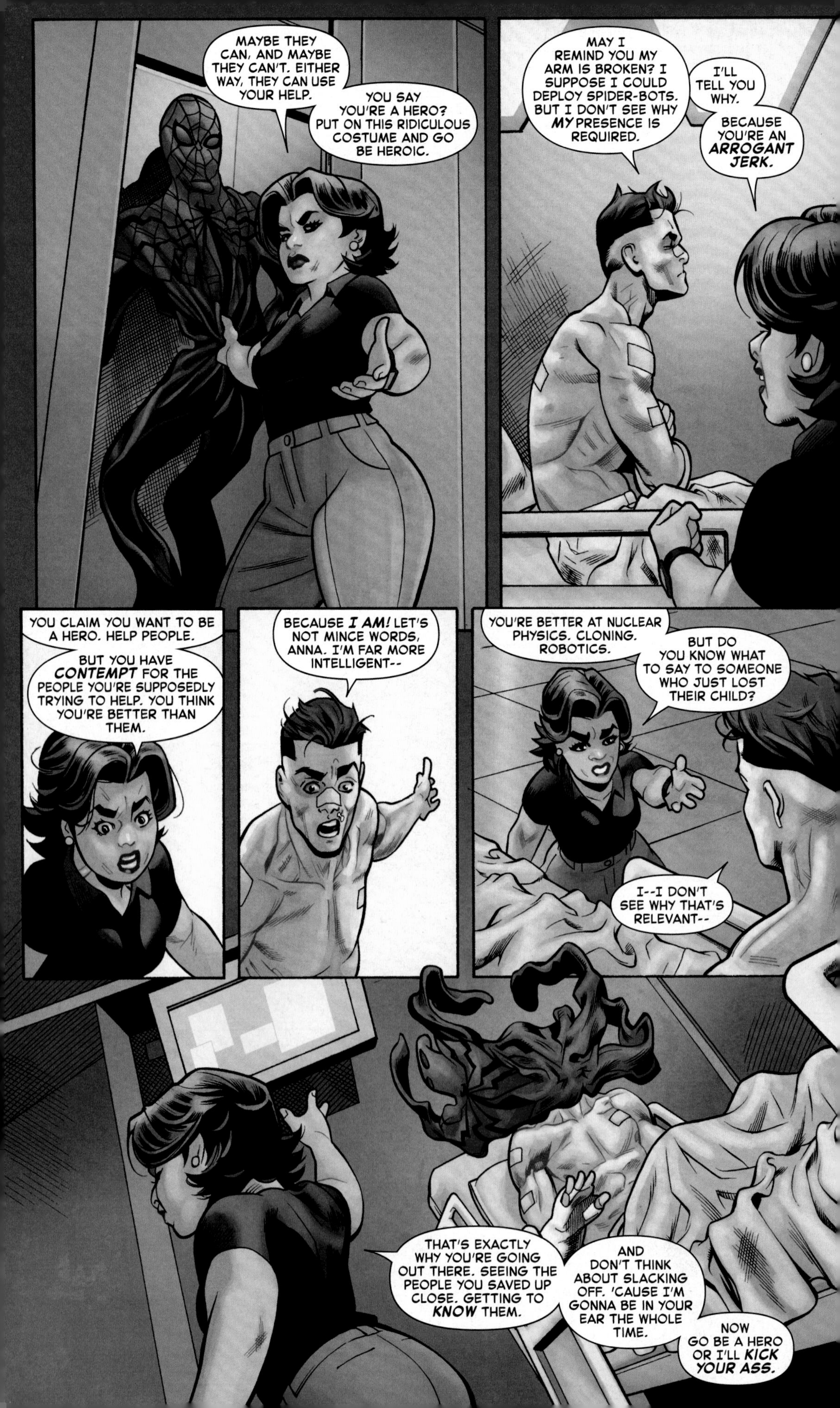
MAYBE THEY CAN, AND MAYBE THEY CAN'T. EITHER WAY, THEY CAN USE YOUR HELP.
YOU SAY YOU'RE A HERO? PUT ON THIS RIDICULOUS COSTUME AND GO BE HEROIC.
MAY I REMIND YOU MY ARM IS BROKEN? I SUPPOSE I COULD DEPLOY SPIDER-BOTS. BUT I DON'T SEE WHY MY PRESENCE IS REQUIRED.
I'LL TELL YOU WHY.
BECAUSE YOU'RE AN ARROGANT JERK.
YOU CLAIM YOU WANT TO BE A HERO. HELP PEOPLE.
BUT YOU HAVE CONTEMPT FOR THE PEOPLE YOU'RE SUPPOSEDLY TRYING TO HELP. YOU THINK YOU'RE BETTER THAN THEM.
BECAUSE I AM! LET'S NOT MINCE WORDS, ANNA. I'M FAR MORE INTELLIGENT--
YOU'RE BETTER AT NUCLEAR PHYSICS. CLONING. ROBOTICS.
BUT DO YOU KNOW WHAT TO SAY TO SOMEONE WHO JUST LOST THEIR CHILD?
I--I DON'T SEE WHY THAT'S RELEVANT--
THAT'S EXACTLY WHY YOU'RE GOING OUT THERE. SEEING THE PEOPLE YOU SAVED UP CLOSE. GETTING TO KNOW THEM.
AND DON'T THINK ABOUT SLACKING OFF. 'CAUSE I'M GONNA BE IN YOUR EAR THE WHOLE TIME.
NOW GO BE A HERO OR I'LL KICK YOUR ASS.

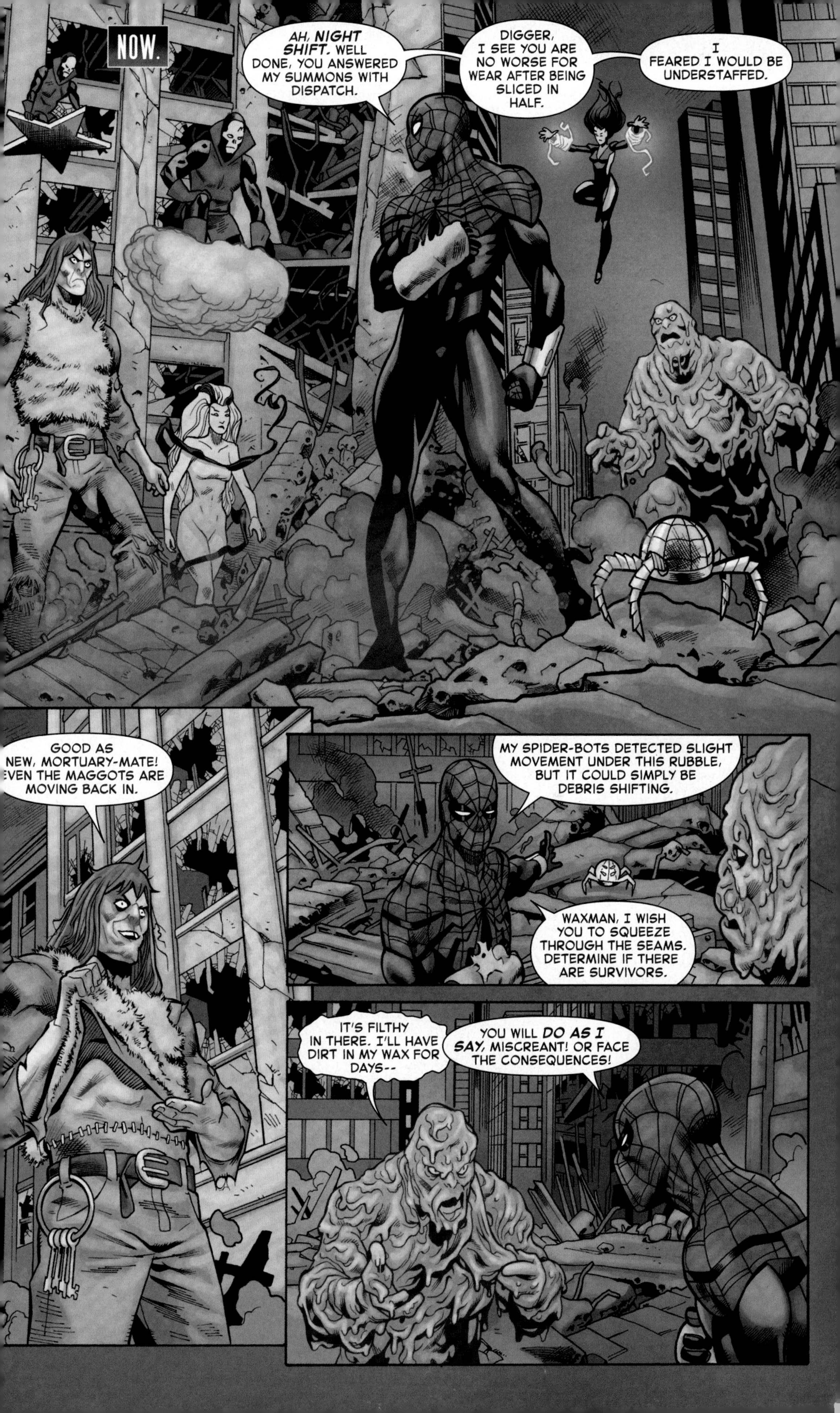
NOW.
AH, NIGHT SHIFT. WELL DONE, YOU ANSWERED MY SUMMONS WITH DISPATCH.
DIGGER, I SEE YOU ARE NO WORSE FOR WEAR AFTER BEING SLICED IN HALF.
I FEARED I WOULD BE UNDERSTAFFED.
GOOD AS NEW, MORTUARY-MATE! EVEN THE MAGGOTS ARE MOVING BACK IN.
MY SPIDER-BOTS DETECTED SLIGHT MOVEMENT UNDER THIS RUBBLE, BUT IT COULD SIMPLY BE DEBRIS SHIFTING.
WAXMAN, I WISH YOU TO SQUEEZE THROUGH THE SEAMS. DETERMINE IF THERE ARE SURVIVORS.
IT'S FILTHY IN THERE. I'LL HAVE DIRT IN MY WAX FOR DAYS--
YOU WILL DO AS I SAY, MISCREANT! OR FACE THE CONSEQUENCES!

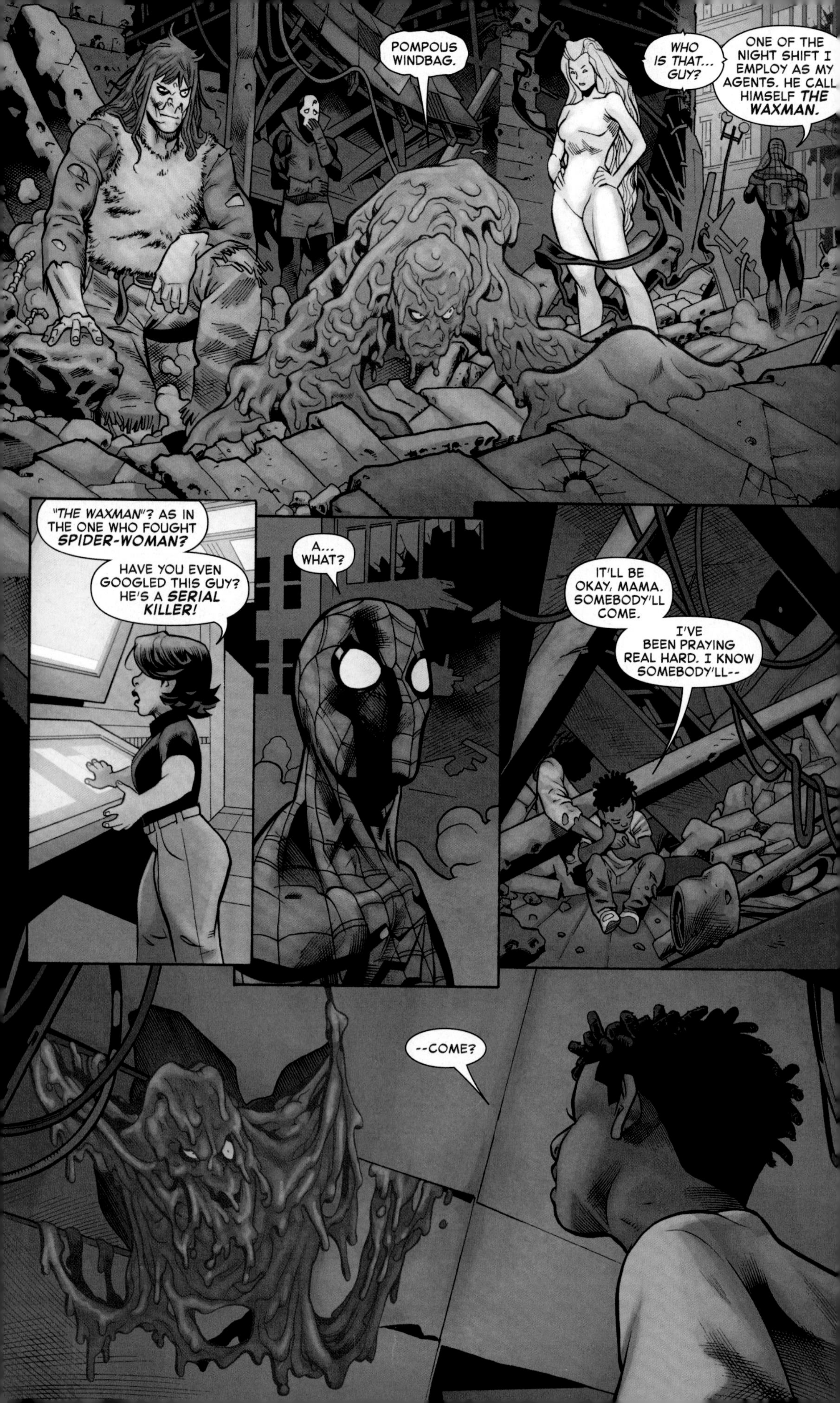
POMPOUS WINDBAG.
WHO IS THAT... GUY?
ONE OF THE NIGHT SHIFT I EMPLOY AS MY AGENTS. HE CALL HIMSELF THE WAXMAN.
"THE WAXMAN"? AS IN THE ONE WHO FOUGHT SPIDER-WOMAN?
HAVE YOU EVEN GOOGLED THIS GUY? HE'S A SERIAL KILLER!
A... WHAT?
IT'LL BE OKAY, MAMA. SOMEBODY'LL COME.
I'VE BEEN PRAYING REAL HARD. I KNOW SOMEBODY'LL--
--COME?

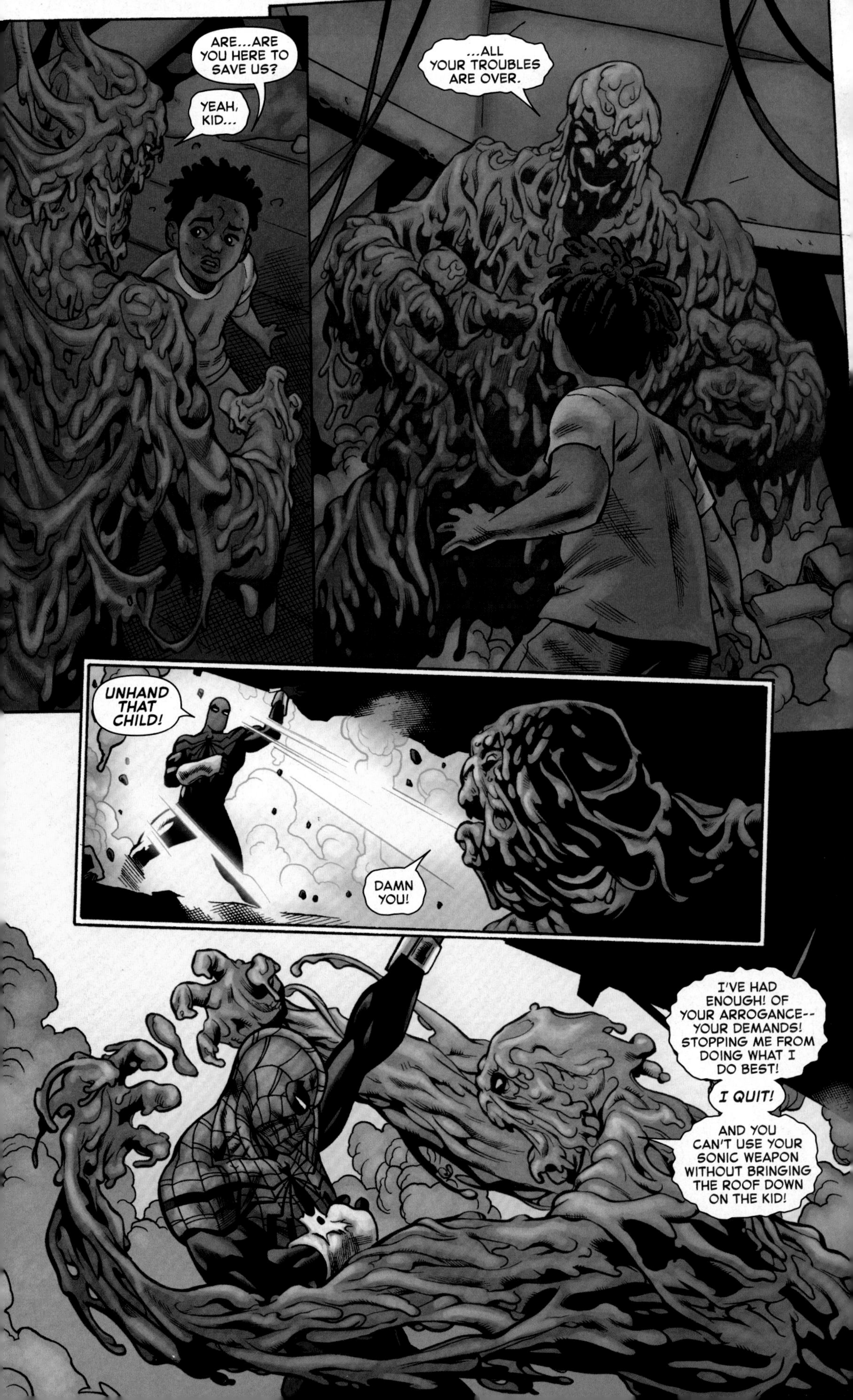

ARE...ARE YOU HERE TO SAVE US?
YEAH, KID...
...ALL YOUR TROUBLES ARE OVER.
UNHAND THAT CHILD!
DAMN YOU!
I'VE HAD ENOUGH! OF YOUR ARROGANCE-- YOUR DEMANDS! STOPPING ME FROM DOING WHAT I DO BEST!
I QUIT!
AND YOU CAN'T USE YOUR SONIC WEAPON WITHOUT BRINGING THE ROOF DOWN ON THE KID!

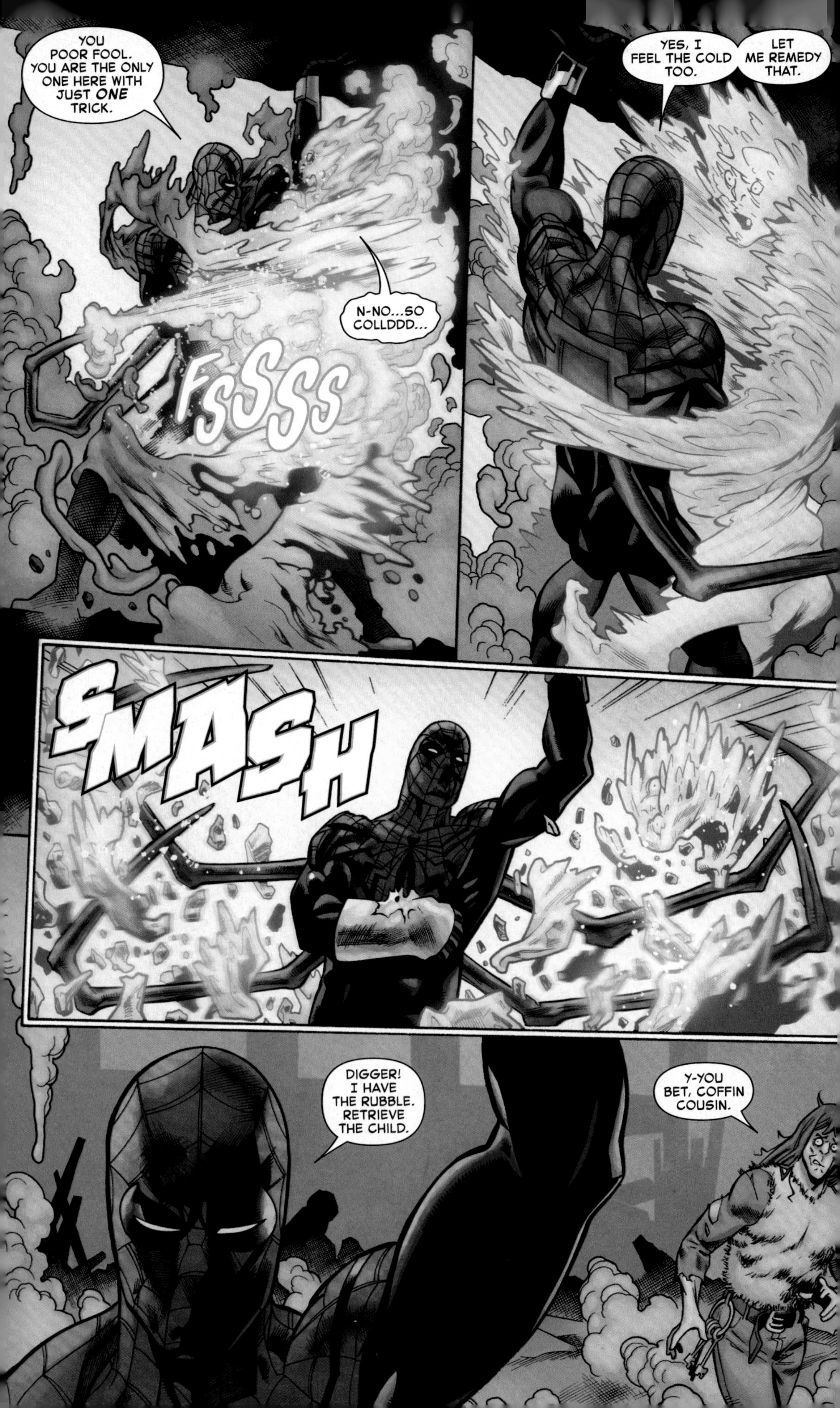
YOU POOR FOOL. YOU ARE THE ONLY ONE HERE WITH JUST ONE TRICK.
N-NO...SO COLLDDD...
FSSSSS
YES, I FEEL THE COLD TOO.
LET ME REMEDY THAT.
SMASH
DIGGER! I HAVE THE RUBBLE. RETRIEVE THE CHILD.
Y-YOU BET, COFFIN COUSIN.

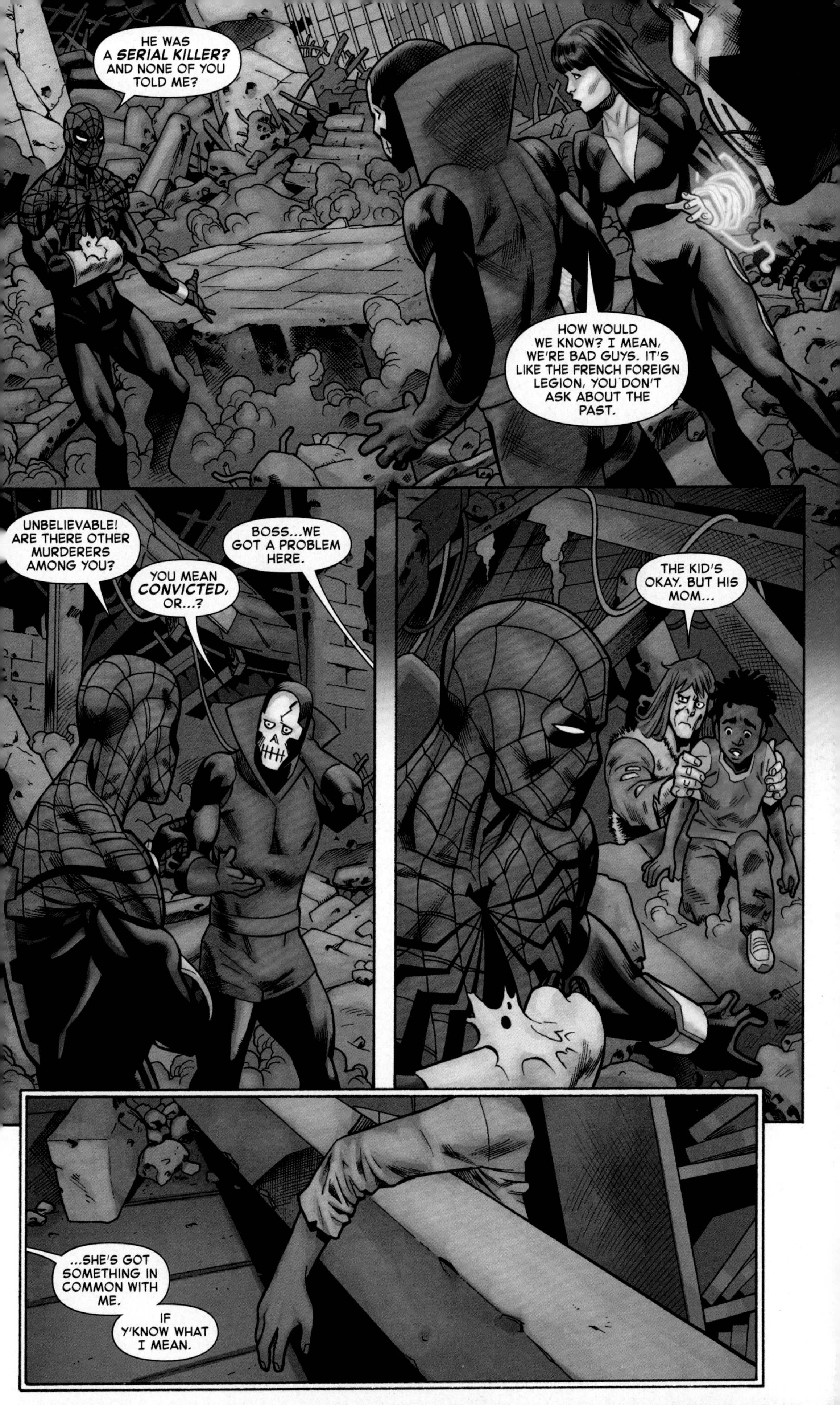
HE WAS A SERIAL KILLER? AND NONE OF YOU TOLD ME?
HOW WOULD WE KNOW? I MEAN, WE'RE BAD GUYS. IT'S LIKE THE FRENCH FOREIGN LEGION, YOU DON'T ASK ABOUT THE PAST.
UNBELIEVABLE! ARE THERE OTHER MURDERERS AMONG YOU?
YOU MEAN CONVICTED, OR...?
BOSS...WE GOT A PROBLEM HERE.
THE KID'S OKAY. BUT HIS MOM...
...SHE'S GOT SOMETHING IN COMMON WITH ME.
IF Y'KNOW WHAT I MEAN.

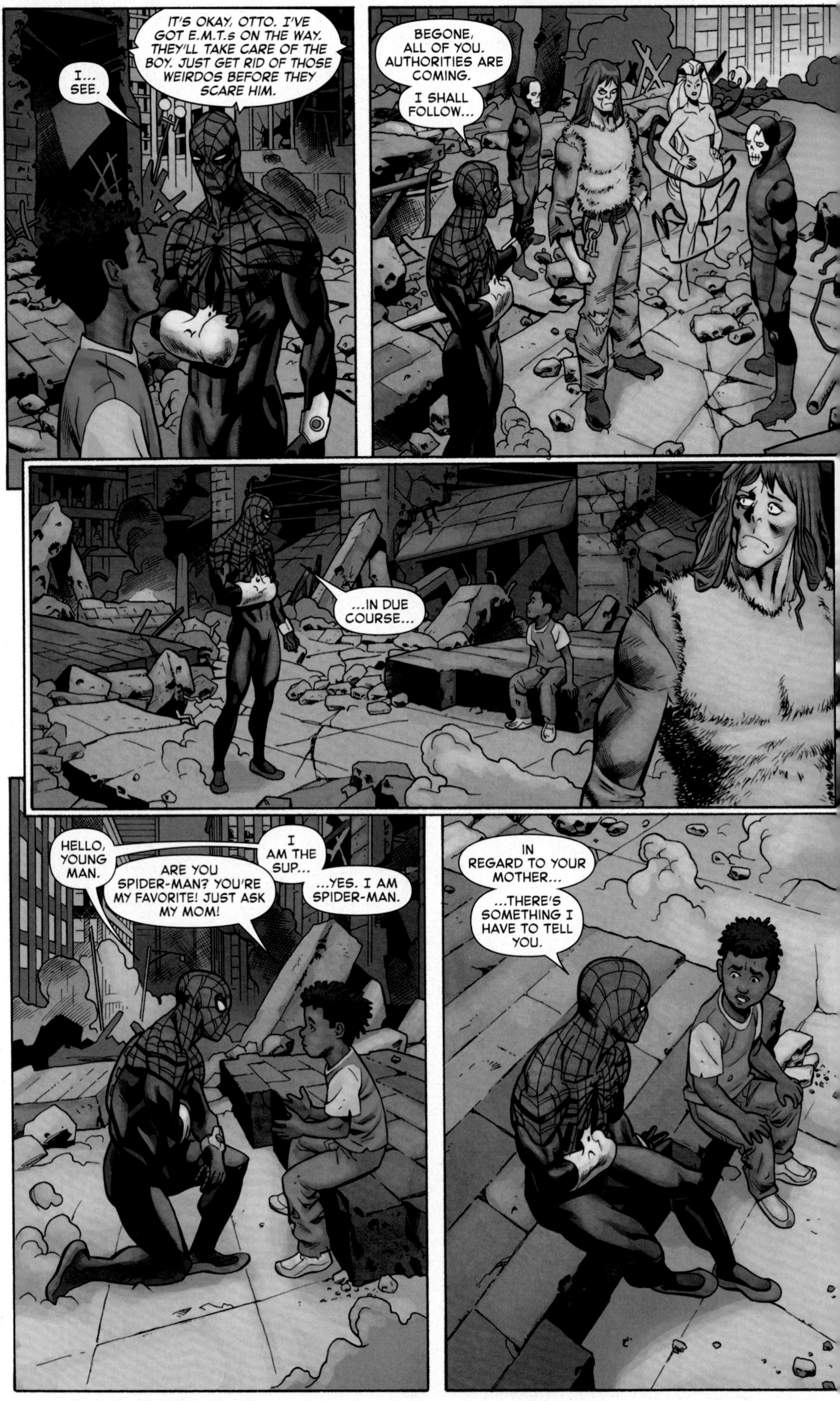
IT'S OKAY, OTTO. I'VE GOT E.M.T.s ON THE WAY. THEY'LL TAKE CARE OF THE BOY. JUST GET RID OF THOSE WEIRDOS BEFORE THEY SCARE HIM.
I... SEE.
BEGONE, ALL OF YOU. AUTHORITIES ARE COMING.
I SHALL FOLLOW...
...IN DUE COURSE...
HELLO, YOUNG MAN.
ARE YOU SPIDER-MAN? YOU'RE MY FAVORITE! JUST ASK MY MOM!
I AM THE SUP...
...YES. I AM SPIDER-MAN.
IN REGARD TO YOUR MOTHER...
...THERE'S SOMETHING I HAVE TO TELL YOU.

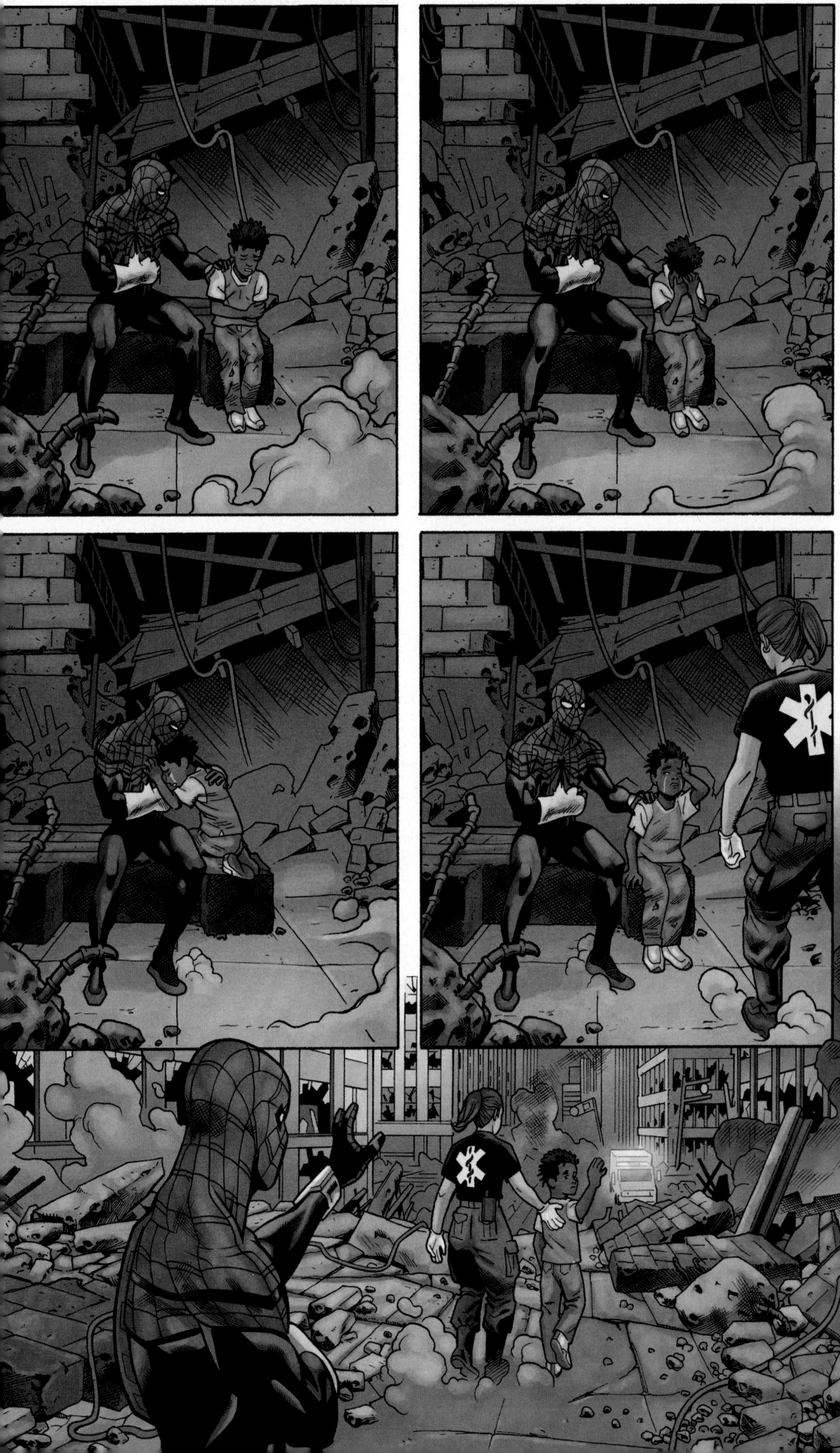

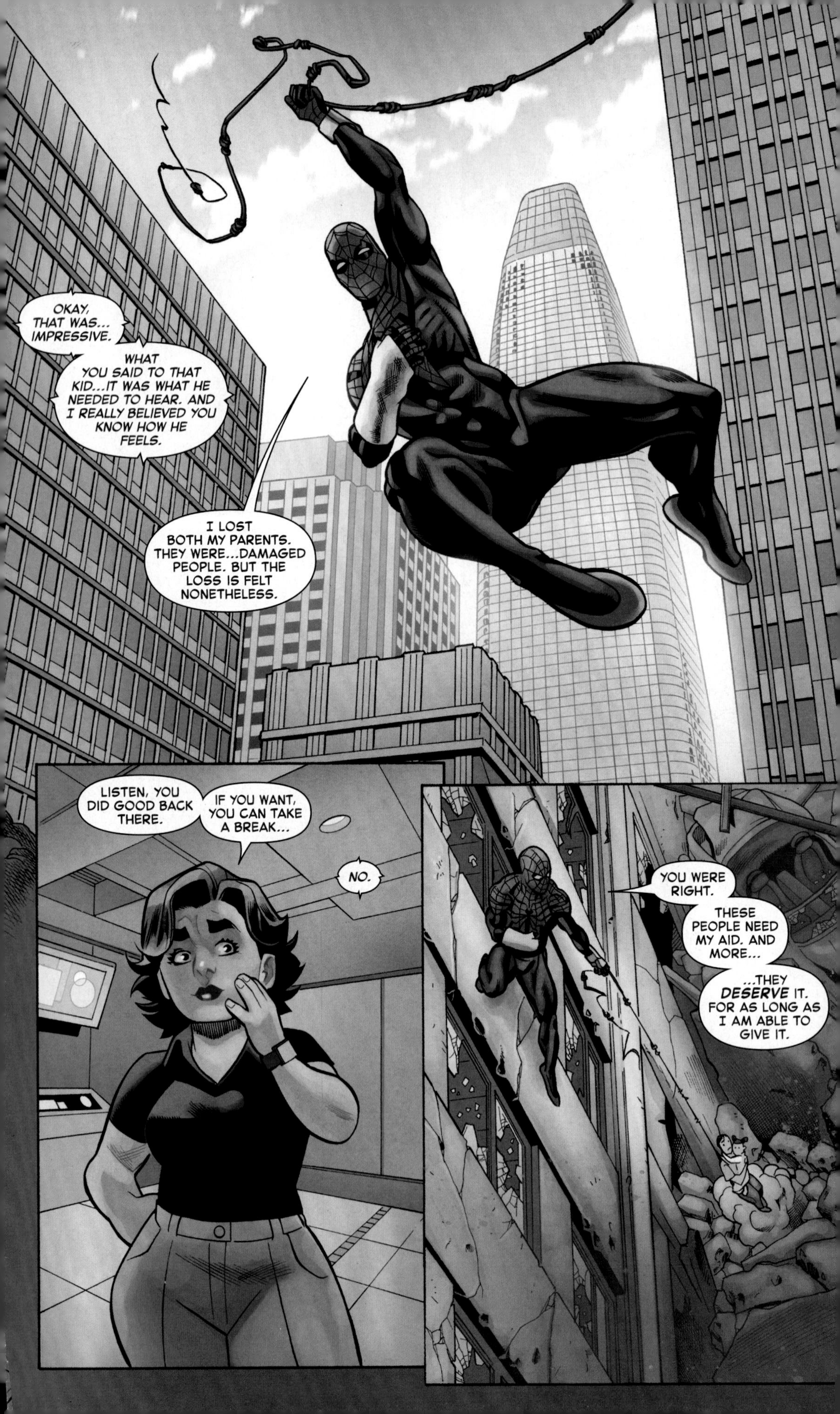

OKAY, THAT WAS... IMPRESSIVE.
WHAT YOU SAID TO THAT KID...IT WAS WHAT HE NEEDED TO HEAR. AND I REALLY BELIEVED YOU KNOW HOW HE FEELS.
I LOST BOTH MY PARENTS. THEY WERE...DAMAGED PEOPLE. BUT THE LOSS IS FELT NONETHELESS.
LISTEN, YOU DID GOOD BACK THERE.
IF YOU WANT, YOU CAN TAKE A BREAK...
NO.
YOU WERE RIGHT.
THESE PEOPLE NEED MY AID. AND MORE...
...THEY *DESERVE* IT. FOR AS LONG AS I AM ABLE TO GIVE IT.

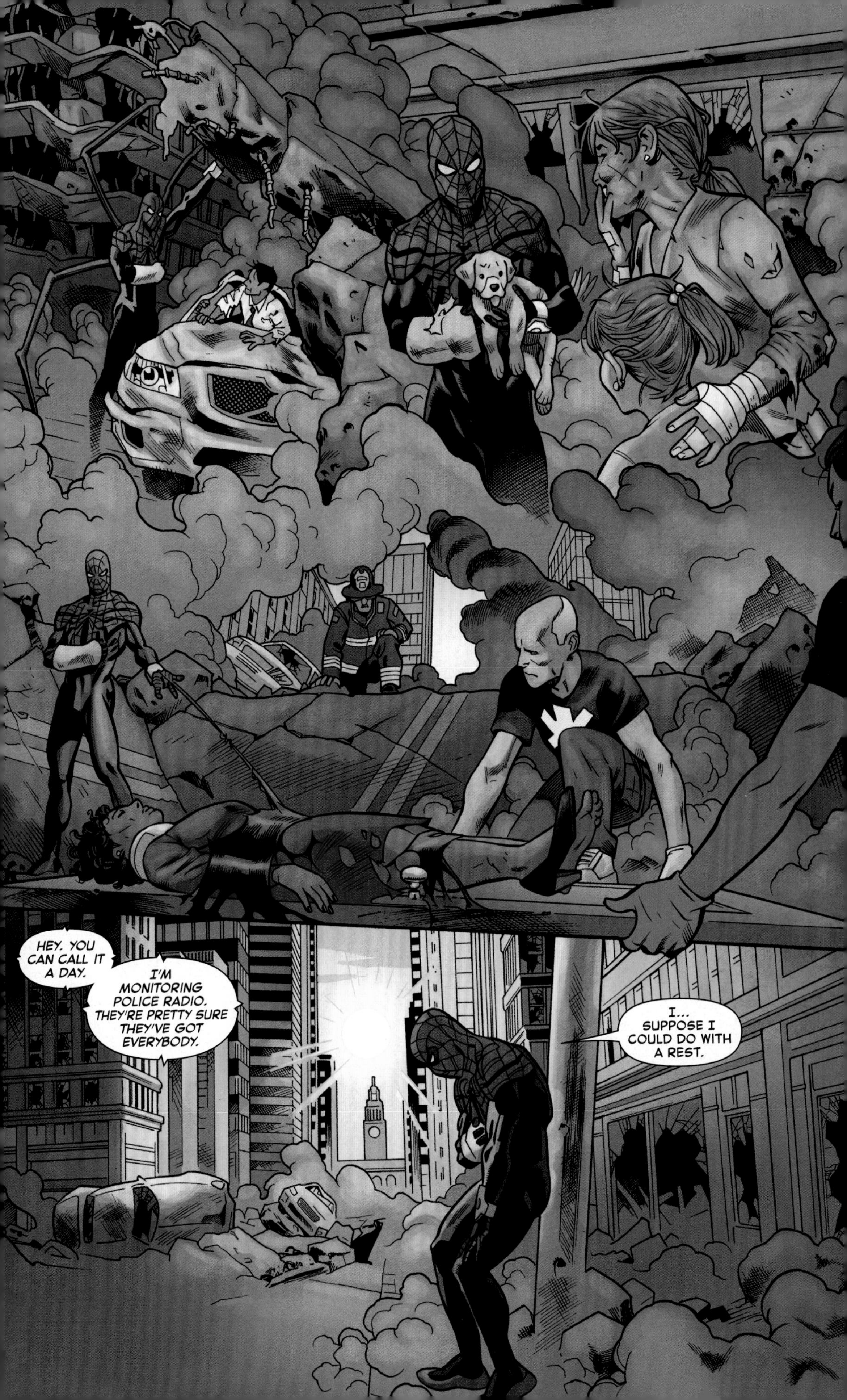
HEY. YOU CAN CALL IT A DAY.
I'M MONITORING POLICE RADIO. THEY'RE PRETTY SURE THEY'VE GOT EVERYBODY.
I... SUPPOSE I COULD DO WITH A REST.

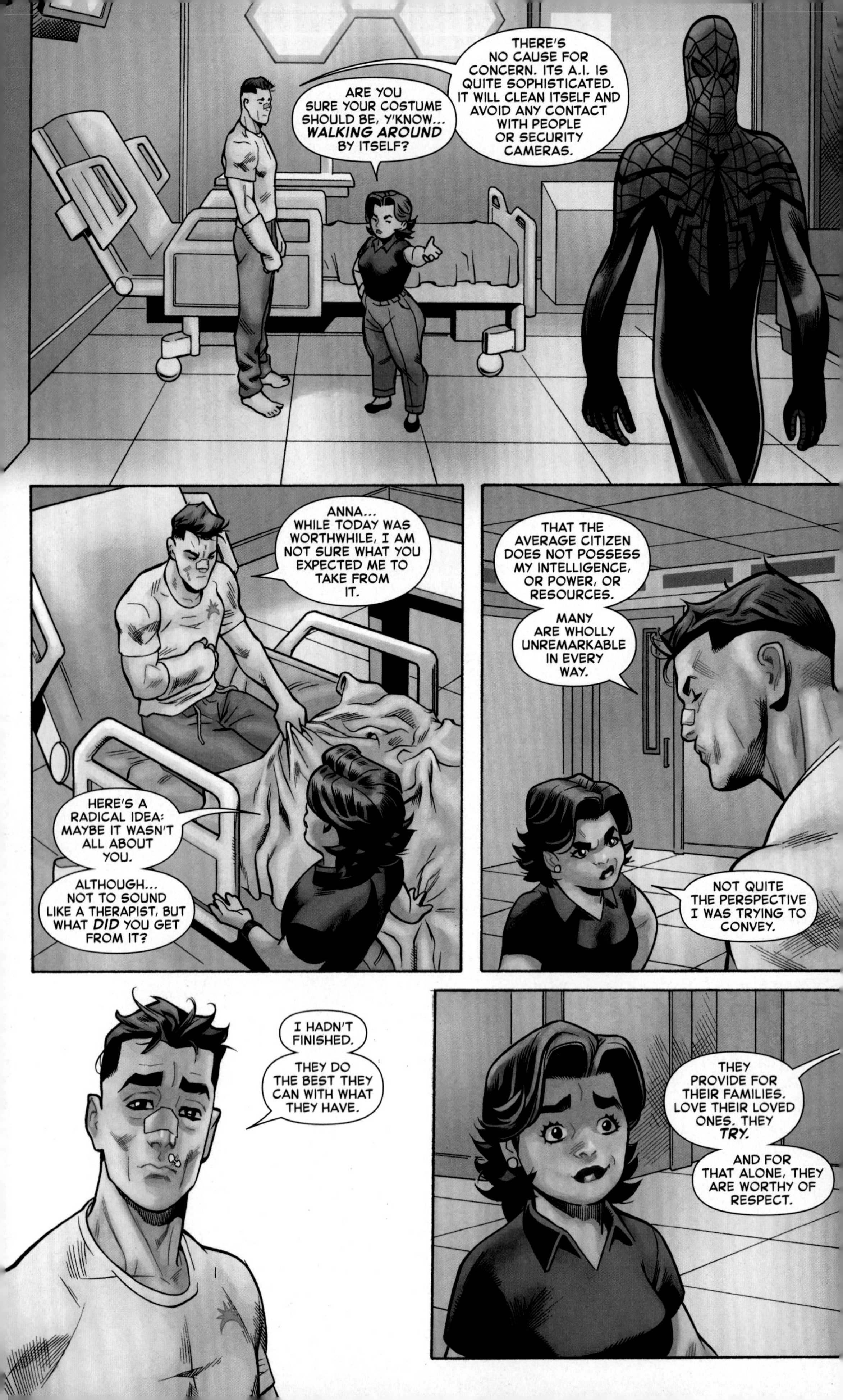
ARE YOU SURE YOUR COSTUME SHOULD BE, Y'KNOW... *WALKING AROUND* BY ITSELF?
THERE'S NO CAUSE FOR CONCERN. ITS A.I. IS QUITE SOPHISTICATED. IT WILL CLEAN ITSELF AND AVOID ANY CONTACT WITH PEOPLE OR SECURITY CAMERAS.
ANNA... WHILE TODAY WAS WORTHWHILE, I AM NOT SURE WHAT YOU EXPECTED ME TO TAKE FROM IT.
HERE'S A RADICAL IDEA: MAYBE IT WASN'T ALL ABOUT YOU.
ALTHOUGH... NOT TO SOUND LIKE A THERAPIST, BUT WHAT *DID* YOU GET FROM IT?
THAT THE AVERAGE CITIZEN DOES NOT POSSESS MY INTELLIGENCE, OR POWER, OR RESOURCES.
MANY ARE WHOLLY UNREMARKABLE IN EVERY WAY.
NOT QUITE THE PERSPECTIVE I WAS TRYING TO CONVEY.
I HADN'T FINISHED.
THEY DO THE BEST THEY CAN WITH WHAT THEY HAVE.
THEY PROVIDE FOR THEIR FAMILIES. LOVE THEIR LOVED ONES. THEY *TRY.*
AND FOR THAT ALONE, THEY ARE WORTHY OF RESPECT.

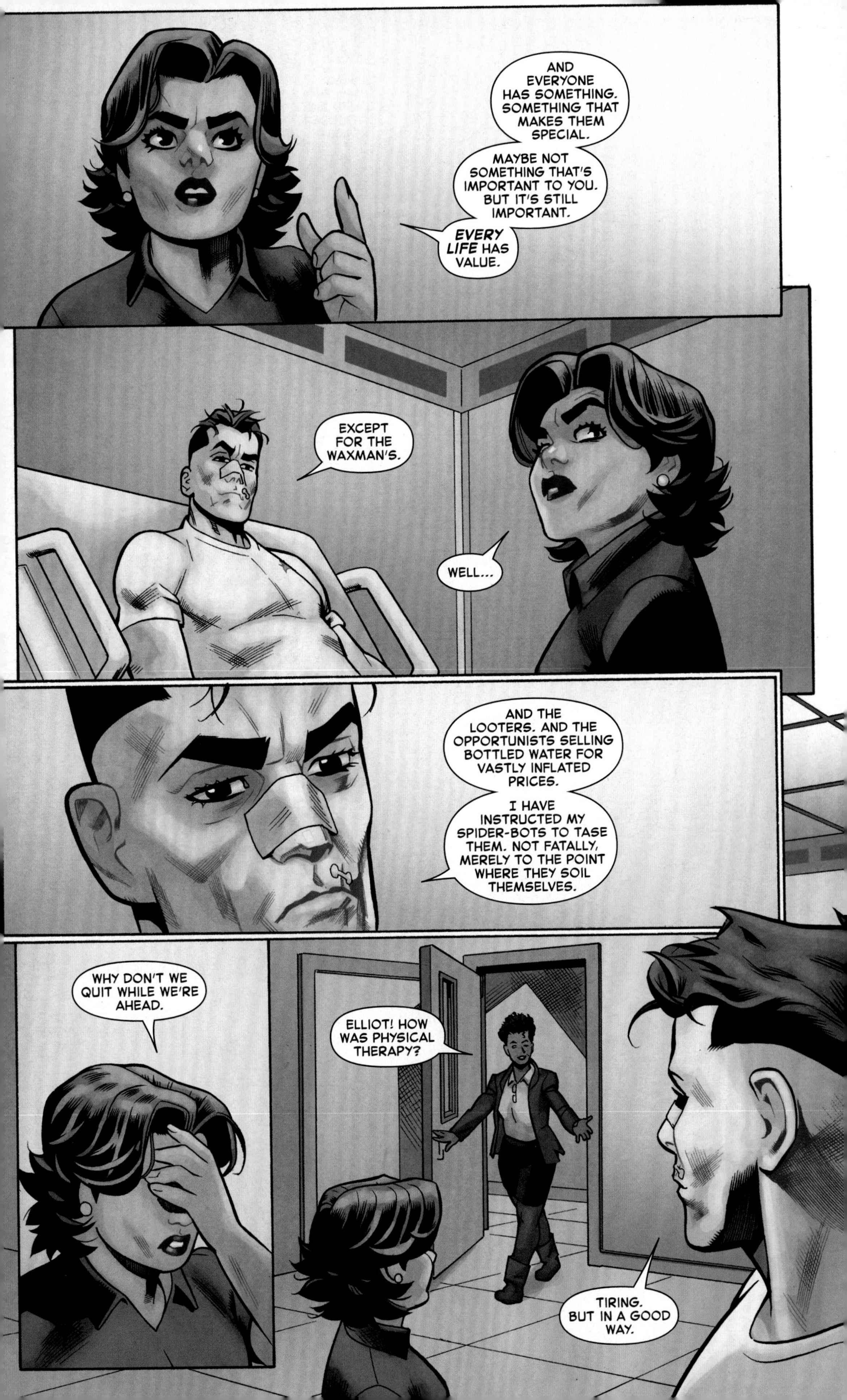
AND EVERYONE HAS SOMETHING. SOMETHING THAT MAKES THEM SPECIAL.
MAYBE NOT SOMETHING THAT'S IMPORTANT TO YOU. BUT IT'S STILL IMPORTANT.
EVERY LIFE HAS VALUE.
EXCEPT FOR THE WAXMAN'S.
WELL...
AND THE LOOTERS. AND THE OPPORTUNISTS SELLING BOTTLED WATER FOR VASTLY INFLATED PRICES.
I HAVE INSTRUCTED MY SPIDER-BOTS TO TASE THEM. NOT FATALLY, MERELY TO THE POINT WHERE THEY SOIL THEMSELVES.
WHY DON'T WE QUIT WHILE WE'RE AHEAD.
ELLIOT! HOW WAS PHYSICAL THERAPY?
TIRING. BUT IN A GOOD WAY.

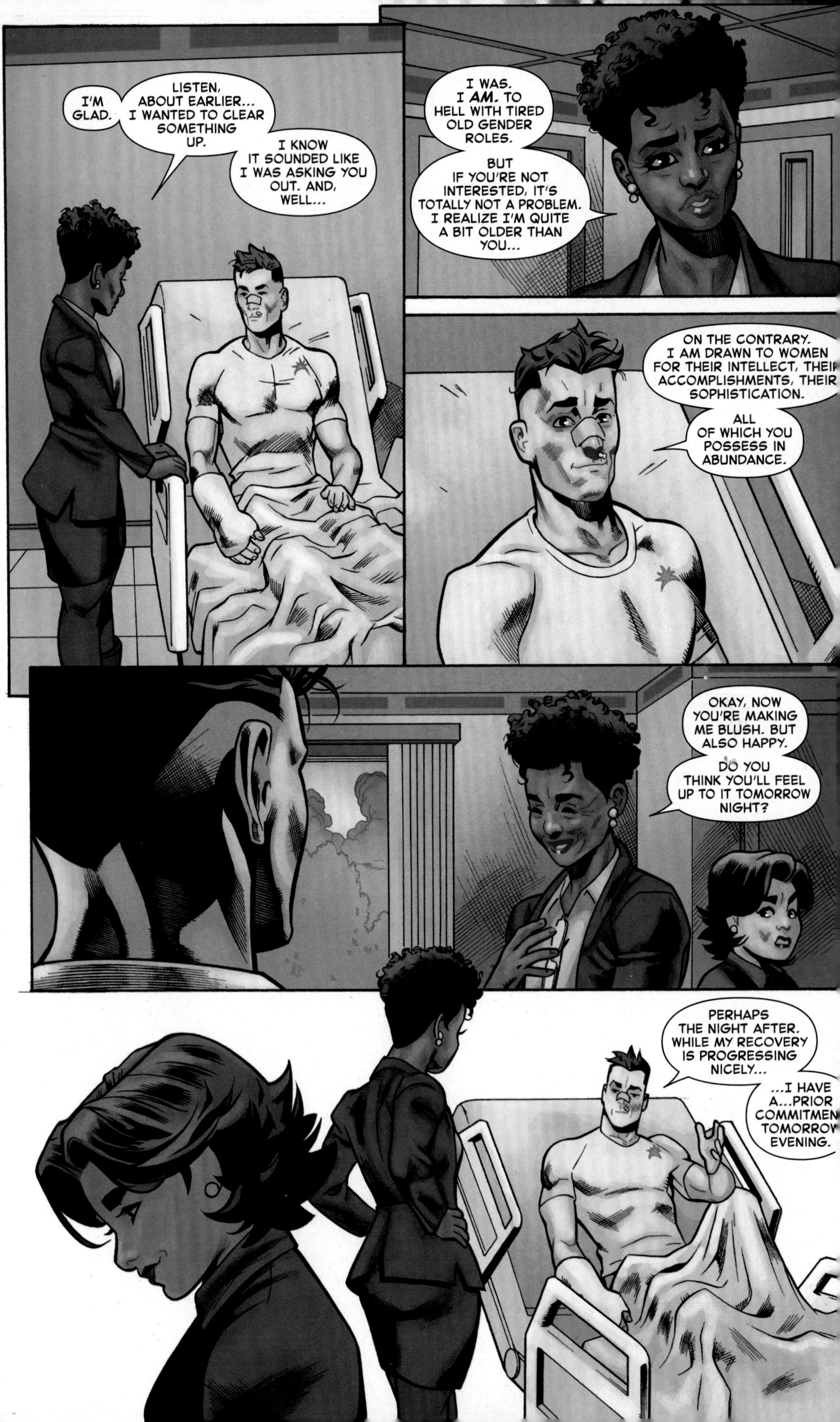
LISTEN, ABOUT EARLIER... I WANTED TO CLEAR SOMETHING UP.
I'M GLAD.
I KNOW IT SOUNDED LIKE I WAS ASKING YOU OUT. AND, WELL...
I WAS. I AM. TO HELL WITH TIRED OLD GENDER ROLES.
BUT IF YOU'RE NOT INTERESTED, IT'S TOTALLY NOT A PROBLEM. I REALIZE I'M QUITE A BIT OLDER THAN YOU...
ON THE CONTRARY. I AM DRAWN TO WOMEN FOR THEIR INTELLECT, THEIR ACCOMPLISHMENTS, THEIR SOPHISTICATION.
ALL OF WHICH YOU POSSESS IN ABUNDANCE.
OKAY, NOW YOU'RE MAKING ME BLUSH. BUT ALSO HAPPY.
DO YOU THINK YOU'LL FEEL UP TO IT TOMORROW NIGHT?
PERHAPS THE NIGHT AFTER. WHILE MY RECOVERY IS PROGRESSING NICELY...
...I HAVE A...PRIOR COMMITMENT TOMORROW EVENING.

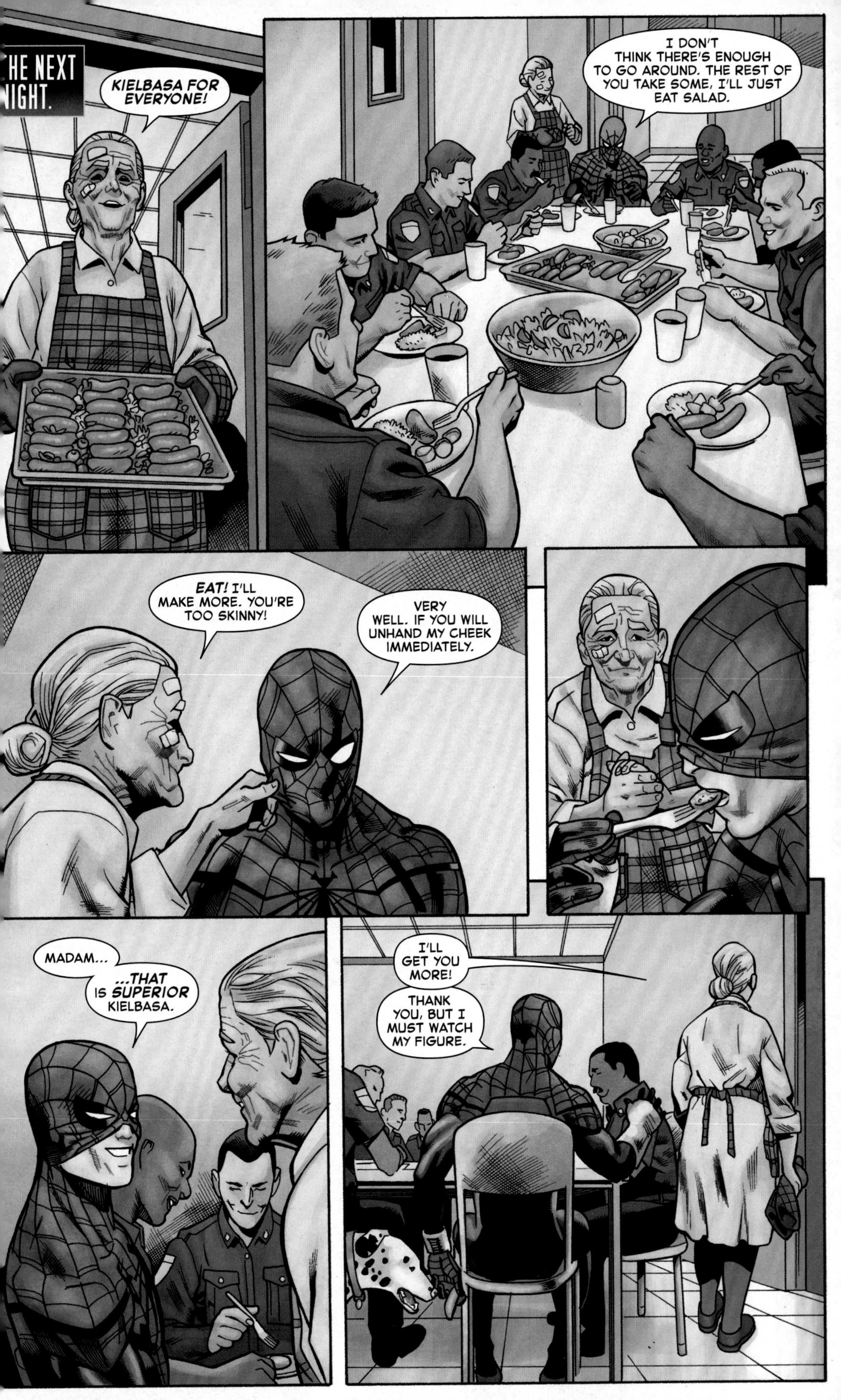
THE NEXT NIGHT.
KIELBASA FOR EVERYONE!
I DON'T THINK THERE'S ENOUGH TO GO AROUND. THE REST OF YOU TAKE SOME, I'LL JUST EAT SALAD.
EAT! I'LL MAKE MORE. YOU'RE TOO SKINNY!
VERY WELL. IF YOU WILL UNHAND MY CHEEK IMMEDIATELY.
MADAM...
...THAT IS SUPERIOR KIELBASA.
I'LL GET YOU MORE!
THANK YOU, BUT I MUST WATCH MY FIGURE.

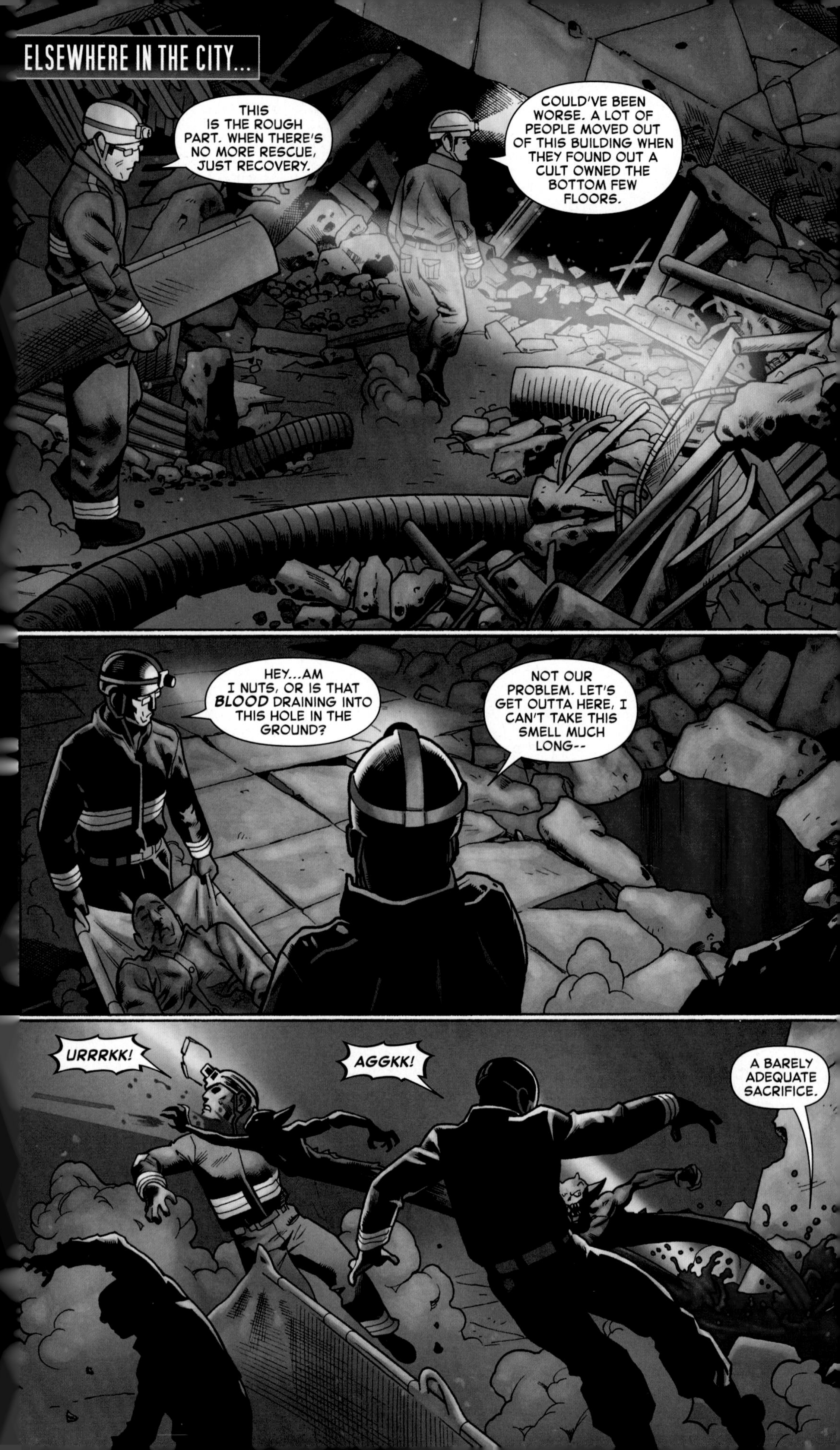
ELSEWHERE IN THE CITY...
THIS IS THE ROUGH PART. WHEN THERE'S NO MORE RESCUE, JUST RECOVERY.
COULD'VE BEEN WORSE. A LOT OF PEOPLE MOVED OUT OF THIS BUILDING WHEN THEY FOUND OUT A CULT OWNED THE BOTTOM FEW FLOORS.
HEY...AM I NUTS, OR IS THAT *BLOOD* DRAINING INTO THIS HOLE IN THE GROUND?
NOT OUR PROBLEM. LET'S GET OUTTA HERE, I CAN'T TAKE THIS SMELL MUCH LONG--
URRRKK!
AGGKK!
A BARELY ADEQUATE SACRIFICE.

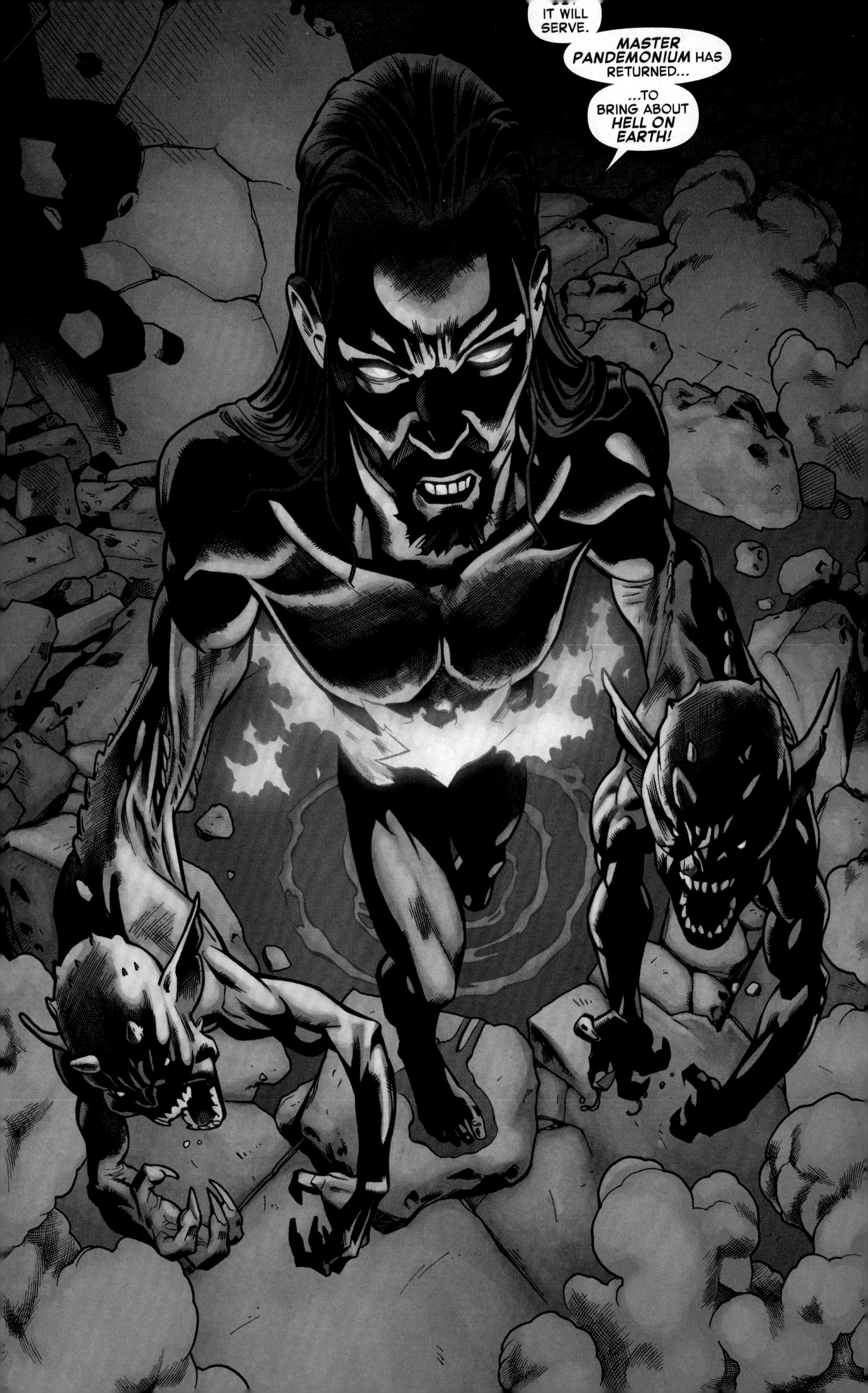
IT WILL SERVE.
MASTER PANDEMONIUM HAS RETURNED...
...TO BRING ABOUT HELL ON EARTH!

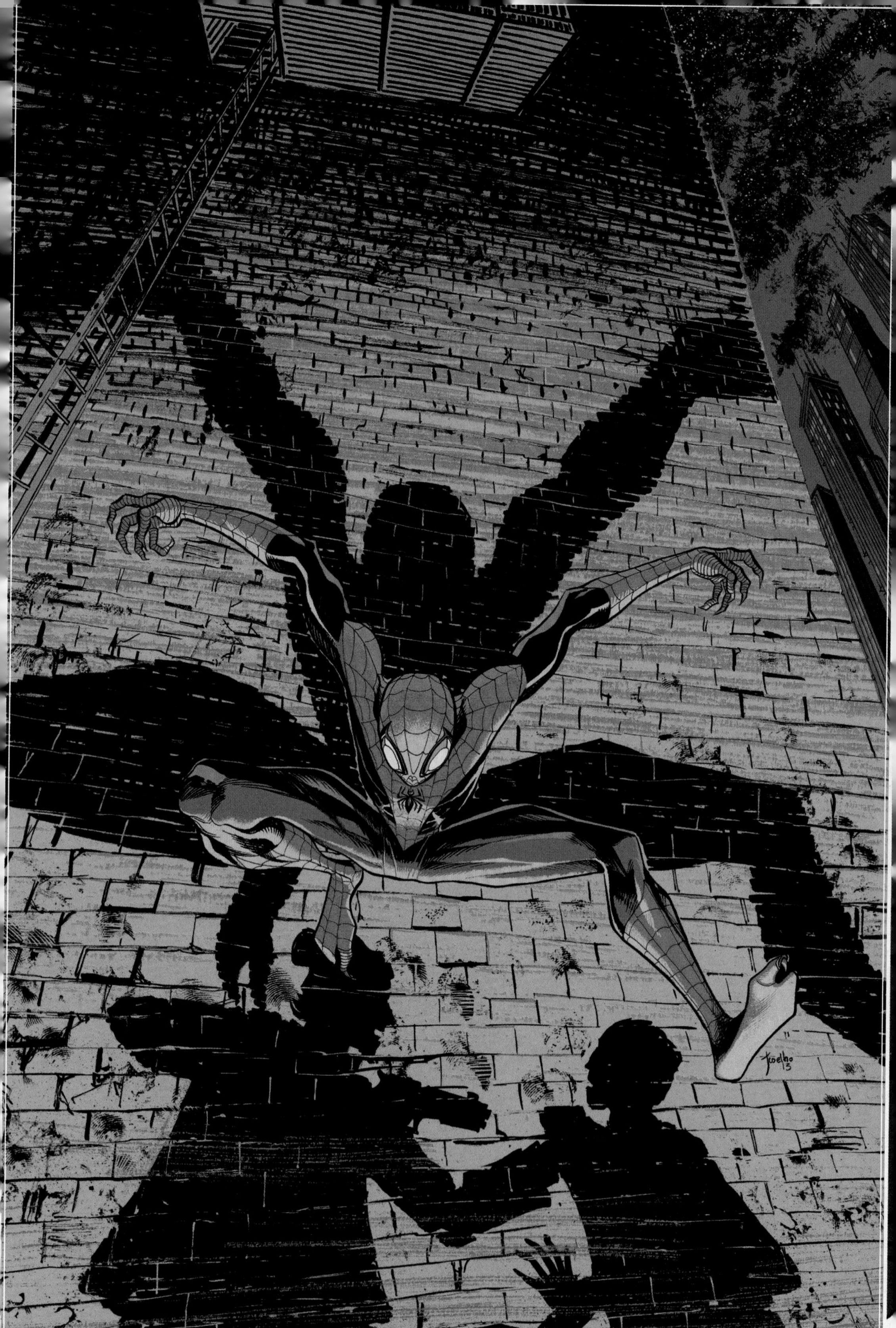

5

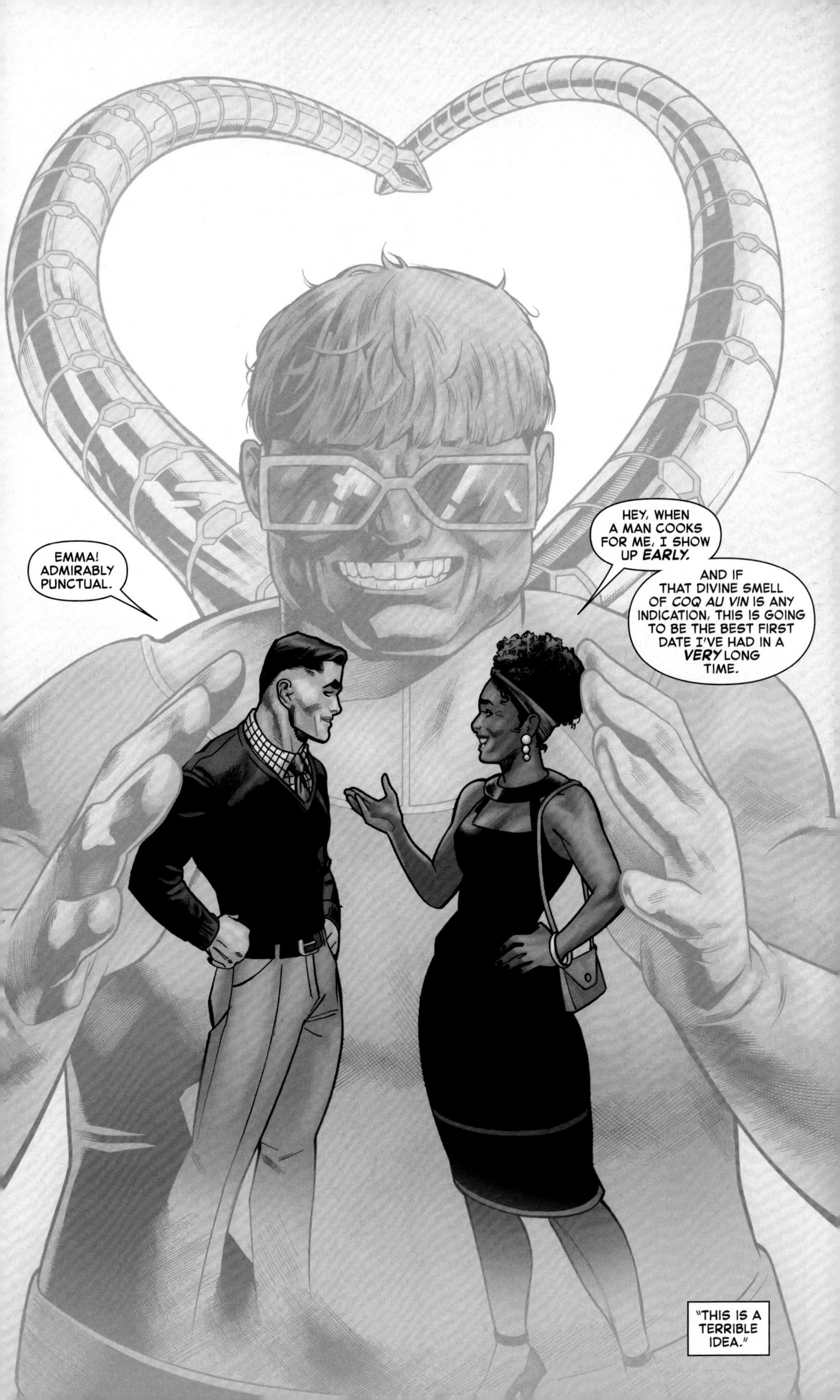
EMMA! ADMIRABLY PUNCTUAL.
HEY, WHEN A MAN COOKS FOR ME, I SHOW UP EARLY.
AND IF THAT DIVINE SMELL OF COQ AU VIN IS ANY INDICATION, THIS IS GOING TO BE THE BEST FIRST DATE I'VE HAD IN A VERY LONG TIME.
"THIS IS A TERRIBLE IDEA."

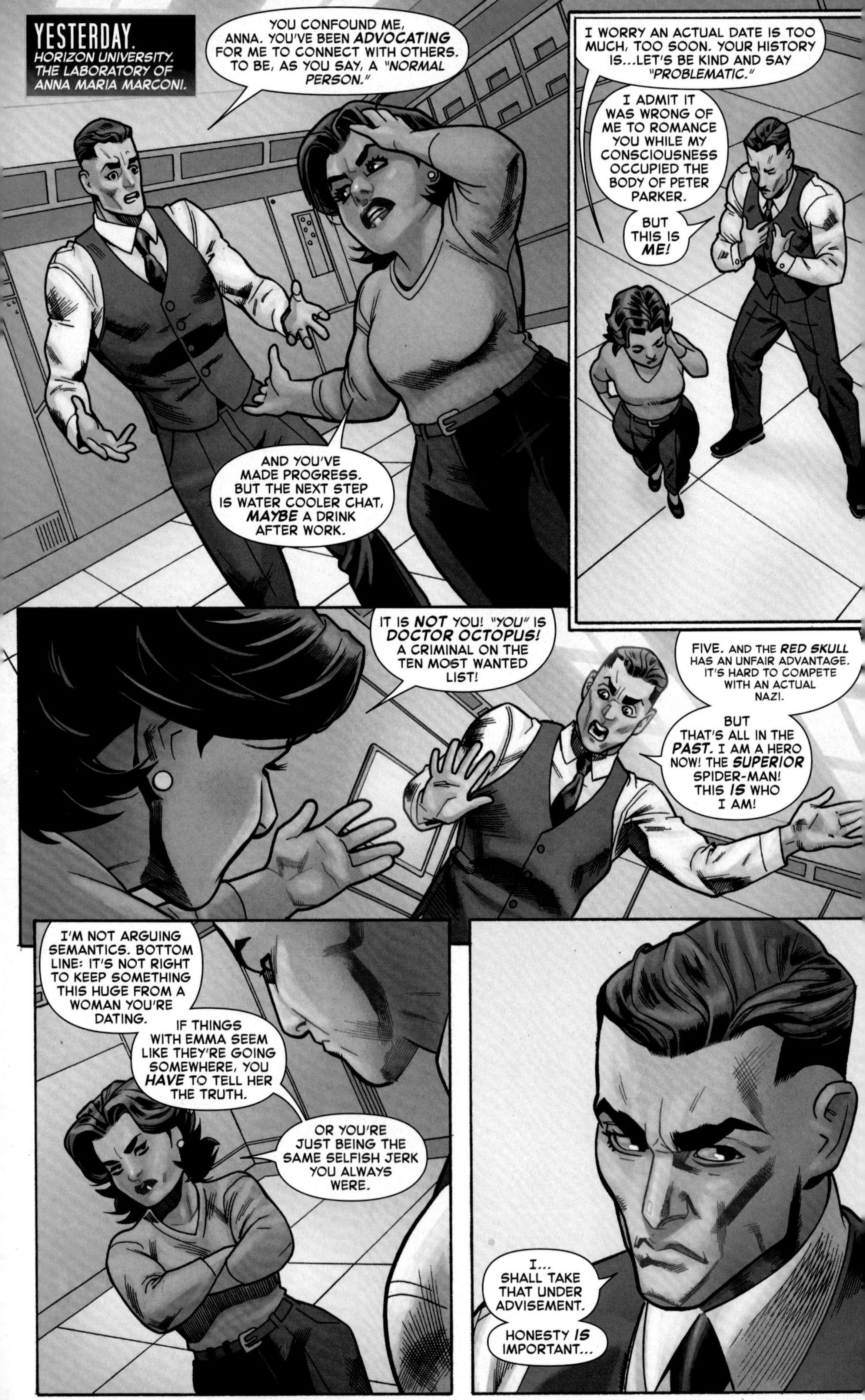
YESTERDAY.
HORIZON UNIVERSITY. THE LABORATORY OF ANNA MARIA MARCONI.
YOU CONFOUND ME, ANNA. YOU'VE BEEN ADVOCATING FOR ME TO CONNECT WITH OTHERS. TO BE, AS YOU SAY, A "NORMAL PERSON."
AND YOU'VE MADE PROGRESS. BUT THE NEXT STEP IS WATER COOLER CHAT, MAYBE A DRINK AFTER WORK.
I WORRY AN ACTUAL DATE IS TOO MUCH, TOO SOON. YOUR HISTORY IS...LET'S BE KIND AND SAY "PROBLEMATIC."
I ADMIT IT WAS WRONG OF ME TO ROMANCE YOU WHILE MY CONSCIOUSNESS OCCUPIED THE BODY OF PETER PARKER.
BUT THIS IS ME!
IT IS NOT YOU! "YOU" IS DOCTOR OCTOPUS! A CRIMINAL ON THE TEN MOST WANTED LIST!
FIVE. AND THE RED SKULL HAS AN UNFAIR ADVANTAGE. IT'S HARD TO COMPETE WITH AN ACTUAL NAZI.
BUT THAT'S ALL IN THE PAST. I AM A HERO NOW! THE SUPERIOR SPIDER-MAN! THIS IS WHO I AM!
I'M NOT ARGUING SEMANTICS. BOTTOM LINE: IT'S NOT RIGHT TO KEEP SOMETHING THIS HUGE FROM A WOMAN YOU'RE DATING.
IF THINGS WITH EMMA SEEM LIKE THEY'RE GOING SOMEWHERE, YOU HAVE TO TELL HER THE TRUTH.
OR YOU'RE JUST BEING THE SAME SELFISH JERK YOU ALWAYS WERE.
I... SHALL TAKE THAT UNDER ADVISEMENT.
HONESTY IS IMPORTANT...

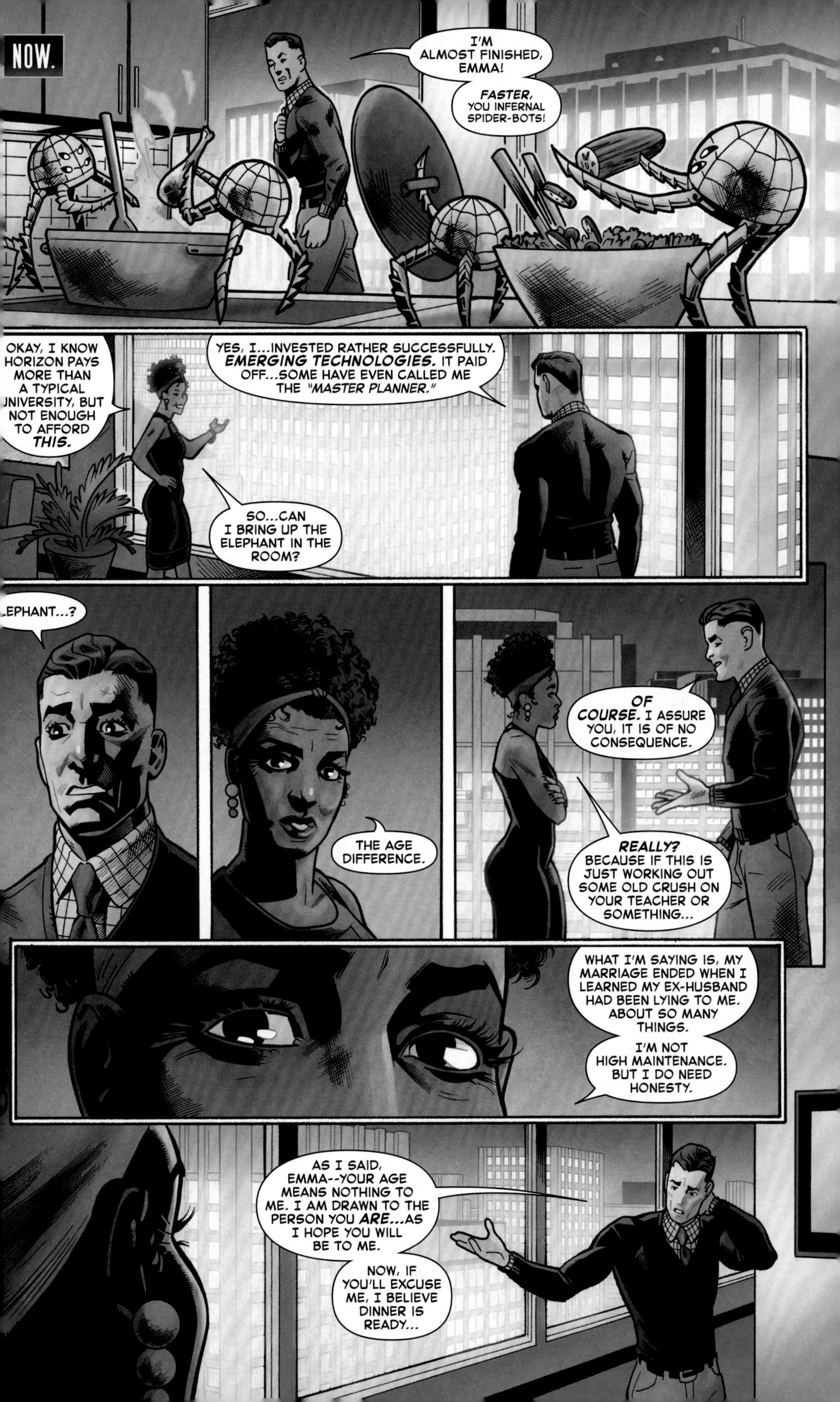
NOW.
I'M ALMOST FINISHED, EMMA!
FASTER, YOU INFERNAL SPIDER-BOTS!
OKAY, I KNOW HORIZON PAYS MORE THAN A TYPICAL UNIVERSITY, BUT NOT ENOUGH TO AFFORD THIS.
YES, I...INVESTED RATHER SUCCESSFULLY. EMERGING TECHNOLOGIES. IT PAID OFF...SOME HAVE EVEN CALLED ME THE "MASTER PLANNER."
SO...CAN I BRING UP THE ELEPHANT IN THE ROOM?
EPHANT...?
THE AGE DIFFERENCE.
OF COURSE. I ASSURE YOU, IT IS OF NO CONSEQUENCE.
REALLY? BECAUSE IF THIS IS JUST WORKING OUT SOME OLD CRUSH ON YOUR TEACHER OR SOMETHING...
WHAT I'M SAYING IS, MY MARRIAGE ENDED WHEN I LEARNED MY EX-HUSBAND HAD BEEN LYING TO ME. ABOUT SO MANY THINGS.
I'M NOT HIGH MAINTENANCE. BUT I DO NEED HONESTY.
AS I SAID, EMMA--YOUR AGE MEANS NOTHING TO ME. I AM DRAWN TO THE PERSON YOU ARE...AS I HOPE YOU WILL BE TO ME.
NOW, IF YOU'LL EXCUSE ME, I BELIEVE DINNER IS READY...

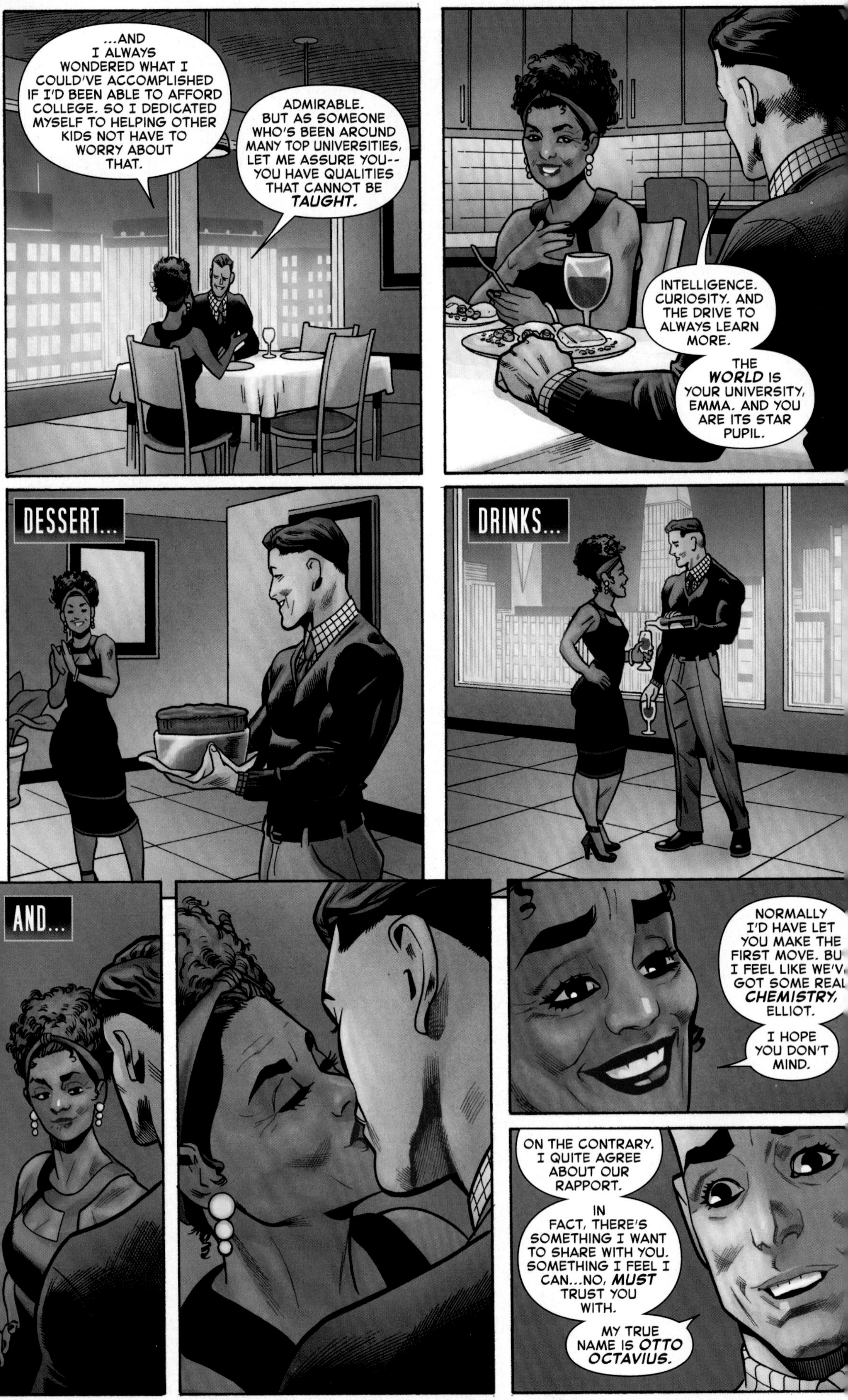
...AND I ALWAYS WONDERED WHAT I COULD'VE ACCOMPLISHED IF I'D BEEN ABLE TO AFFORD COLLEGE. SO I DEDICATED MYSELF TO HELPING OTHER KIDS NOT HAVE TO WORRY ABOUT THAT.
ADMIRABLE. BUT AS SOMEONE WHO'S BEEN AROUND MANY TOP UNIVERSITIES, LET ME ASSURE YOU-- YOU HAVE QUALITIES THAT CANNOT BE TAUGHT.
INTELLIGENCE. CURIOSITY. AND THE DRIVE TO ALWAYS LEARN MORE.
THE WORLD IS YOUR UNIVERSITY, EMMA. AND YOU ARE ITS STAR PUPIL.
DESSERT...
DRINKS...
AND...
NORMALLY I'D HAVE LET YOU MAKE THE FIRST MOVE. BU I FEEL LIKE WE'V GOT SOME REAL CHEMISTRY, ELLIOT.
I HOPE YOU DON'T MIND.
ON THE CONTRARY. I QUITE AGREE ABOUT OUR RAPPORT.
IN FACT, THERE'S SOMETHING I WANT TO SHARE WITH YOU. SOMETHING I FEEL I CAN...NO, MUST TRUST YOU WITH.
MY TRUE NAME IS OTTO OCTAVIUS.

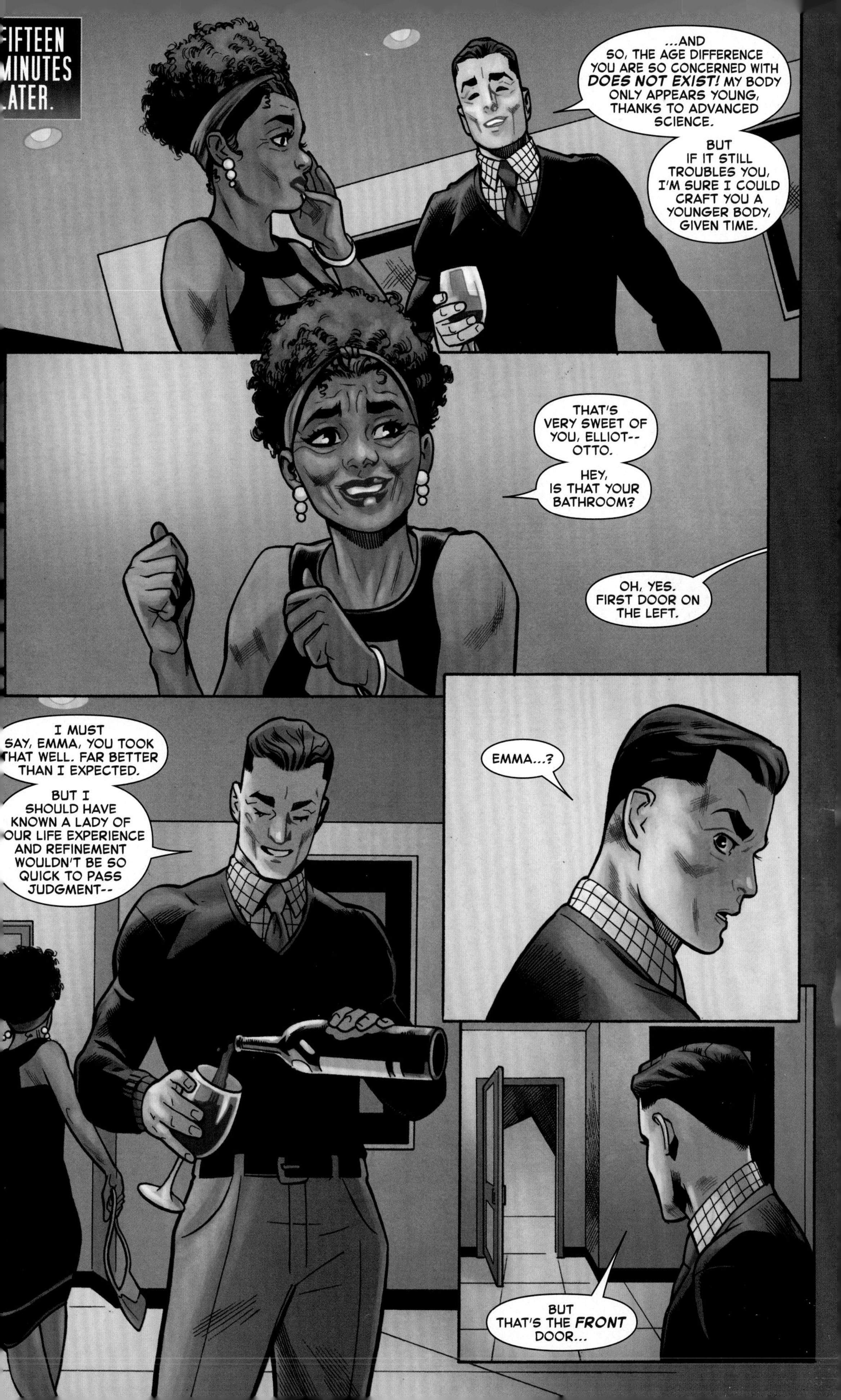

FIFTEEN MINUTES LATER.
...AND SO, THE AGE DIFFERENCE YOU ARE SO CONCERNED WITH ***DOES NOT EXIST!*** MY BODY ONLY APPEARS YOUNG, THANKS TO ADVANCED SCIENCE.
BUT IF IT STILL TROUBLES YOU, I'M SURE I COULD CRAFT YOU A YOUNGER BODY, GIVEN TIME.
THAT'S VERY SWEET OF YOU, ELLIOT--OTTO.
HEY, IS THAT YOUR BATHROOM?
OH, YES. FIRST DOOR ON THE LEFT.
I MUST SAY, EMMA, YOU TOOK THAT WELL. FAR BETTER THAN I EXPECTED.
BUT I SHOULD HAVE KNOWN A LADY OF OUR LIFE EXPERIENCE AND REFINEMENT WOULDN'T BE SO QUICK TO PASS JUDGMENT--
EMMA...?
BUT THAT'S THE ***FRONT*** DOOR...

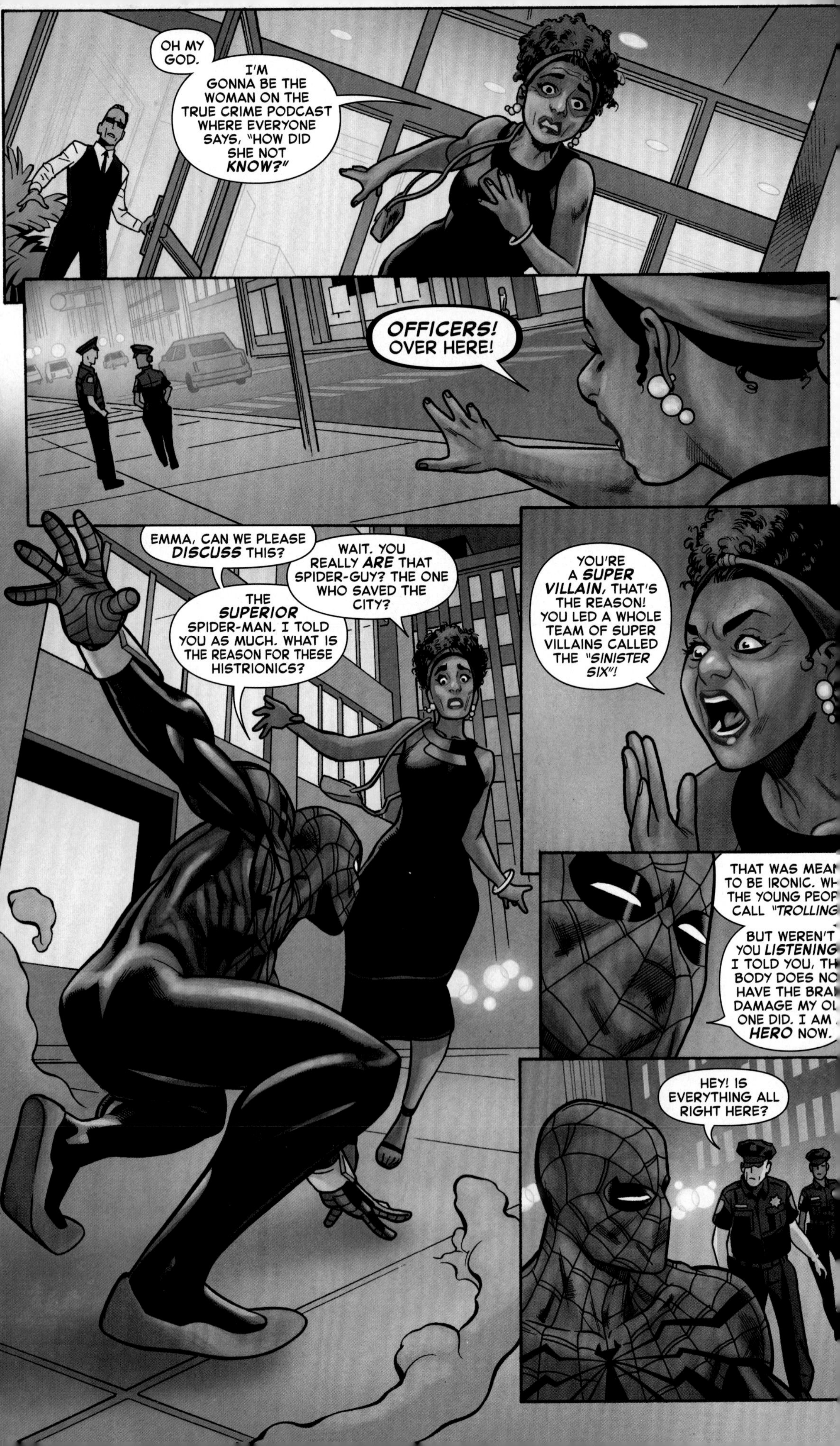
OH MY GOD.
I'M GONNA BE THE WOMAN ON THE TRUE CRIME PODCAST WHERE EVERYONE SAYS, "HOW DID SHE NOT KNOW?"
OFFICERS! OVER HERE!
EMMA, CAN WE PLEASE DISCUSS THIS?
WAIT. YOU REALLY ARE THAT SPIDER-GUY? THE ONE WHO SAVED THE CITY?
THE SUPERIOR SPIDER-MAN. I TOLD YOU AS MUCH. WHAT IS THE REASON FOR THESE HISTRIONICS?
YOU'RE A SUPER VILLAIN, THAT'S THE REASON! YOU LED A WHOLE TEAM OF SUPER VILLAINS CALLED THE "SINISTER SIX"!
THAT WAS MEA TO BE IRONIC. WH THE YOUNG PEOP CALL "TROLLING
BUT WEREN'T YOU LISTENING I TOLD YOU, TH BODY DOES NO HAVE THE BRA DAMAGE MY OL ONE DID. I AM HERO NOW.
HEY! IS EVERYTHING ALL RIGHT HERE?

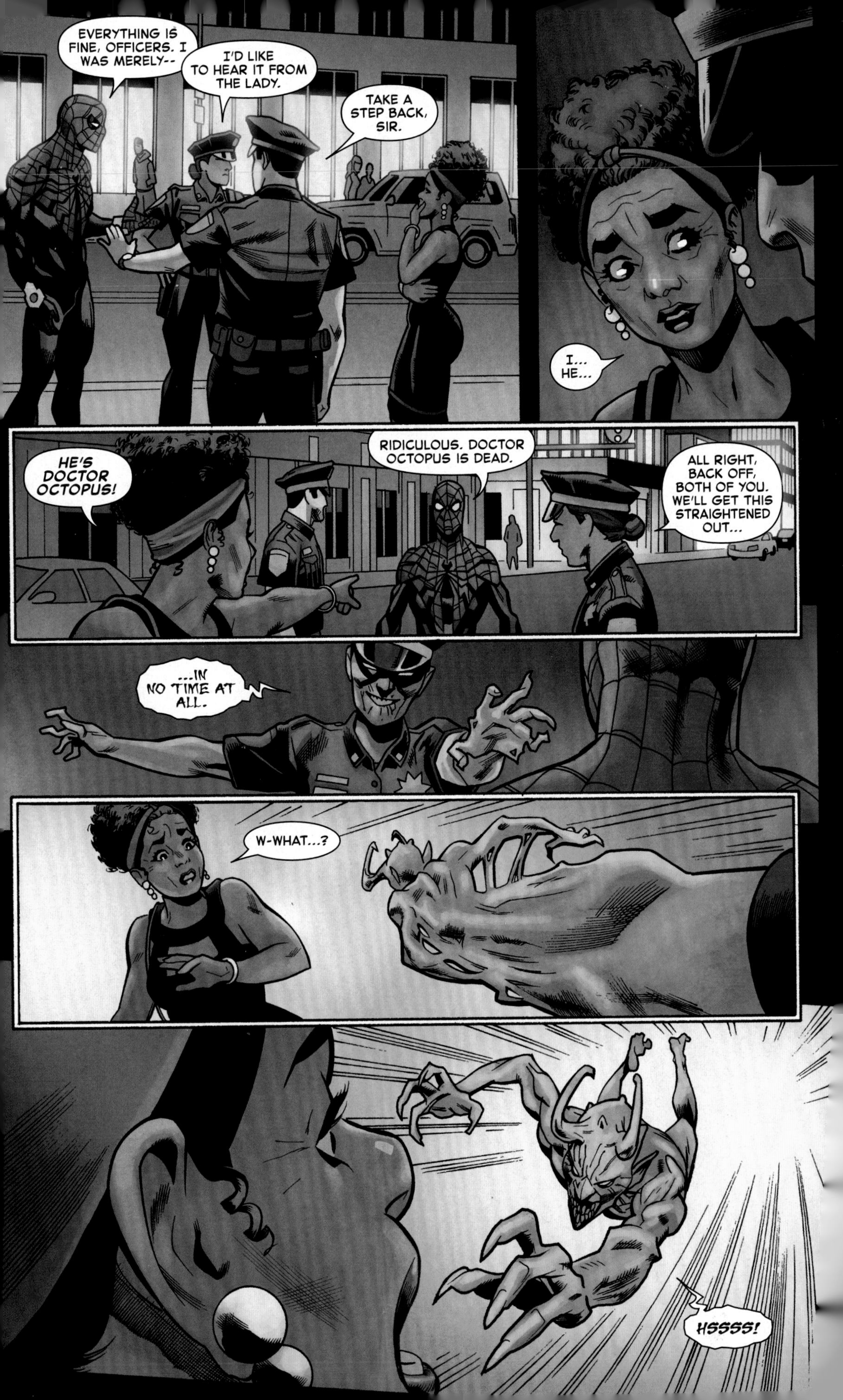
EVERYTHING IS FINE, OFFICERS. I WAS MERELY--
I'D LIKE TO HEAR IT FROM THE LADY.
TAKE A STEP BACK, SIR.
I... HE...
HE'S DOCTOR OCTOPUS!
RIDICULOUS. DOCTOR OCTOPUS IS DEAD.
ALL RIGHT, BACK OFF, BOTH OF YOU. WE'LL GET THIS STRAIGHTENED OUT...
...IN NO TIME AT ALL.
W-WHAT...?
HSSSS!

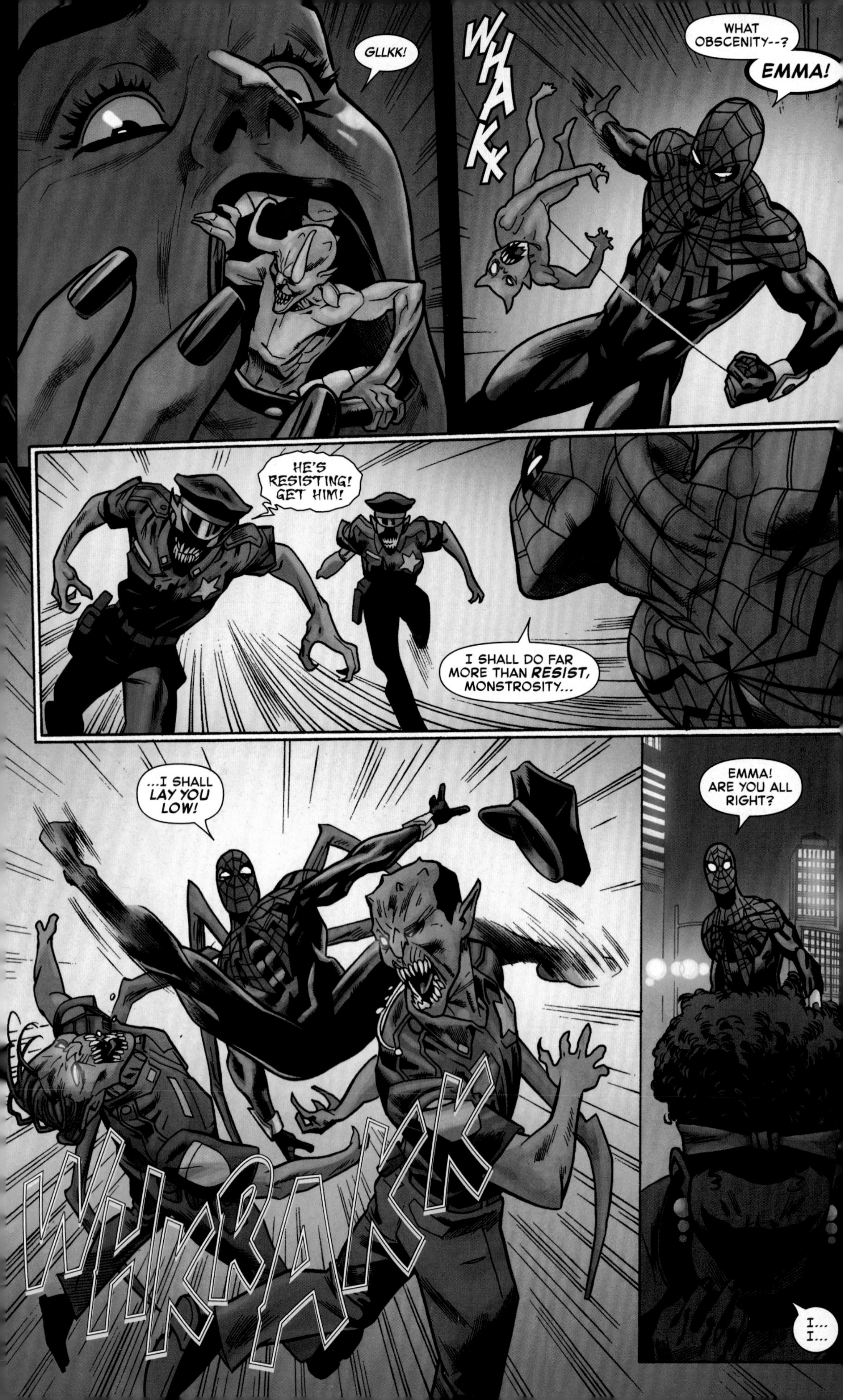

GLLKK!
WHAKK
WHAT OBSCENITY--?
EMMA!
HE'S RESISTING! GET HIM!
I SHALL DO FAR MORE THAN RESIST, MONSTROSITY...
...I SHALL LAY YOU LOW!
WHKRAKK
EMMA! ARE YOU ALL RIGHT?
I... I...

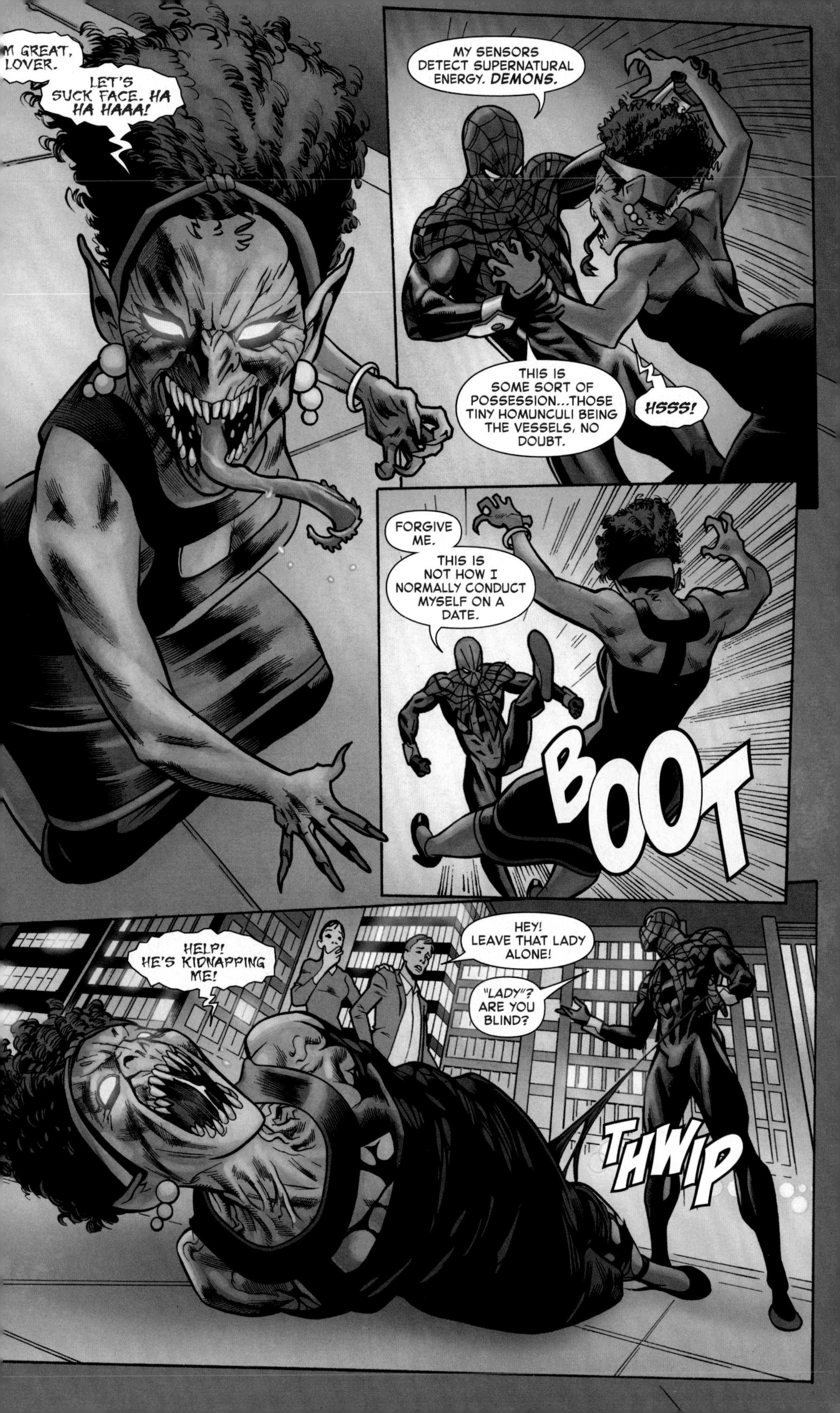
M GREAT, LOVER.
LET'S SUCK FACE. HA HA HAAA!
MY SENSORS DETECT SUPERNATURAL ENERGY. DEMONS.
THIS IS SOME SORT OF POSSESSION...THOSE TINY HOMUNCULI BEING THE VESSELS, NO DOUBT.
HSSS!
FORGIVE ME.
THIS IS NOT HOW I NORMALLY CONDUCT MYSELF ON A DATE.
BOOT
HELP! HE'S KIDNAPPING ME!
HEY! LEAVE THAT LADY ALONE!
"LADY"? ARE YOU BLIND?
THWIP

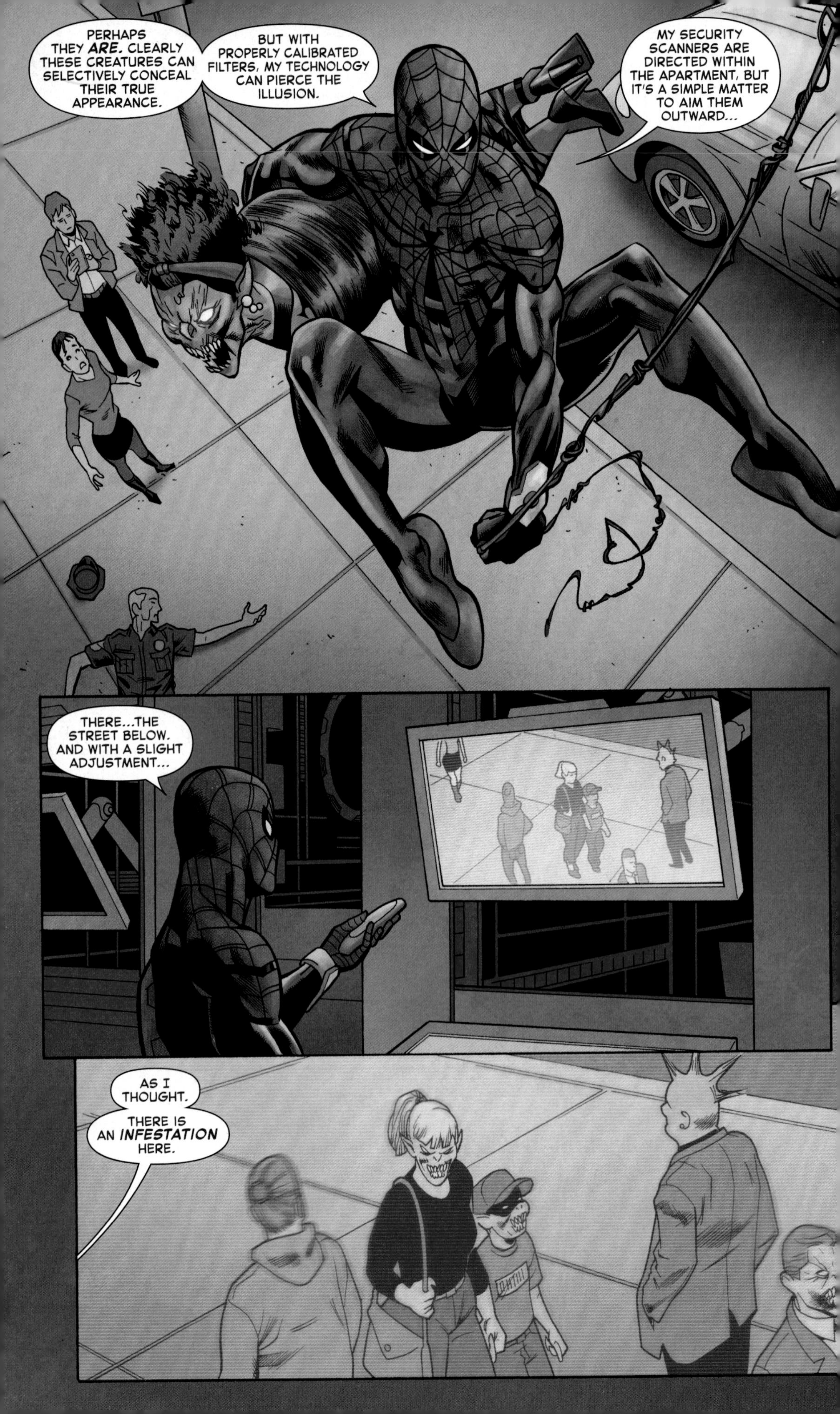
PERHAPS THEY ARE. CLEARLY THESE CREATURES CAN SELECTIVELY CONCEAL THEIR TRUE APPEARANCE.
BUT WITH PROPERLY CALIBRATED FILTERS, MY TECHNOLOGY CAN PIERCE THE ILLUSION.
MY SECURITY SCANNERS ARE DIRECTED WITHIN THE APARTMENT, BUT IT'S A SIMPLE MATTER TO AIM THEM OUTWARD...
THERE...THE STREET BELOW. AND WITH A SLIGHT ADJUSTMENT...
AS I THOUGHT.
THERE IS AN INFESTATION HERE.

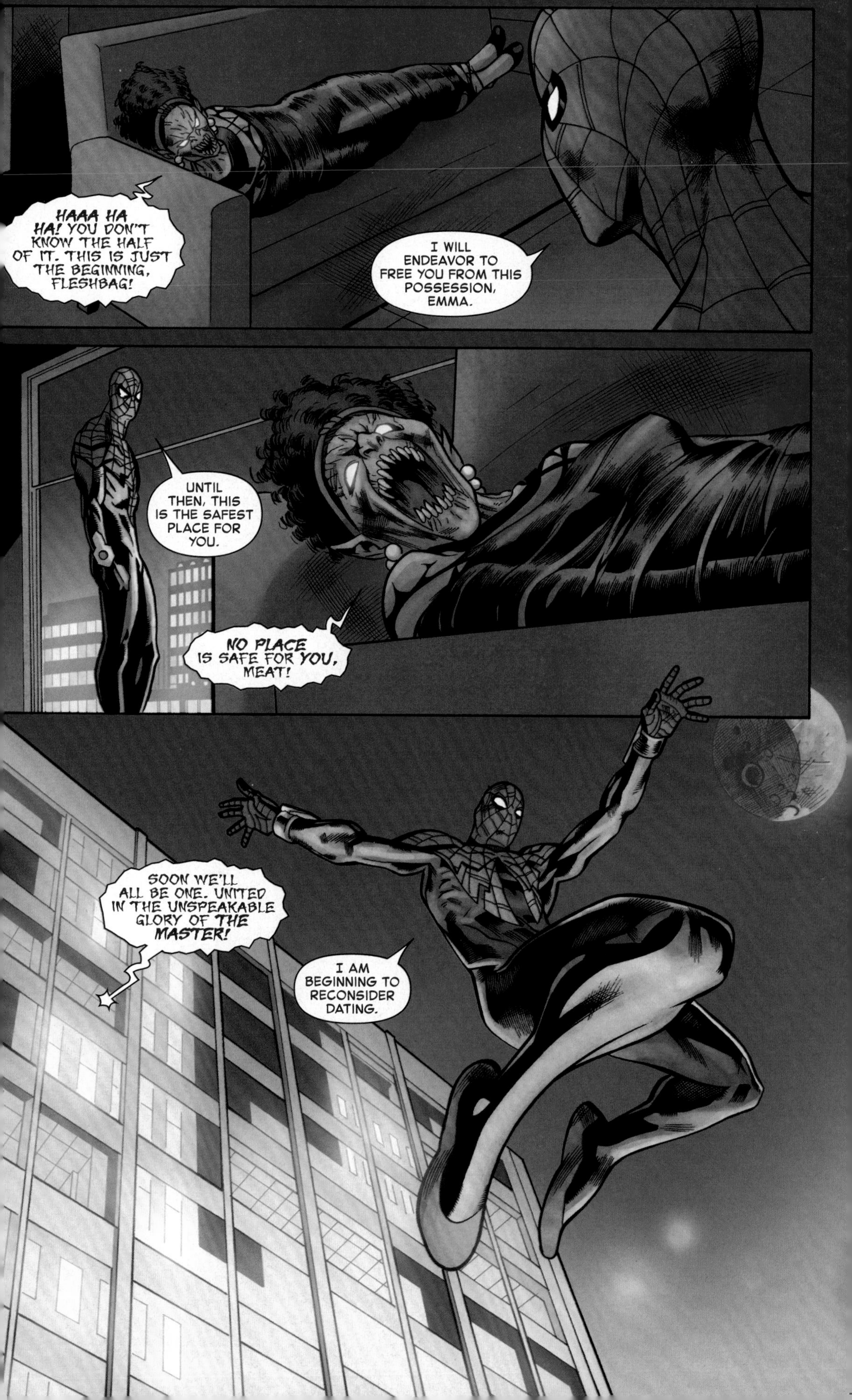
HAAAA HA HA! YOU DON'T KNOW THE HALF OF IT. THIS IS JUST THE BEGINNING, FLESHBAG!
I WILL ENDEAVOR TO FREE YOU FROM THIS POSSESSION, EMMA.
UNTIL THEN, THIS IS THE SAFEST PLACE FOR YOU.
NO PLACE IS SAFE FOR YOU, MEAT!
SOON WE'LL ALL BE ONE. UNITED IN THE UNSPEAKABLE GLORY OF THE MASTER!
I AM BEGINNING TO RECONSIDER DATING.

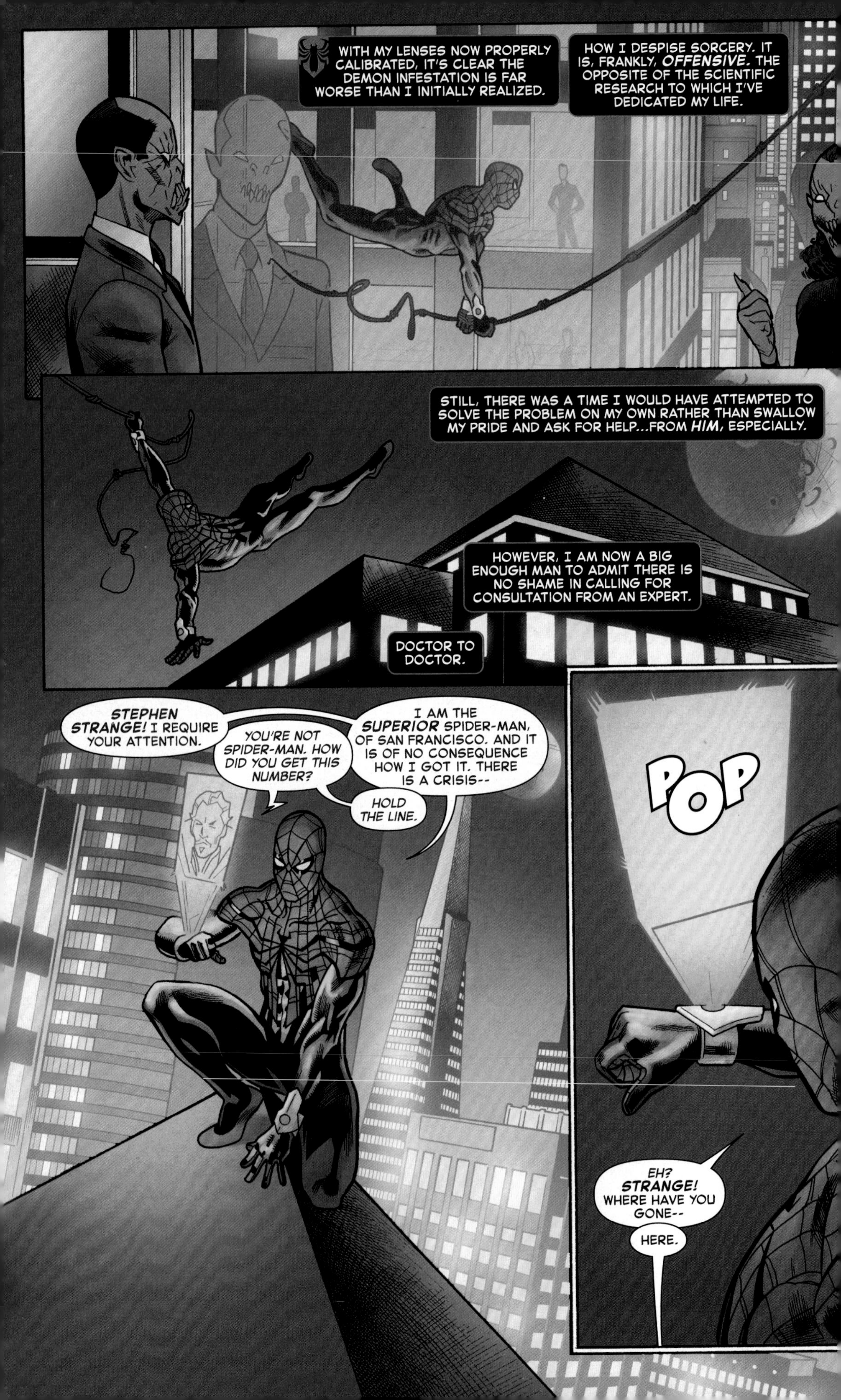

WITH MY LENSES NOW PROPERLY CALIBRATED, IT'S CLEAR THE DEMON INFESTATION IS FAR WORSE THAN I INITIALLY REALIZED.
HOW I DESPISE SORCERY. IT IS, FRANKLY, OFFENSIVE. THE OPPOSITE OF THE SCIENTIFIC RESEARCH TO WHICH I'VE DEDICATED MY LIFE.
STILL, THERE WAS A TIME I WOULD HAVE ATTEMPTED TO SOLVE THE PROBLEM ON MY OWN RATHER THAN SWALLOW MY PRIDE AND ASK FOR HELP...FROM HIM, ESPECIALLY.
HOWEVER, I AM NOW A BIG ENOUGH MAN TO ADMIT THERE IS NO SHAME IN CALLING FOR CONSULTATION FROM AN EXPERT.
DOCTOR TO DOCTOR.
STEPHEN STRANGE! I REQUIRE YOUR ATTENTION.
YOU'RE NOT SPIDER-MAN. HOW DID YOU GET THIS NUMBER?
I AM THE SUPERIOR SPIDER-MAN, OF SAN FRANCISCO. AND IT IS OF NO CONSEQUENCE HOW I GOT IT. THERE IS A CRISIS--
HOLD THE LINE.
POP
EH? STRANGE! WHERE HAVE YOU GONE--
HERE.

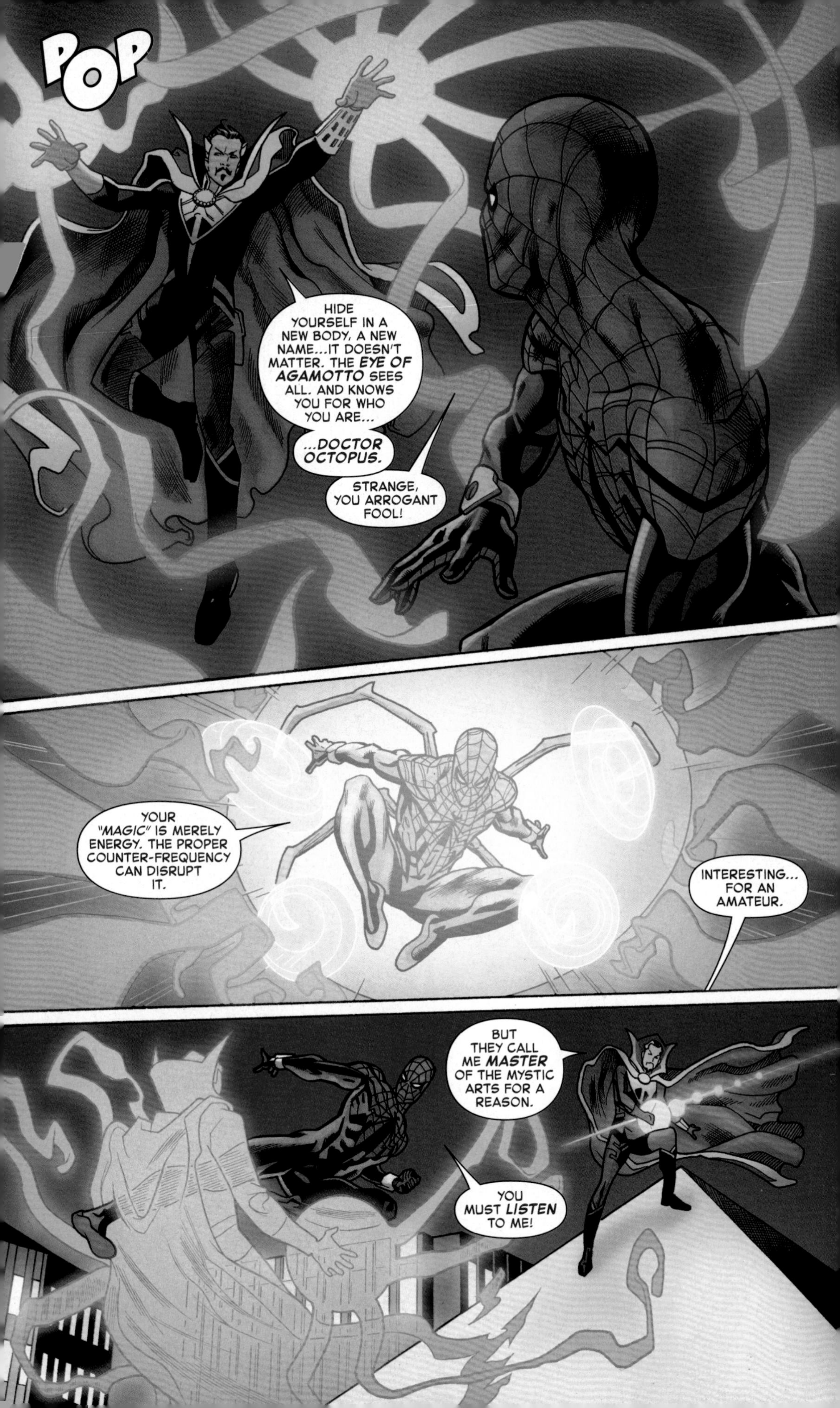
POP
HIDE YOURSELF IN A NEW BODY, A NEW NAME...IT DOESN'T MATTER. THE EYE OF AGAMOTTO SEES ALL. AND KNOWS YOU FOR WHO YOU ARE...
...DOCTOR OCTOPUS.
STRANGE, YOU ARROGANT FOOL!
YOUR "MAGIC" IS MERELY ENERGY. THE PROPER COUNTER-FREQUENCY CAN DISRUPT IT.
INTERESTING... FOR AN AMATEUR.
BUT THEY CALL ME MASTER OF THE MYSTIC ARTS FOR A REASON.
YOU MUST LISTEN TO ME!

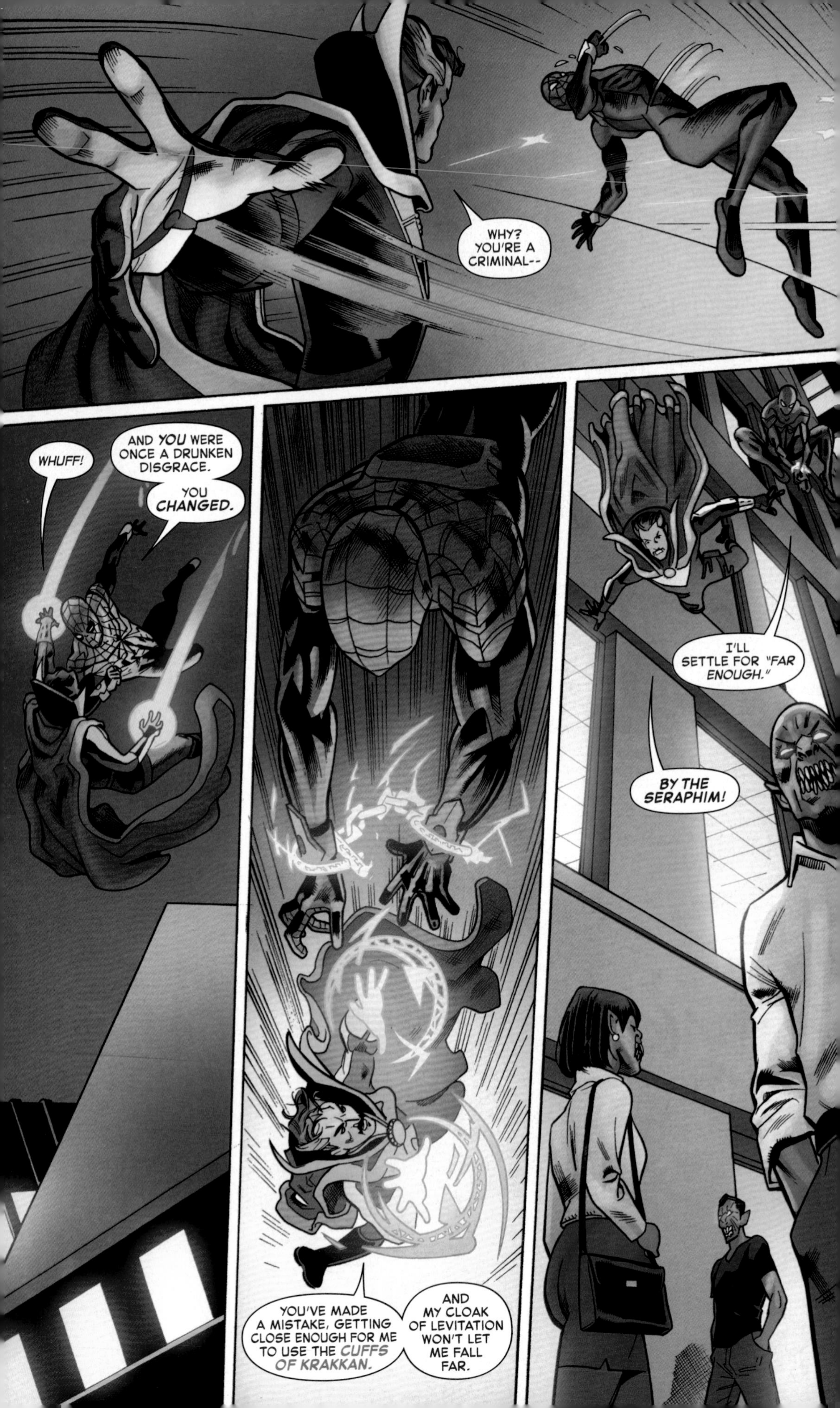
WHY? YOU'RE A CRIMINAL--
WHUFF!
AND YOU WERE ONCE A DRUNKEN DISGRACE.
YOU CHANGED.
YOU'VE MADE A MISTAKE, GETTING CLOSE ENOUGH FOR ME TO USE THE CUFFS OF KRAKKAN.
AND MY CLOAK OF LEVITATION WON'T LET ME FALL FAR.
I'LL SETTLE FOR "FAR ENOUGH."
BY THE SERAPHIM!

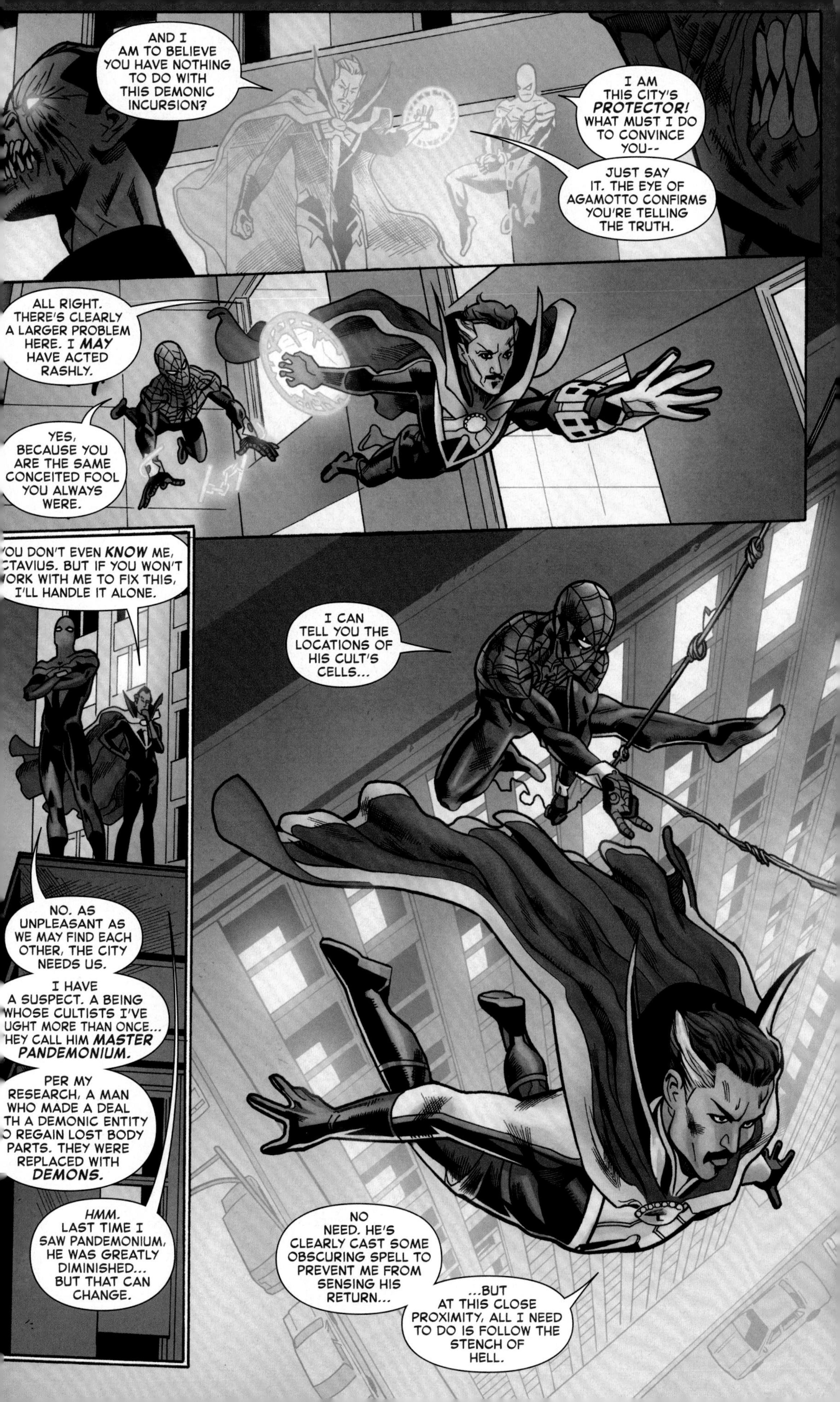

AND I AM TO BELIEVE YOU HAVE NOTHING TO DO WITH THIS DEMONIC INCURSION?
I AM THIS CITY'S *PROTECTOR!* WHAT MUST I DO TO CONVINCE YOU--
JUST SAY IT. THE EYE OF AGAMOTTO CONFIRMS YOU'RE TELLING THE TRUTH.
ALL RIGHT. THERE'S CLEARLY A LARGER PROBLEM HERE. I *MAY* HAVE ACTED RASHLY.
YES, BECAUSE YOU ARE THE SAME CONCEITED FOOL YOU ALWAYS WERE.
YOU DON'T EVEN *KNOW* ME, OCTAVIUS. BUT IF YOU WON'T WORK WITH ME TO FIX THIS, I'LL HANDLE IT ALONE.
NO. AS UNPLEASANT AS WE MAY FIND EACH OTHER, THE CITY NEEDS US.
I HAVE A SUSPECT. A BEING WHOSE CULTISTS I'VE FOUGHT MORE THAN ONCE... THEY CALL HIM *MASTER PANDEMONIUM.*
PER MY RESEARCH, A MAN WHO MADE A DEAL WITH A DEMONIC ENTITY TO REGAIN LOST BODY PARTS. THEY WERE REPLACED WITH *DEMONS.*
HMM. LAST TIME I SAW PANDEMONIUM, HE WAS GREATLY DIMINISHED... BUT THAT CAN CHANGE.
I CAN TELL YOU THE LOCATIONS OF HIS CULT'S CELLS...
NO NEED. HE'S CLEARLY CAST SOME OBSCURING SPELL TO PREVENT ME FROM SENSING HIS RETURN...
...BUT AT THIS CLOSE PROXIMITY, ALL I NEED TO DO IS FOLLOW THE STENCH OF HELL.

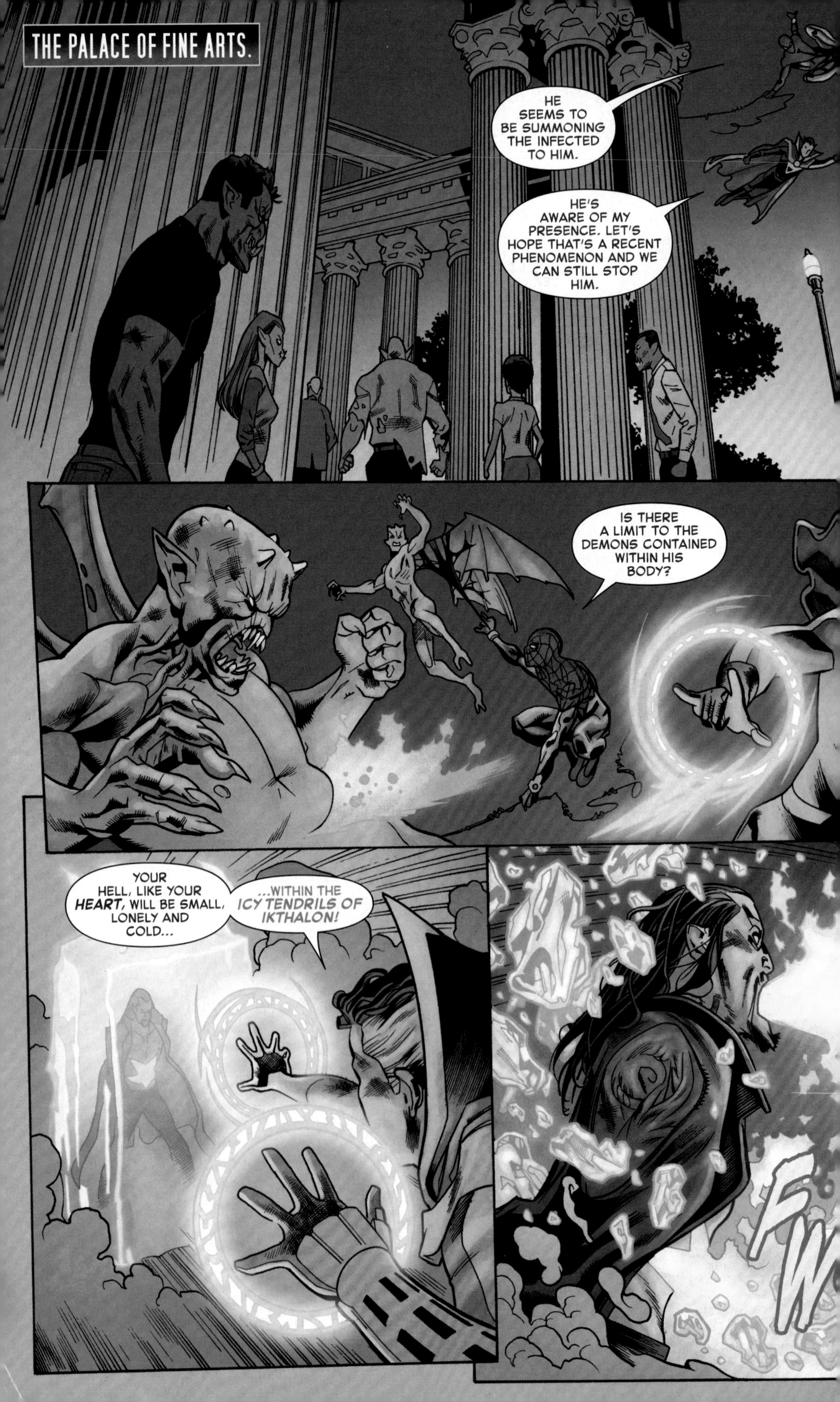
THE PALACE OF FINE ARTS.
HE SEEMS TO BE SUMMONING THE INFECTED TO HIM.
HE'S AWARE OF MY PRESENCE. LET'S HOPE THAT'S A RECENT PHENOMENON AND WE CAN STILL STOP HIM.
IS THERE A LIMIT TO THE DEMONS CONTAINED WITHIN HIS BODY?
YOUR HELL, LIKE YOUR HEART, WILL BE SMALL, LONELY AND COLD...
...WITHIN THE ICY TENDRILS OF IKTHALON!

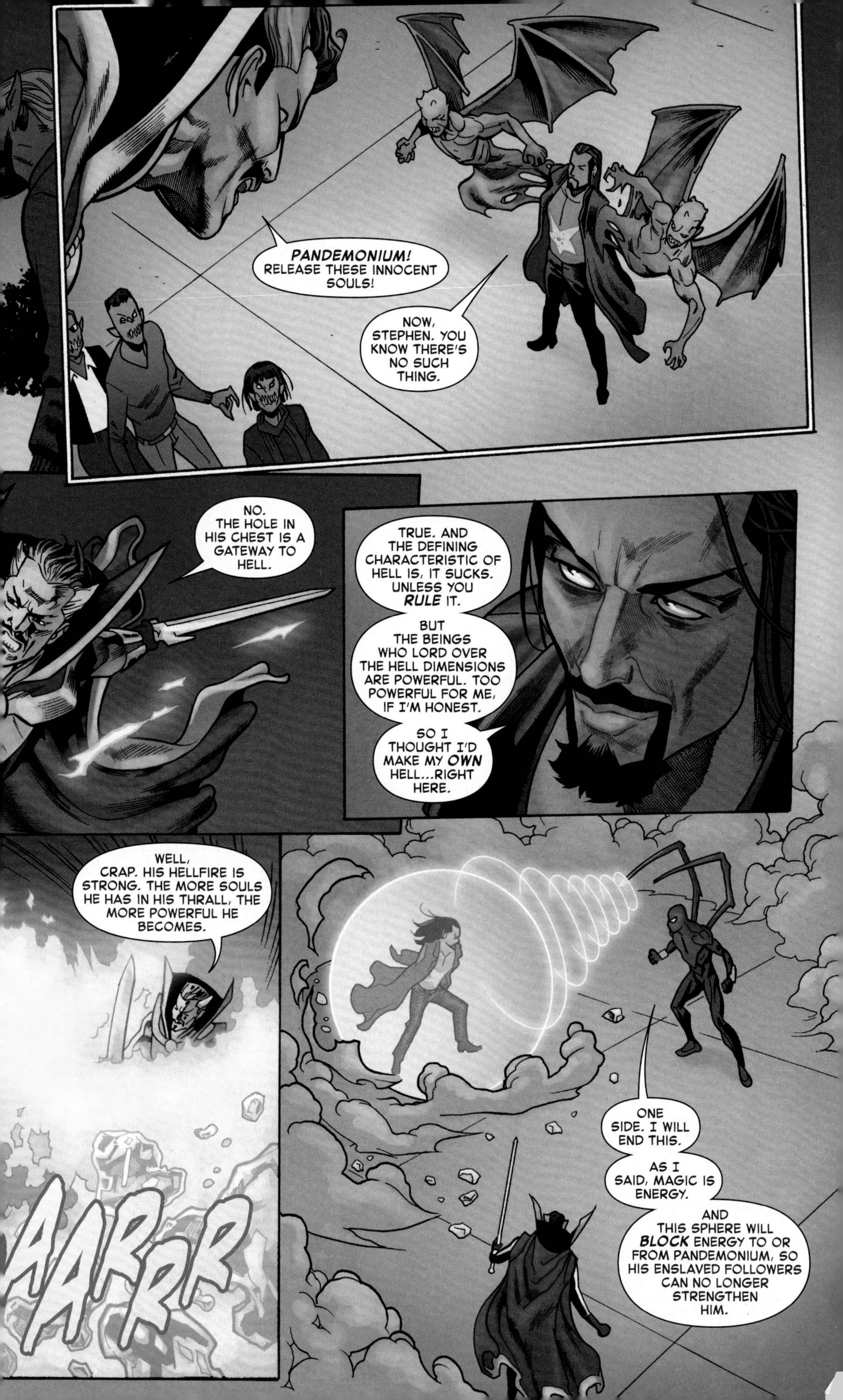
PANDEMONIUM! RELEASE THESE INNOCENT SOULS!
NOW, STEPHEN. YOU KNOW THERE'S NO SUCH THING.
NO. THE HOLE IN HIS CHEST IS A GATEWAY TO HELL.
TRUE. AND THE DEFINING CHARACTERISTIC OF HELL IS, IT SUCKS. UNLESS YOU RULE IT.
BUT THE BEINGS WHO LORD OVER THE HELL DIMENSIONS ARE POWERFUL. TOO POWERFUL FOR ME, IF I'M HONEST.
SO I THOUGHT I'D MAKE MY OWN HELL...RIGHT HERE.
WELL, CRAP. HIS HELLFIRE IS STRONG. THE MORE SOULS HE HAS IN HIS THRALL, THE MORE POWERFUL HE BECOMES.
AARRR
ONE SIDE. I WILL END THIS.
AS I SAID, MAGIC IS ENERGY.
AND THIS SPHERE WILL BLOCK ENERGY TO OR FROM PANDEMONIUM, SO HIS ENSLAVED FOLLOWERS CAN NO LONGER STRENGTHEN HIM.

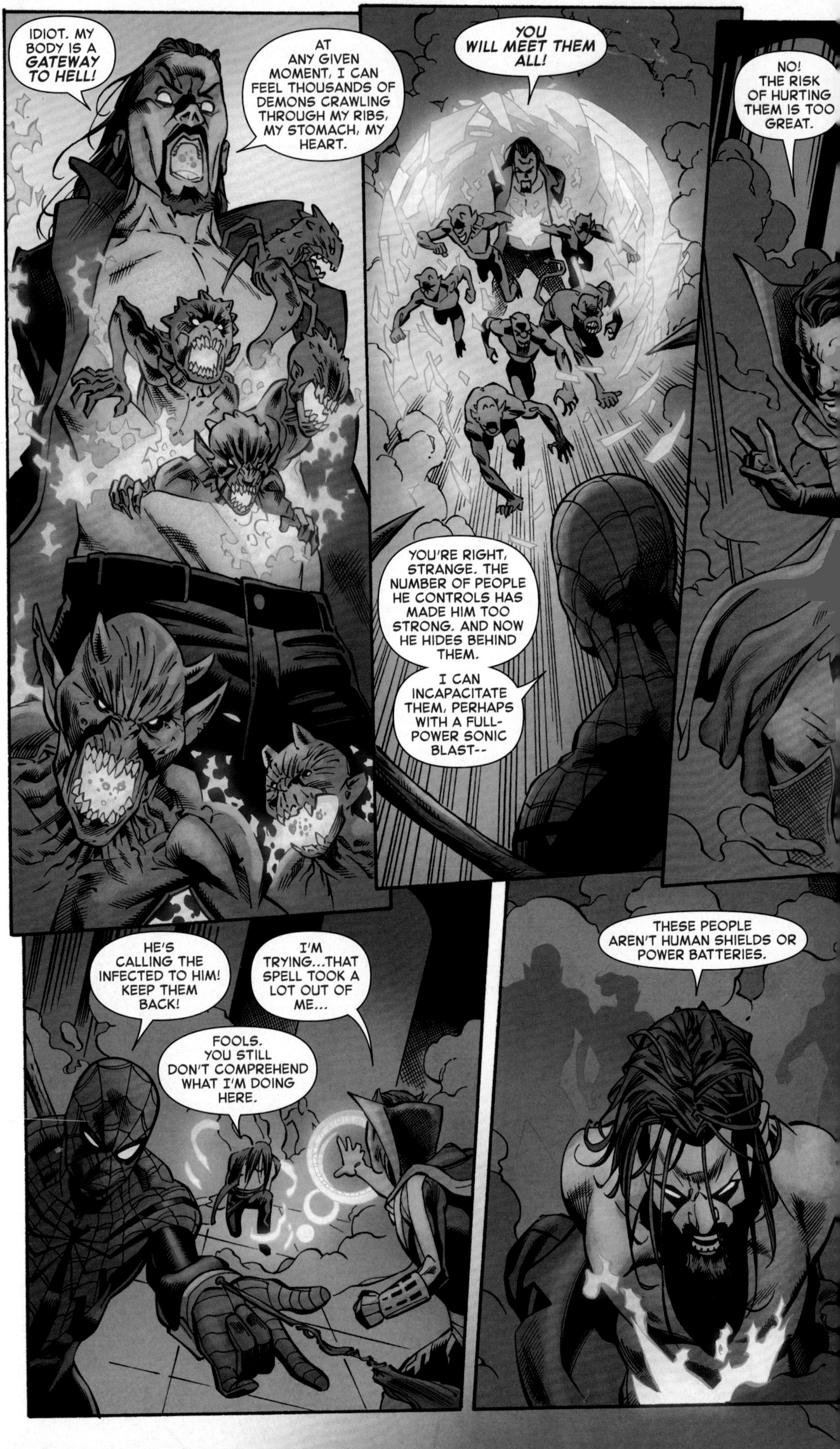
IDIOT. MY BODY IS A *GATEWAY TO HELL!*
AT ANY GIVEN MOMENT, I CAN FEEL THOUSANDS OF DEMONS CRAWLING THROUGH MY RIBS, MY STOMACH, MY HEART.
YOU WILL MEET THEM ALL!
YOU'RE RIGHT, STRANGE. THE NUMBER OF PEOPLE HE CONTROLS HAS MADE HIM TOO STRONG. AND NOW HE HIDES BEHIND THEM.
I CAN INCAPACITATE THEM, PERHAPS WITH A FULL-POWER SONIC BLAST--
NO! THE RISK OF HURTING THEM IS TOO GREAT.
HE'S CALLING THE INFECTED TO HIM! KEEP THEM BACK!
I'M TRYING...THAT SPELL TOOK A LOT OUT OF ME...
FOOLS. YOU STILL DON'T COMPREHEND WHAT I'M DOING HERE.
THESE PEOPLE AREN'T HUMAN SHIELDS OR POWER BATTERIES.

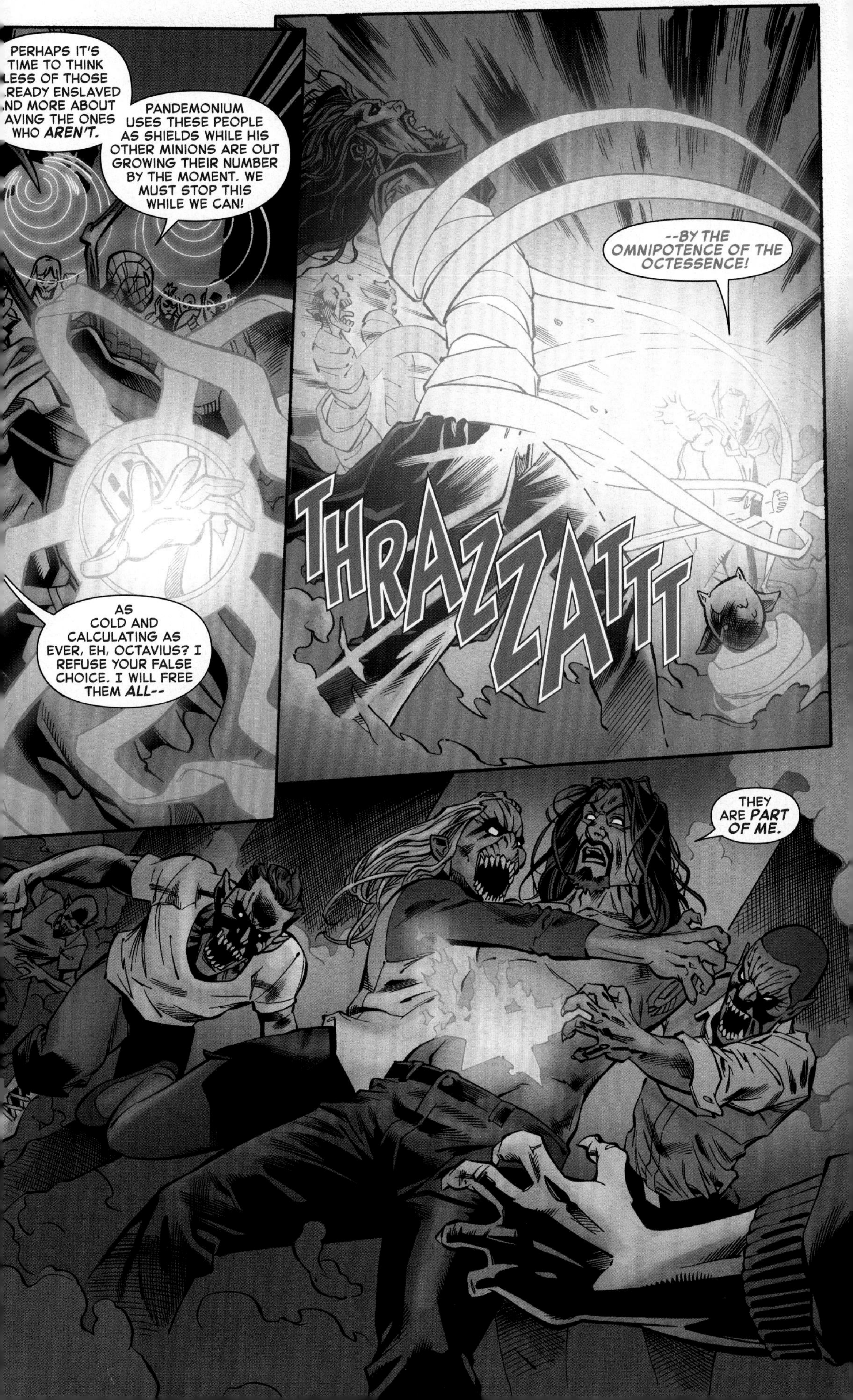
PERHAPS IT'S TIME TO THINK LESS OF THOSE ALREADY ENSLAVED AND MORE ABOUT SAVING THE ONES WHO AREN'T.
PANDEMONIUM USES THESE PEOPLE AS SHIELDS WHILE HIS OTHER MINIONS ARE OUT GROWING THEIR NUMBER BY THE MOMENT. WE MUST STOP THIS WHILE WE CAN!
AS COLD AND CALCULATING AS EVER, EH, OCTAVIUS? I REFUSE YOUR FALSE CHOICE. I WILL FREE THEM ALL--
--BY THE OMNIPOTENCE OF THE OCTESSENCE!
THRAZZATTT
THEY ARE PART OF ME.

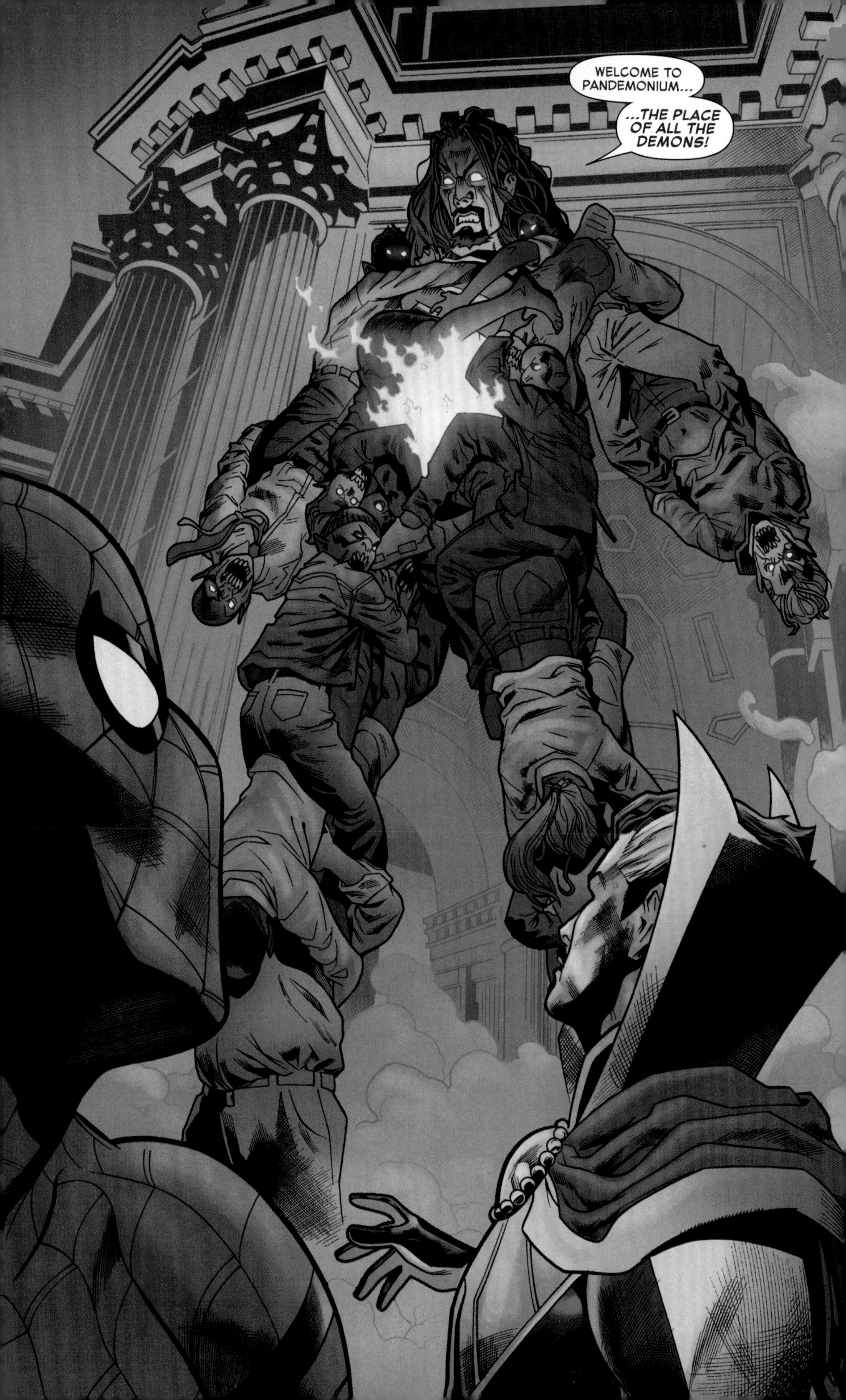
WELCOME TO PANDEMONIUM...
...THE PLACE OF ALL THE DEMONS!

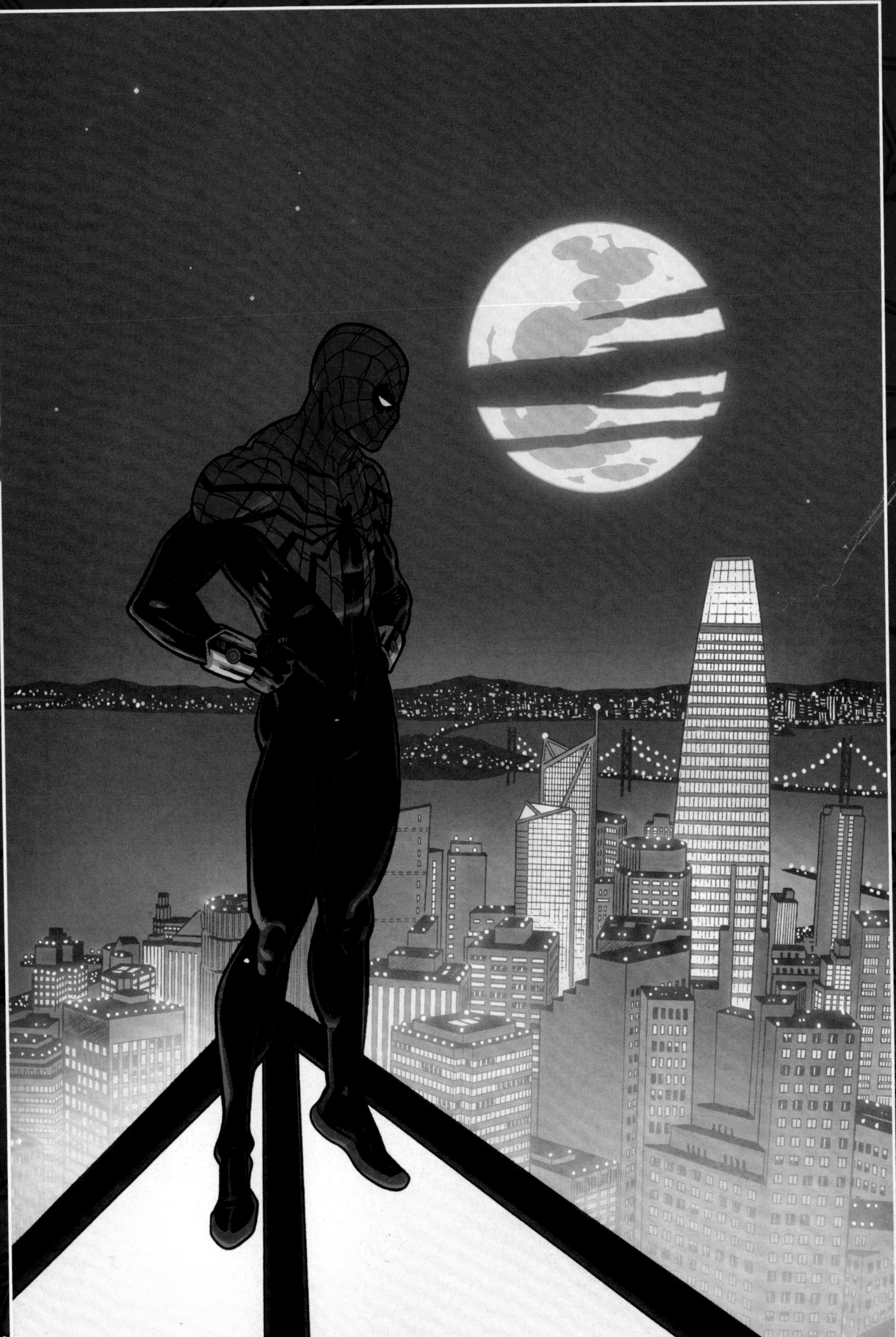

#1 VARIANT
BY MIKE HAWTHORNE & JORDIE BELLAIRE

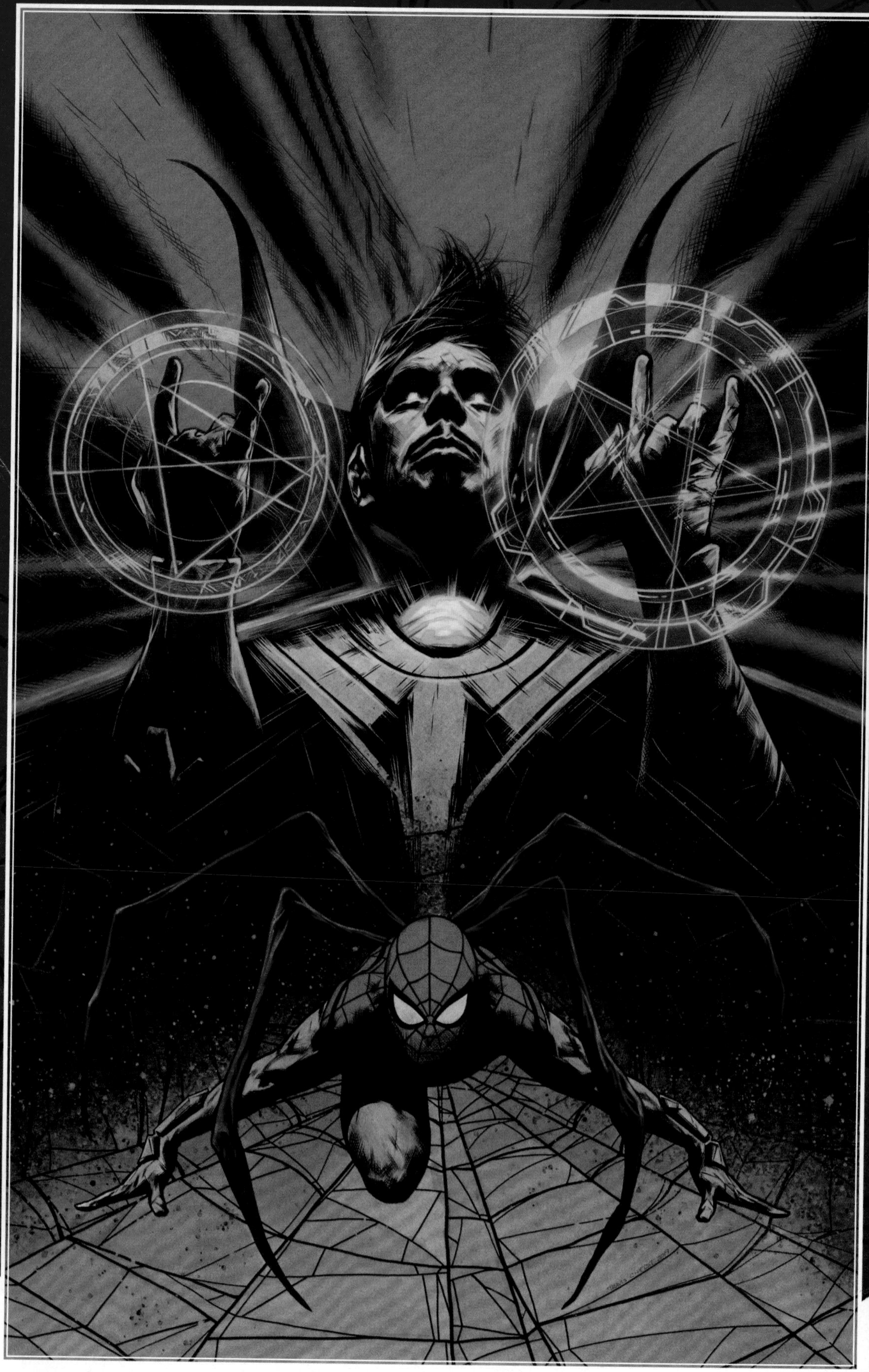

6

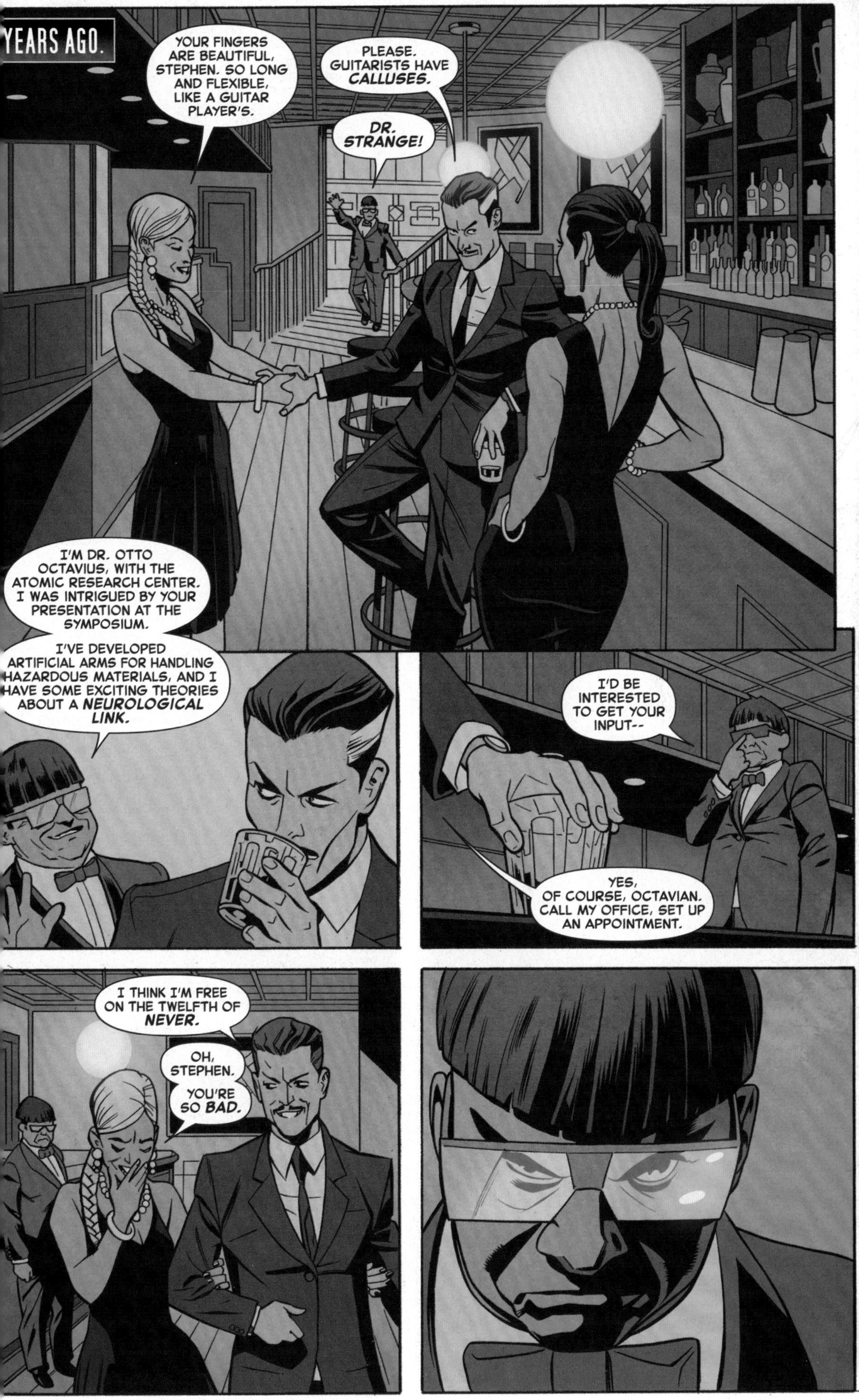

YEARS AGO.
YOUR FINGERS ARE BEAUTIFUL, STEPHEN. SO LONG AND FLEXIBLE, LIKE A GUITAR PLAYER'S.
PLEASE. GUITARISTS HAVE CALLUSES.
DR. STRANGE!
I'M DR. OTTO OCTAVIUS, WITH THE ATOMIC RESEARCH CENTER. I WAS INTRIGUED BY YOUR PRESENTATION AT THE SYMPOSIUM.
I'VE DEVELOPED ARTIFICIAL ARMS FOR HANDLING HAZARDOUS MATERIALS, AND I HAVE SOME EXCITING THEORIES ABOUT A NEUROLOGICAL LINK.
I'D BE INTERESTED TO GET YOUR INPUT--
YES, OF COURSE, OCTAVIAN. CALL MY OFFICE, SET UP AN APPOINTMENT.
I THINK I'M FREE ON THE TWELFTH OF NEVER.
OH, STEPHEN.
YOU'RE SO BAD.

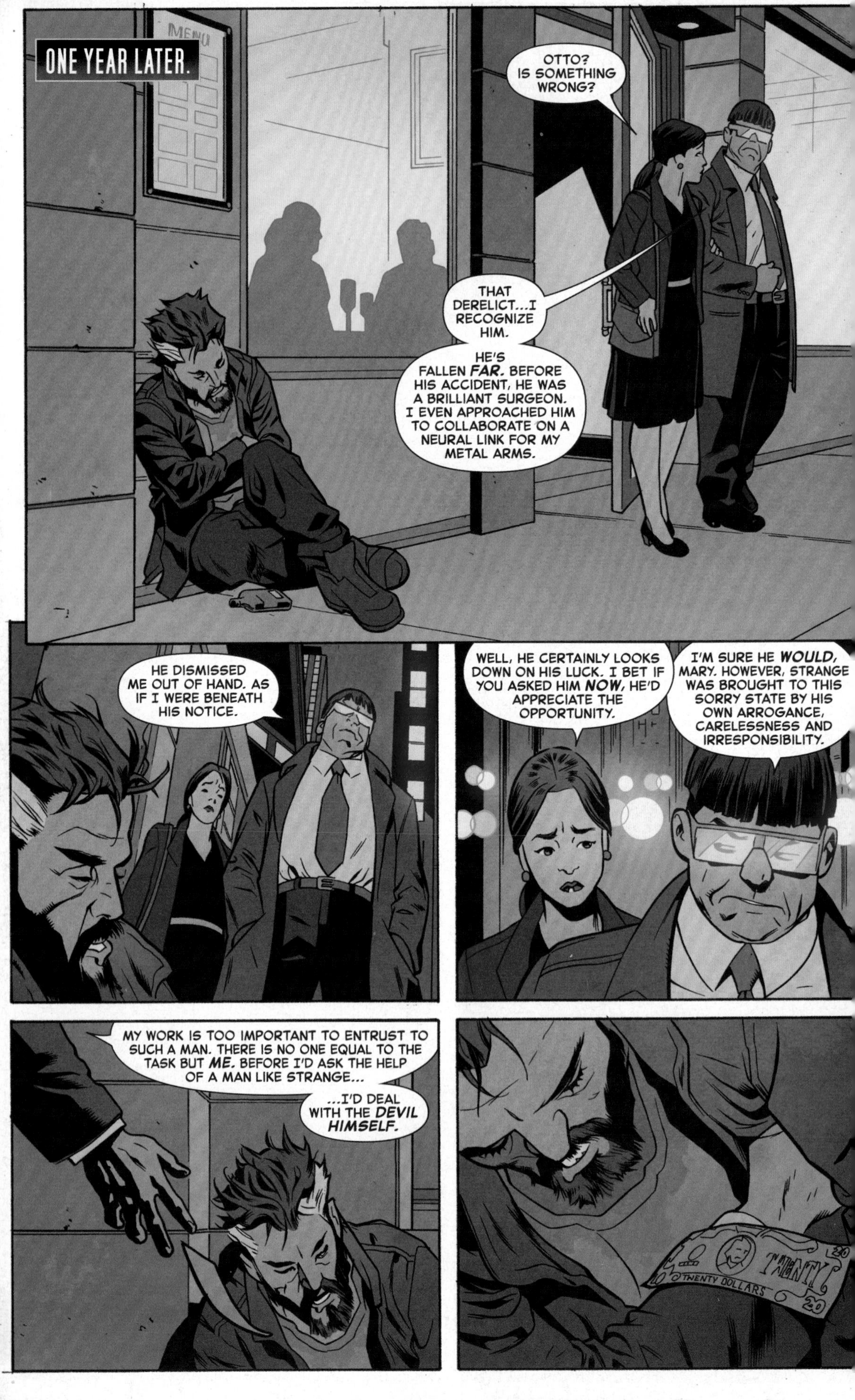

ONE YEAR LATER.
MENU
OTTO? IS SOMETHING WRONG?
THAT DERELICT...I RECOGNIZE HIM.
HE'S FALLEN FAR. BEFORE HIS ACCIDENT, HE WAS A BRILLIANT SURGEON. I EVEN APPROACHED HIM TO COLLABORATE ON A NEURAL LINK FOR MY METAL ARMS.
HE DISMISSED ME OUT OF HAND. AS IF I WERE BENEATH HIS NOTICE.
WELL, HE CERTAINLY LOOKS DOWN ON HIS LUCK. I BET IF YOU ASKED HIM NOW, HE'D APPRECIATE THE OPPORTUNITY.
I'M SURE HE WOULD, MARY. HOWEVER, STRANGE WAS BROUGHT TO THIS SORRY STATE BY HIS OWN ARROGANCE, CARELESSNESS AND IRRESPONSIBILITY.
MY WORK IS TOO IMPORTANT TO ENTRUST TO SUCH A MAN. THERE IS NO ONE EQUAL TO THE TASK BUT ME. BEFORE I'D ASK THE HELP OF A MAN LIKE STRANGE...
...I'D DEAL WITH THE DEVIL HIMSELF.
TWENTY
TWENTY DOLLARS
20
20

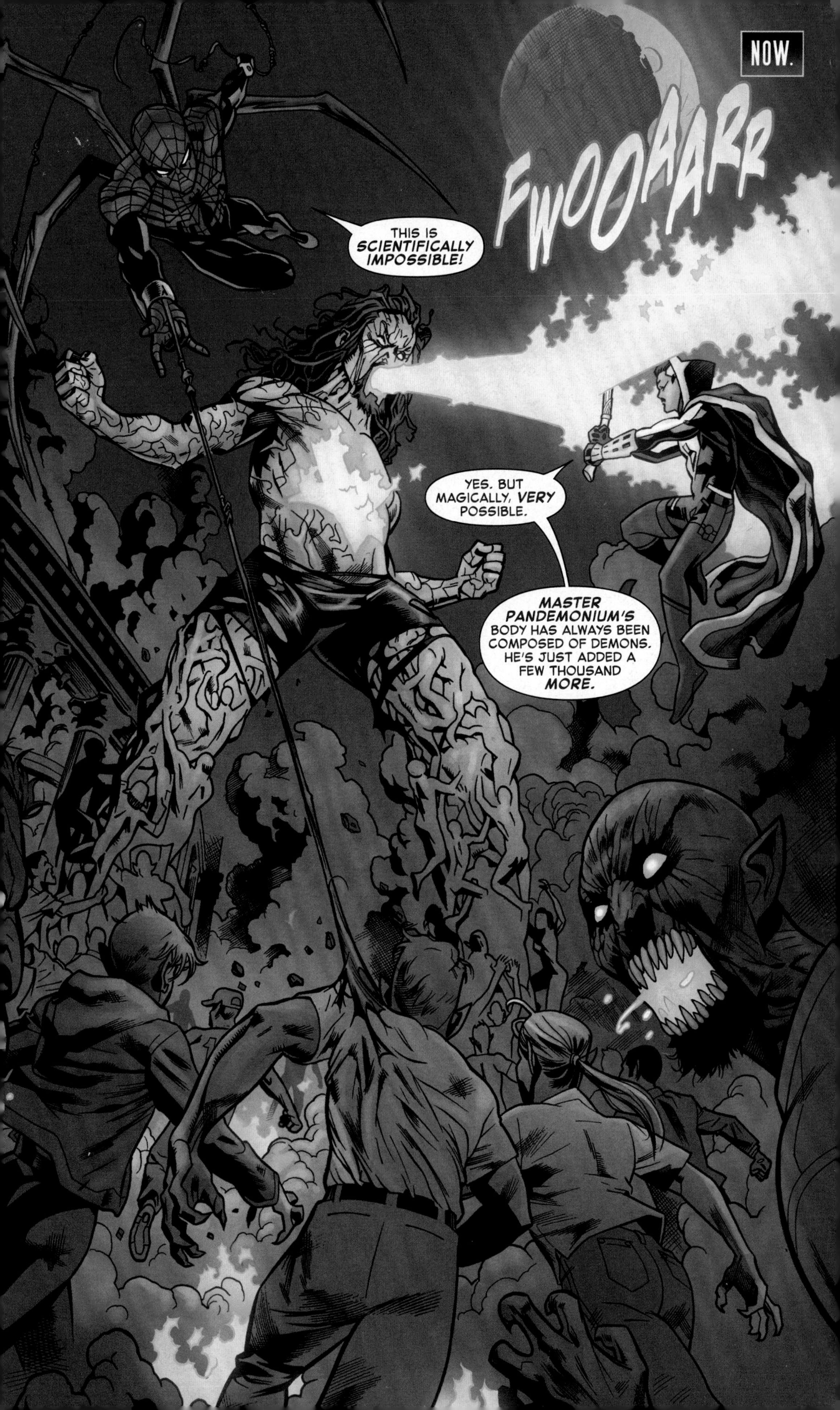
NOW.
FWOOAARR
THIS IS SCIENTIFICALLY IMPOSSIBLE!
YES. BUT MAGICALLY, VERY POSSIBLE.
MASTER PANDEMONIUM'S BODY HAS ALWAYS BEEN COMPOSED OF DEMONS. HE'S JUST ADDED A FEW THOUSAND MORE.

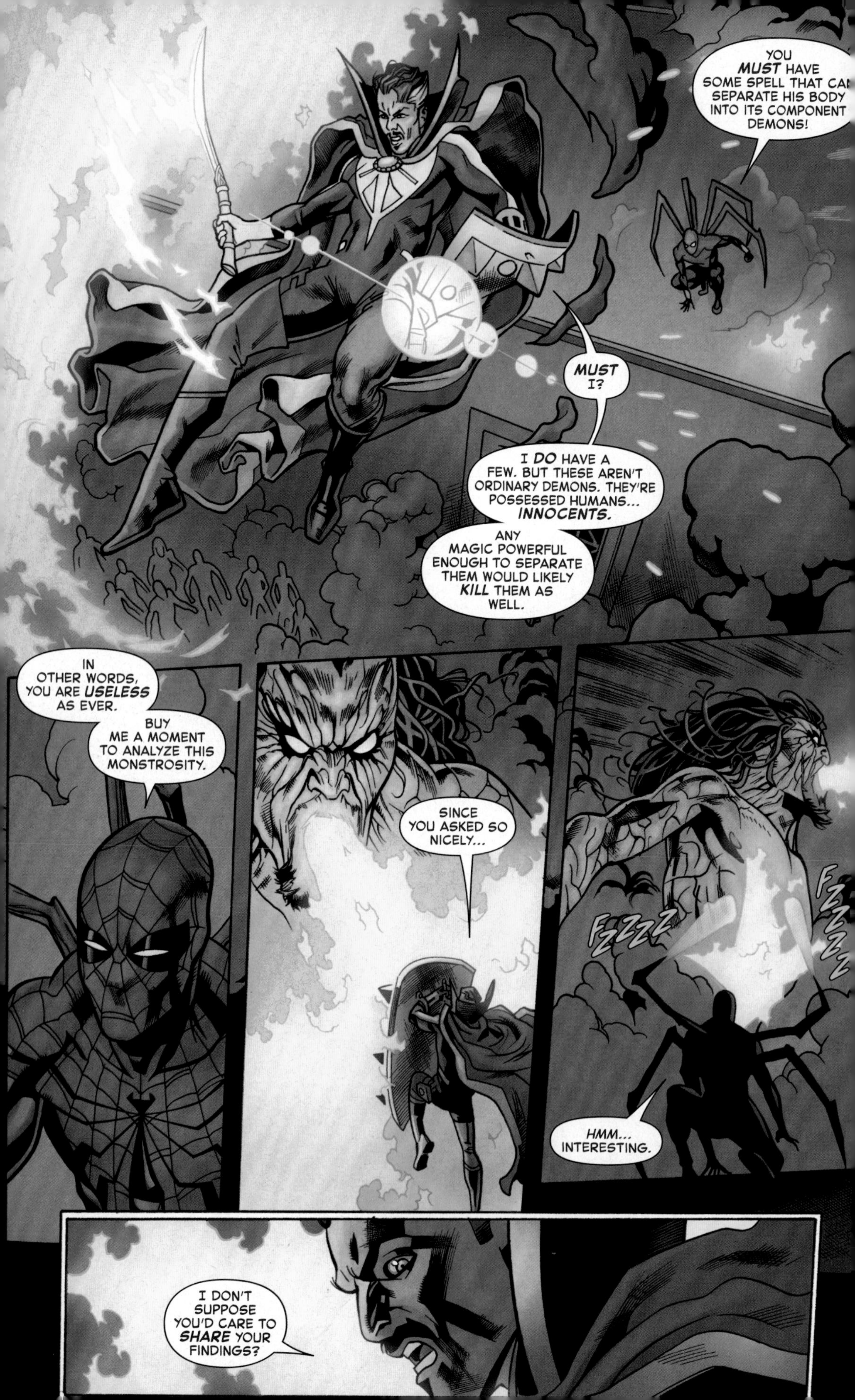
YOU MUST HAVE SOME SPELL THAT CA SEPARATE HIS BODY INTO ITS COMPONENT DEMONS!
MUST I?
I DO HAVE A FEW. BUT THESE AREN'T ORDINARY DEMONS. THEY'RE POSSESSED HUMANS... INNOCENTS.
ANY MAGIC POWERFUL ENOUGH TO SEPARATE THEM WOULD LIKELY KILL THEM AS WELL.
IN OTHER WORDS, YOU ARE USELESS AS EVER.
BUY ME A MOMENT TO ANALYZE THIS MONSTROSITY.
SINCE YOU ASKED SO NICELY...
FZZZZ
FZZZZ
HMM... INTERESTING.
I DON'T SUPPOSE YOU'D CARE TO SHARE YOUR FINDINGS?

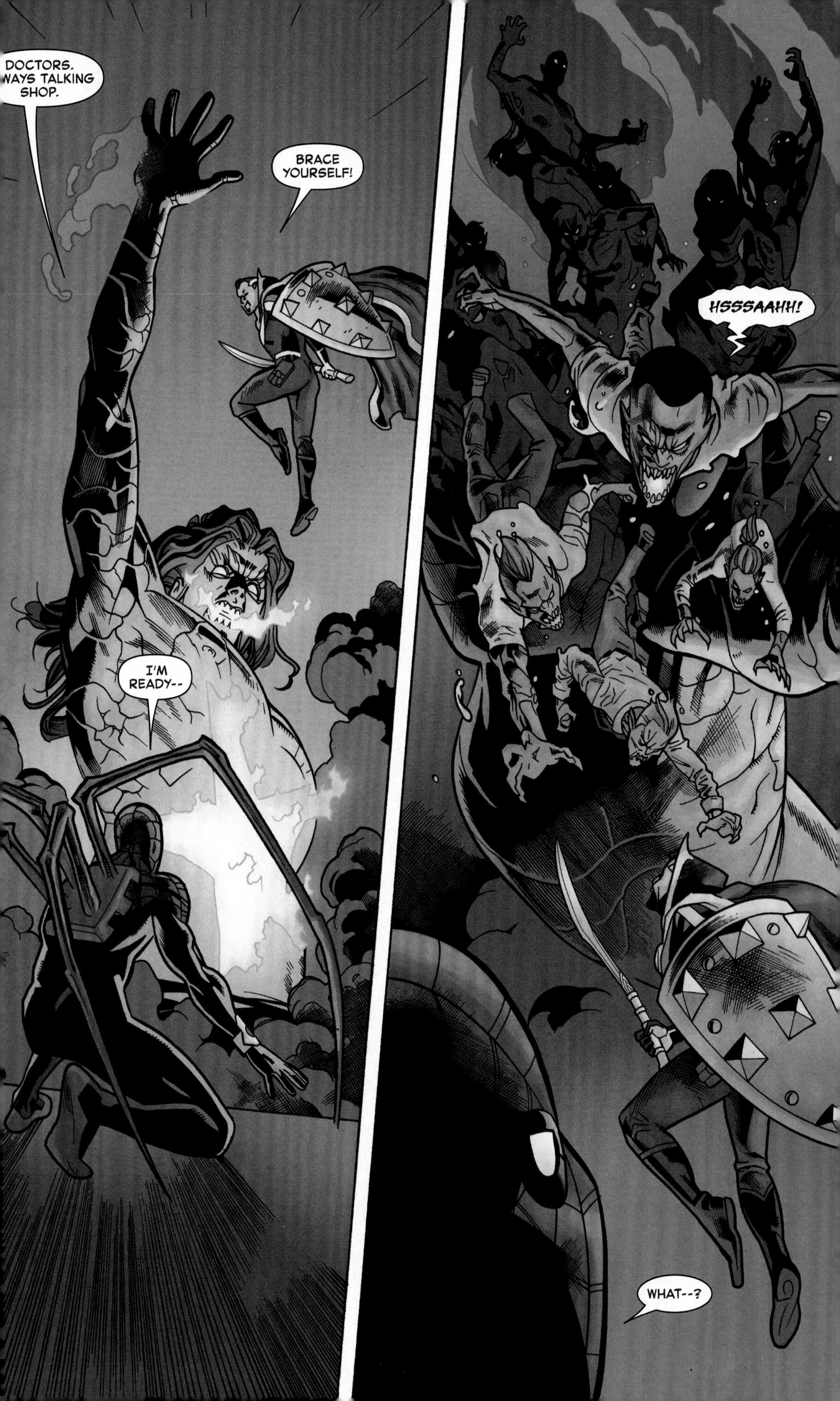
DOCTORS. ...WAYS TALKING SHOP.
BRACE YOURSELF!
I'M READY--
HSSSAAHH!
WHAT--?

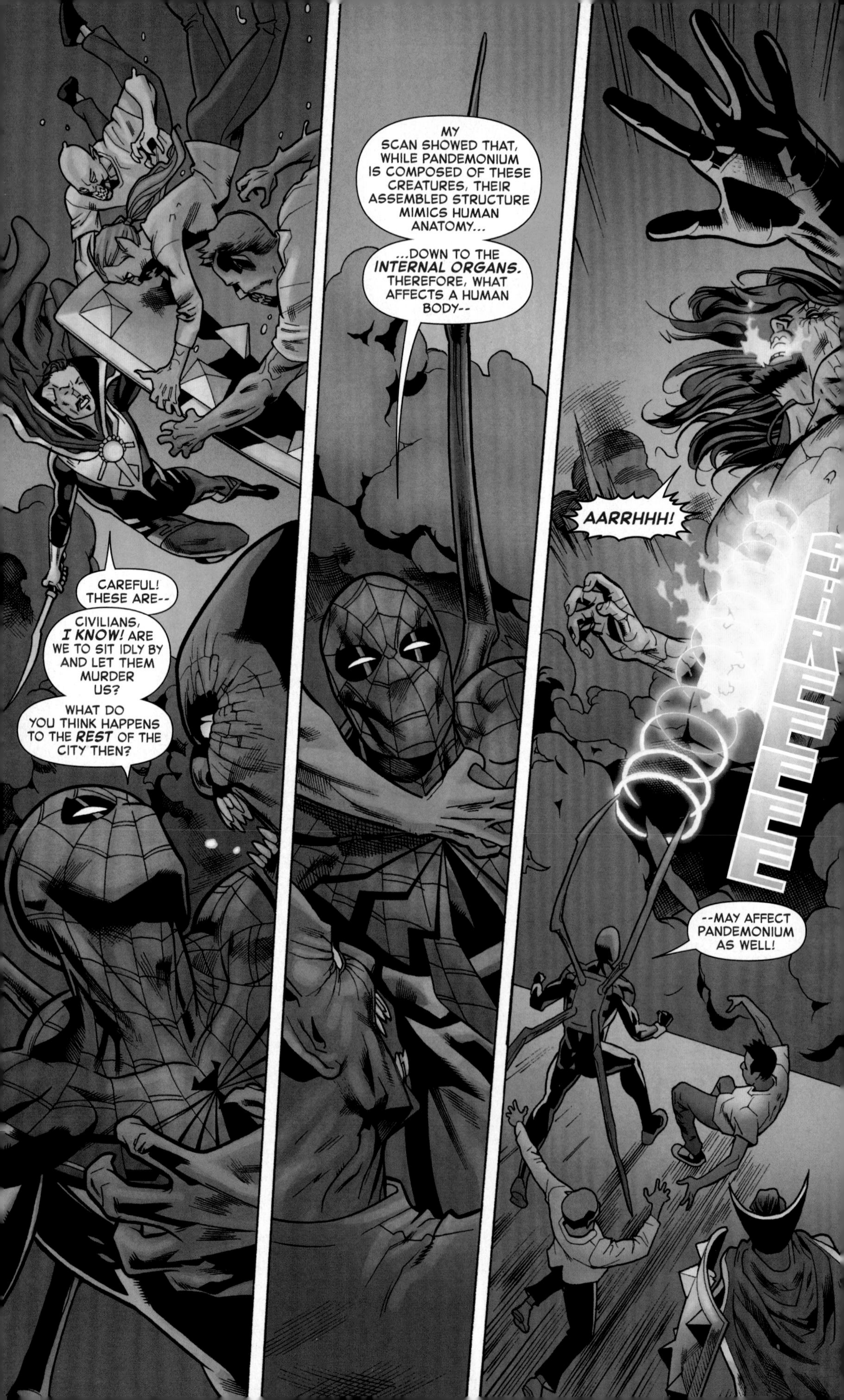
CAREFUL! THESE ARE--
CIVILIANS, I KNOW! ARE WE TO SIT IDLY BY AND LET THEM MURDER US?
WHAT DO YOU THINK HAPPENS TO THE REST OF THE CITY THEN?
MY SCAN SHOWED THAT, WHILE PANDEMONIUM IS COMPOSED OF THESE CREATURES, THEIR ASSEMBLED STRUCTURE MIMICS HUMAN ANATOMY...
...DOWN TO THE INTERNAL ORGANS. THEREFORE, WHAT AFFECTS A HUMAN BODY--
AARRHHH!
SKREEEE
--MAY AFFECT PANDEMONIUM AS WELL!

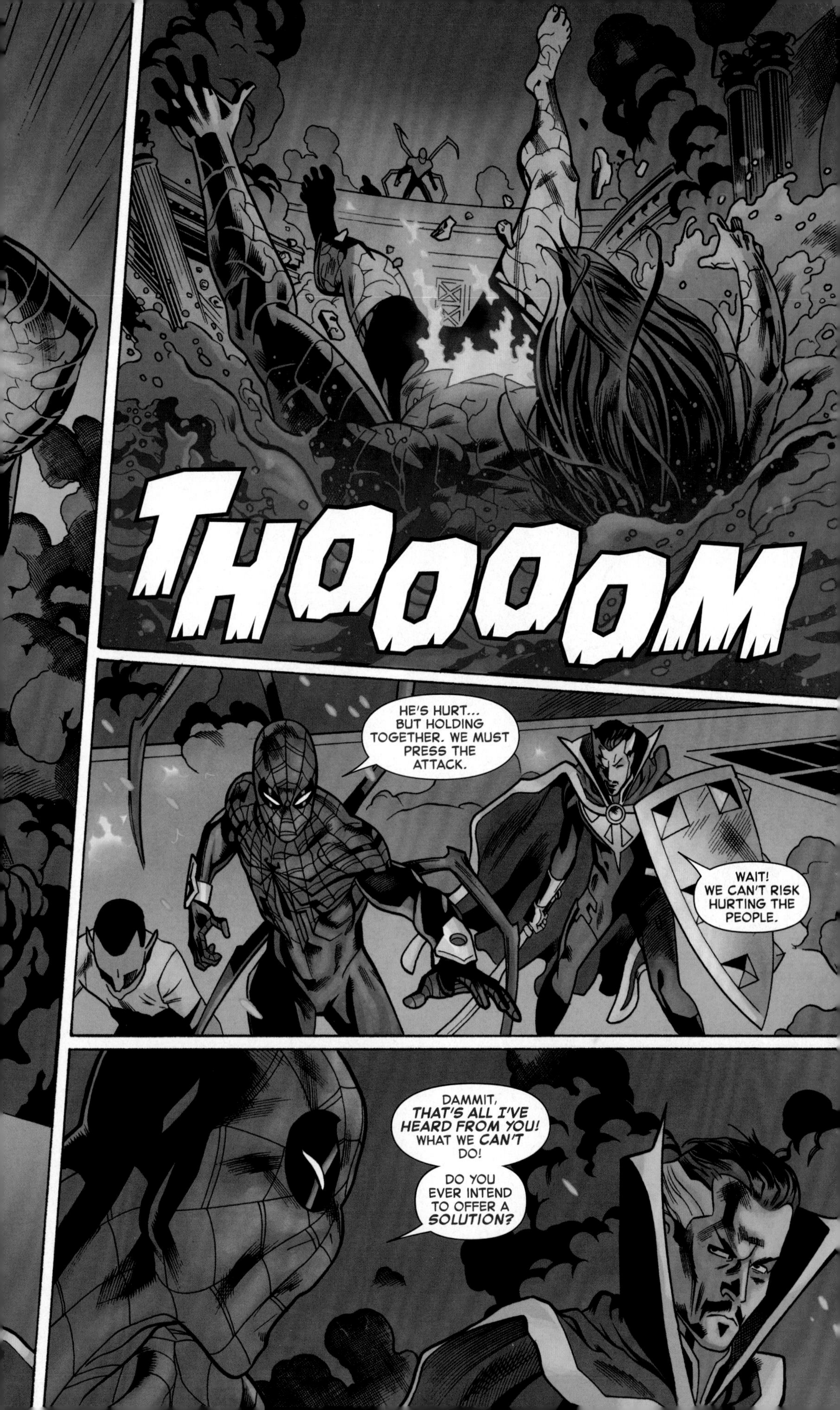
THOOOOM
HE'S HURT... BUT HOLDING TOGETHER. WE MUST PRESS THE ATTACK.
WAIT! WE CAN'T RISK HURTING THE PEOPLE.
DAMMIT, THAT'S ALL I'VE HEARD FROM YOU! WHAT WE CAN'T DO!
DO YOU EVER INTEND TO OFFER A SOLUTION?

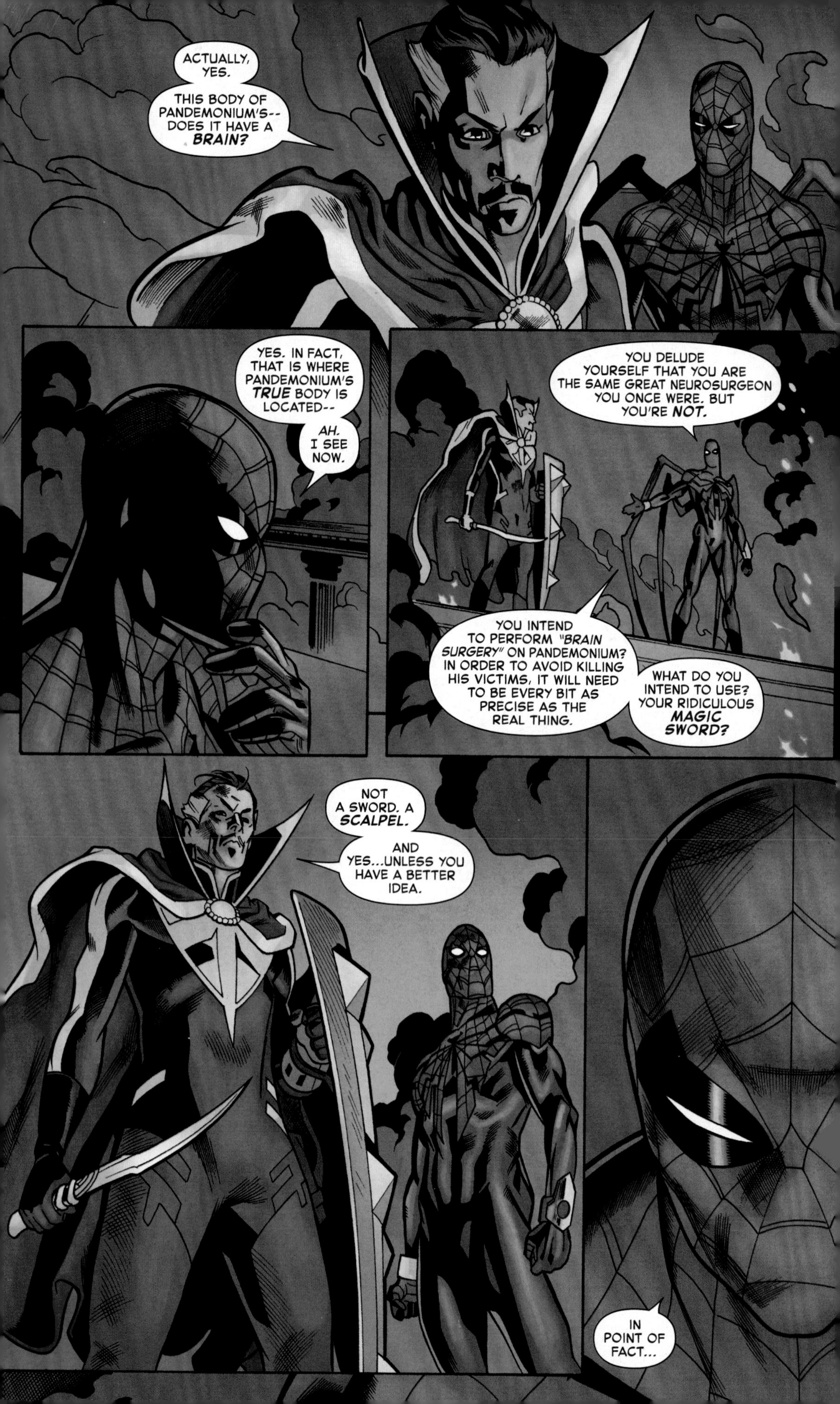
ACTUALLY, YES.
THIS BODY OF PANDEMONIUM'S-- DOES IT HAVE A BRAIN?
YES. IN FACT, THAT IS WHERE PANDEMONIUM'S TRUE BODY IS LOCATED--
AH. I SEE NOW.
YOU DELUDE YOURSELF THAT YOU ARE THE SAME GREAT NEUROSURGEON YOU ONCE WERE. BUT YOU'RE NOT.
YOU INTEND TO PERFORM "BRAIN SURGERY" ON PANDEMONIUM? IN ORDER TO AVOID KILLING HIS VICTIMS, IT WILL NEED TO BE EVERY BIT AS PRECISE AS THE REAL THING.
WHAT DO YOU INTEND TO USE? YOUR RIDICULOUS MAGIC SWORD?
NOT A SWORD. A SCALPEL.
AND YES...UNLESS YOU HAVE A BETTER IDEA.
IN POINT OF FACT...

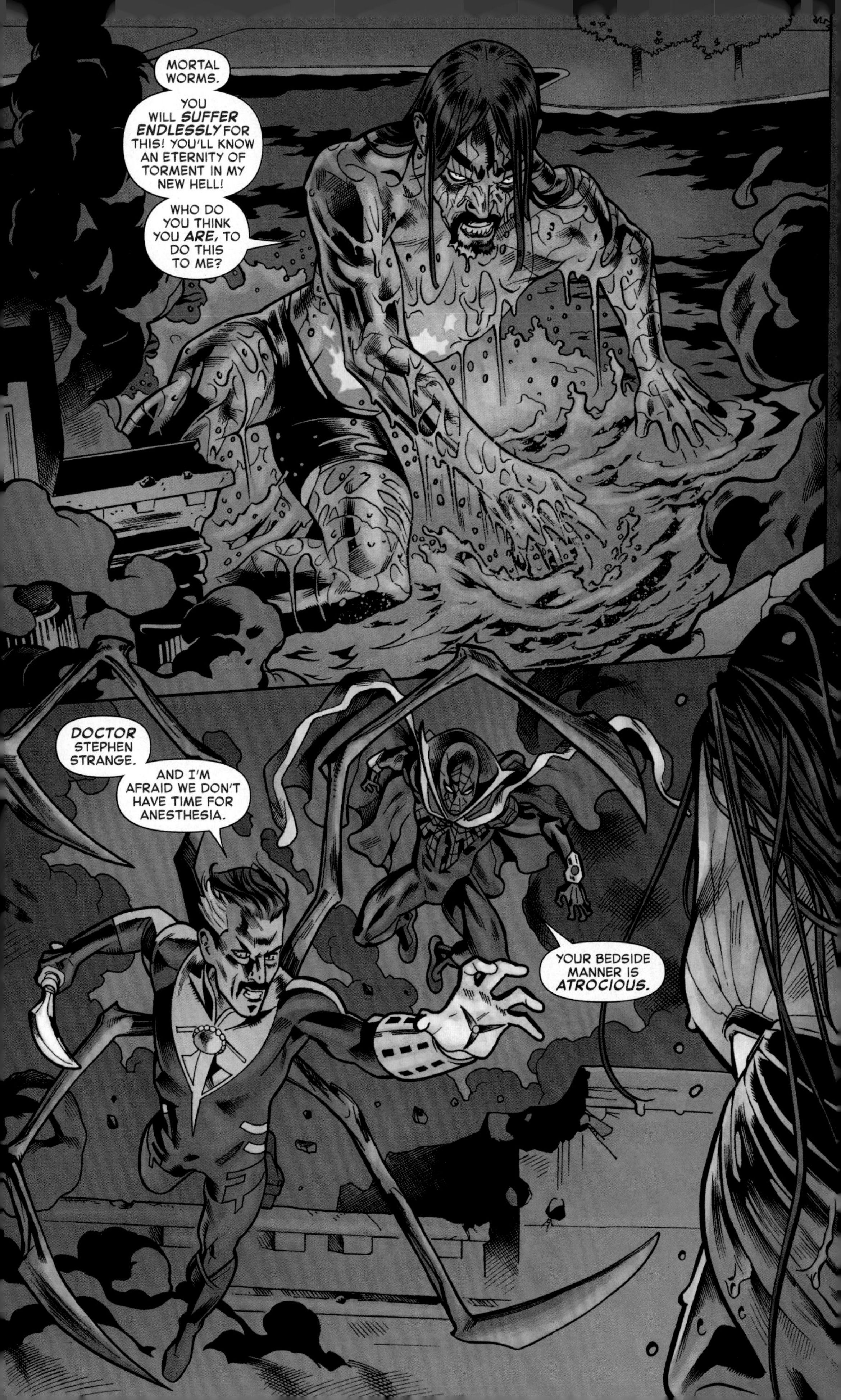
MORTAL WORMS.
YOU WILL SUFFER ENDLESSLY FOR THIS! YOU'LL KNOW AN ETERNITY OF TORMENT IN MY NEW HELL!
WHO DO YOU THINK YOU ARE, TO DO THIS TO ME?
DOCTOR STEPHEN STRANGE.
AND I'M AFRAID WE DON'T HAVE TIME FOR ANESTHESIA.
YOUR BEDSIDE MANNER IS ATROCIOUS.

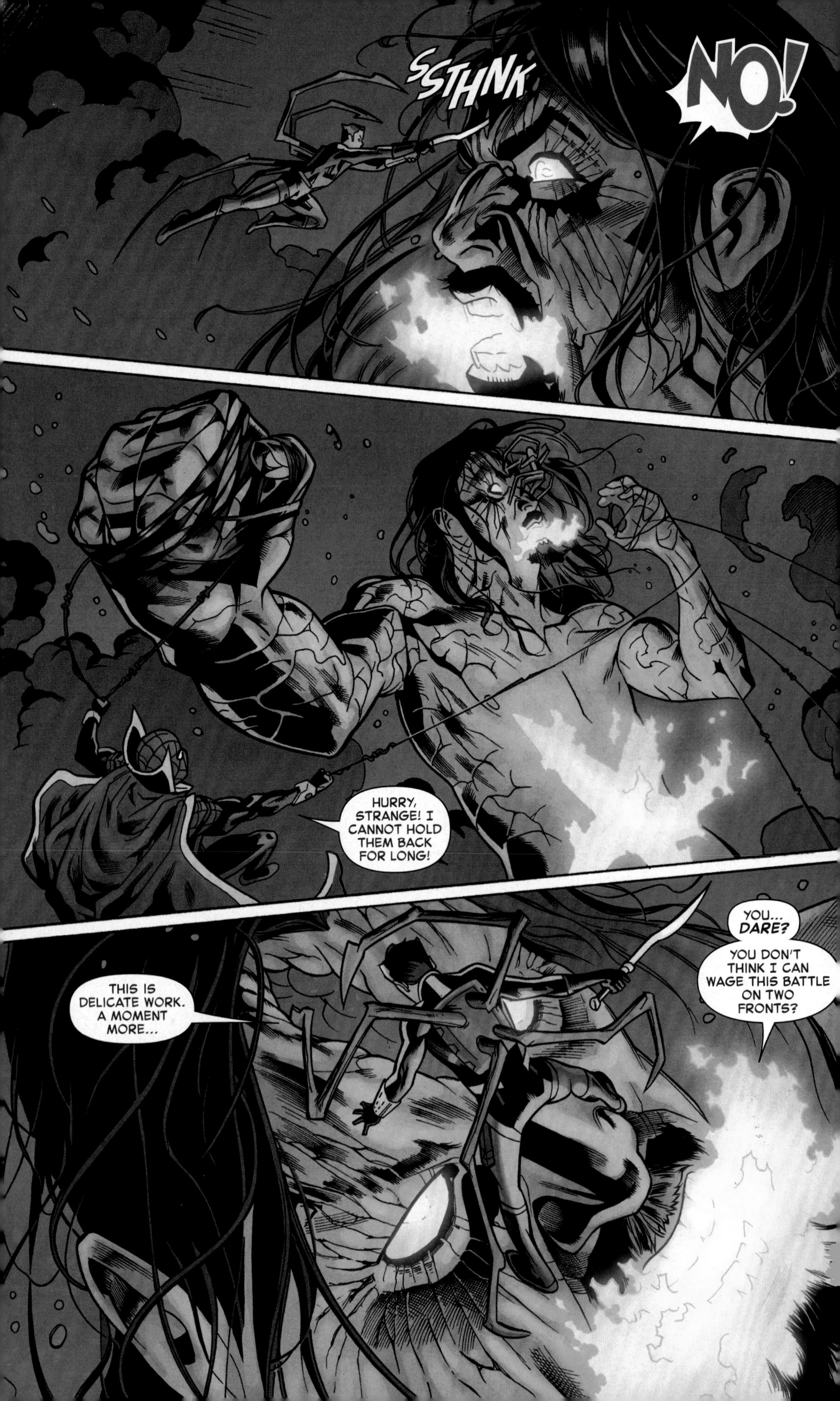
SSTHNK
NO!
HURRY, STRANGE! I CANNOT HOLD THEM BACK FOR LONG!
THIS IS DELICATE WORK. A MOMENT MORE...
YOU... DARE?
YOU DON'T THINK I CAN WAGE THIS BATTLE ON TWO FRONTS?

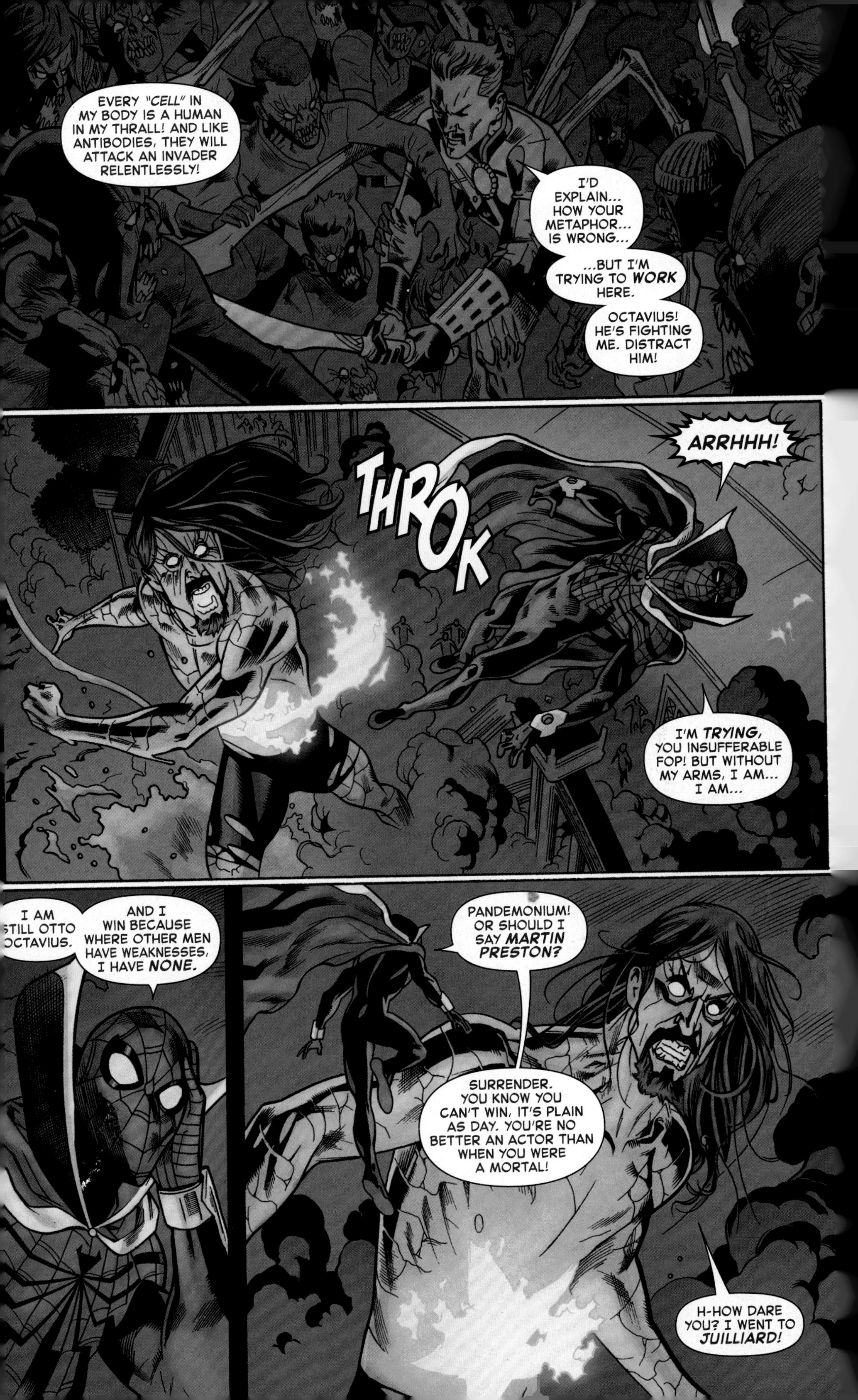
EVERY "CELL" IN MY BODY IS A HUMAN IN MY THRALL! AND LIKE ANTIBODIES, THEY WILL ATTACK AN INVADER RELENTLESSLY!
I'D EXPLAIN... HOW YOUR METAPHOR... IS WRONG...
...BUT I'M TRYING TO WORK HERE.
OCTAVIUS! HE'S FIGHTING ME. DISTRACT HIM!
THROK
ARRHHH!
I'M TRYING, YOU INSUFFERABLE FOP! BUT WITHOUT MY ARMS, I AM... I AM...
I AM STILL OTTO OCTAVIUS.
AND I WIN BECAUSE WHERE OTHER MEN HAVE WEAKNESSES, I HAVE NONE.
PANDEMONIUM! OR SHOULD I SAY MARTIN PRESTON?
SURRENDER. YOU KNOW YOU CAN'T WIN, IT'S PLAIN AS DAY. YOU'RE NO BETTER AN ACTOR THAN WHEN YOU WERE A MORTAL!
H-HOW DARE YOU? I WENT TO JUILLIARD!

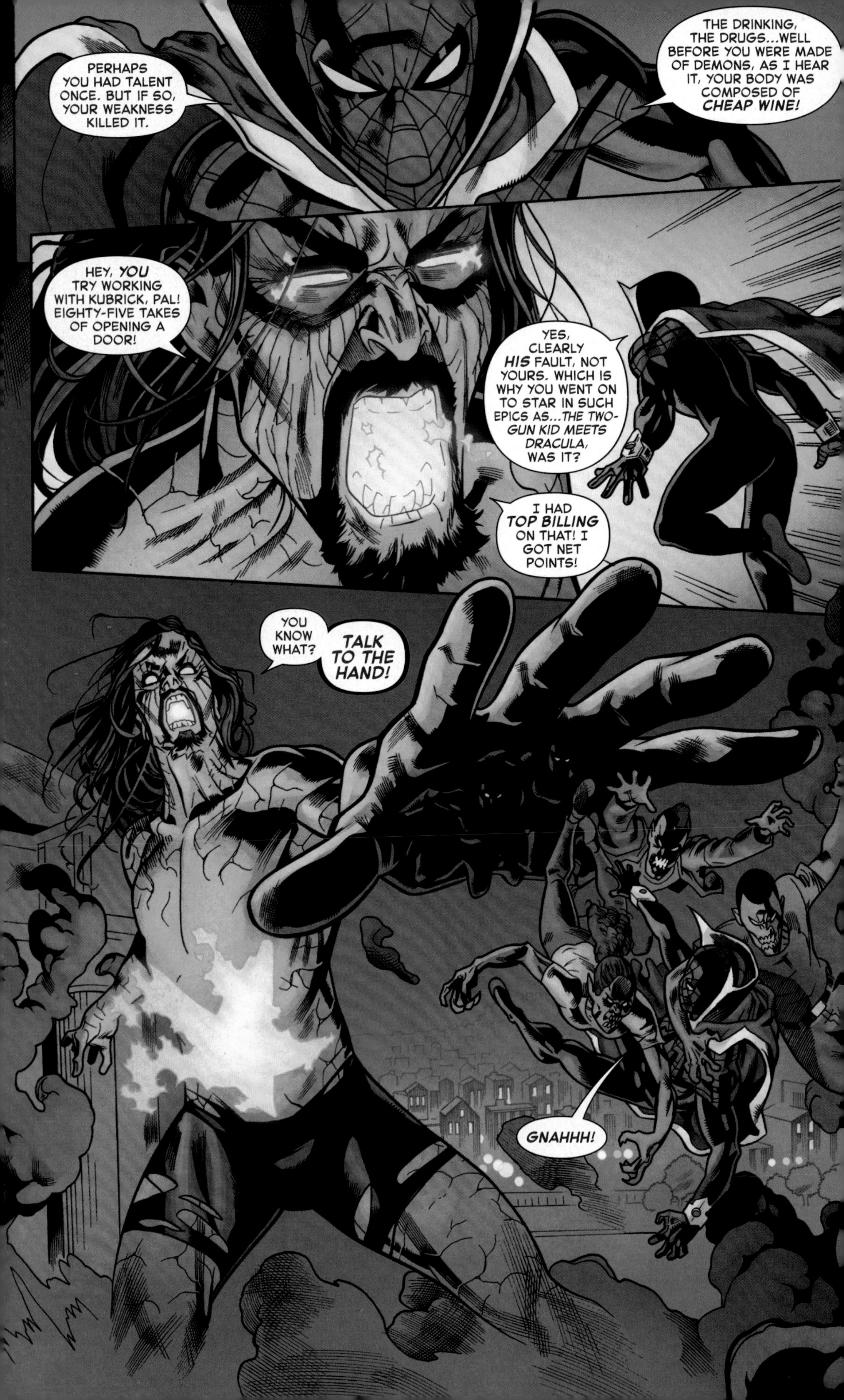
PERHAPS YOU HAD TALENT ONCE. BUT IF SO, YOUR WEAKNESS KILLED IT.
THE DRINKING, THE DRUGS...WELL BEFORE YOU WERE MADE OF DEMONS, AS I HEAR IT, YOUR BODY WAS COMPOSED OF *CHEAP WINE!*
HEY, *YOU* TRY WORKING WITH KUBRICK, PAL! EIGHTY-FIVE TAKES OF OPENING A DOOR!
YES, CLEARLY *HIS* FAULT, NOT YOURS. WHICH IS WHY YOU WENT ON TO STAR IN SUCH EPICS AS...*THE TWO-GUN KID MEETS DRACULA,* WAS IT?
I HAD *TOP BILLING* ON THAT! I GOT NET POINTS!
YOU KNOW WHAT?
TALK TO THE HAND!
GNAHHH!

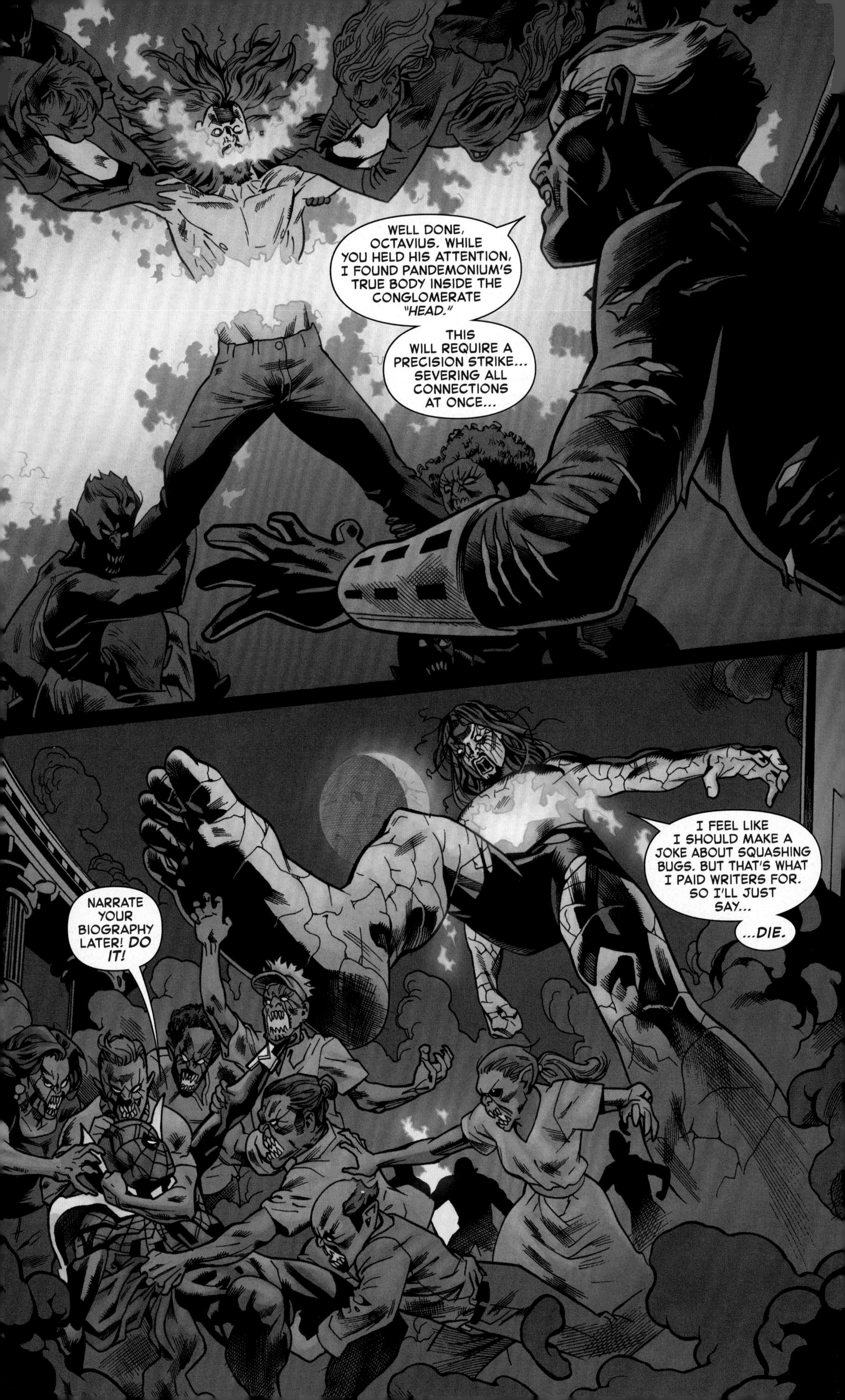
WELL DONE, OCTAVIUS. WHILE YOU HELD HIS ATTENTION, I FOUND PANDEMONIUM'S TRUE BODY INSIDE THE CONGLOMERATE "HEAD."
THIS WILL REQUIRE A PRECISION STRIKE... SEVERING ALL CONNECTIONS AT ONCE...
I FEEL LIKE I SHOULD MAKE A JOKE ABOUT SQUASHING BUGS. BUT THAT'S WHAT I PAID WRITERS FOR. SO I'LL JUST SAY...
...DIE.
NARRATE YOUR BIOGRAPHY LATER! DO IT!

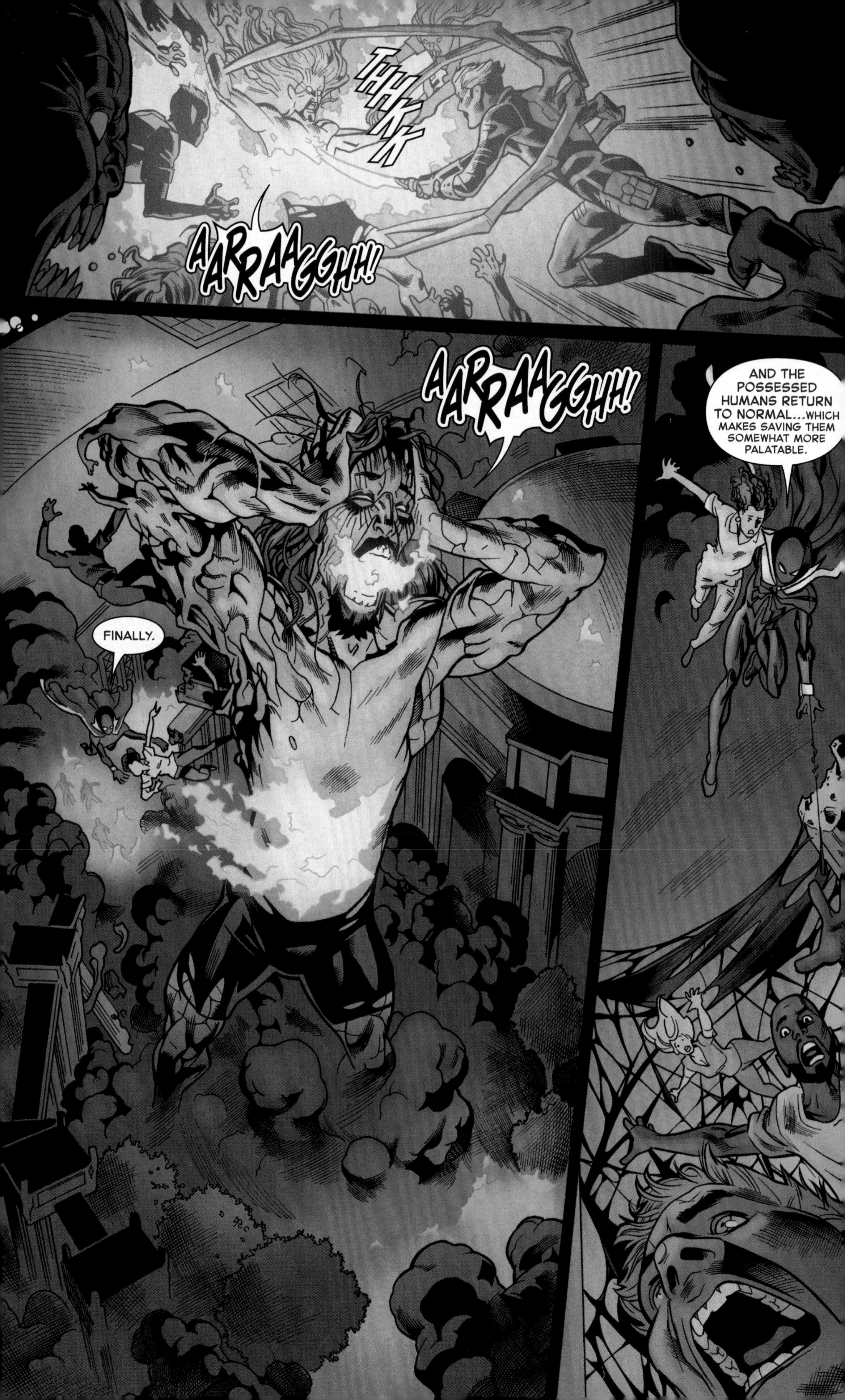
THHKK
AARRAAGGHH!
AARRAAGGHH!
FINALLY.
AND THE POSSESSED HUMANS RETURN TO NORMAL...WHICH MAKES SAVING THEM SOMEWHAT MORE PALATABLE.

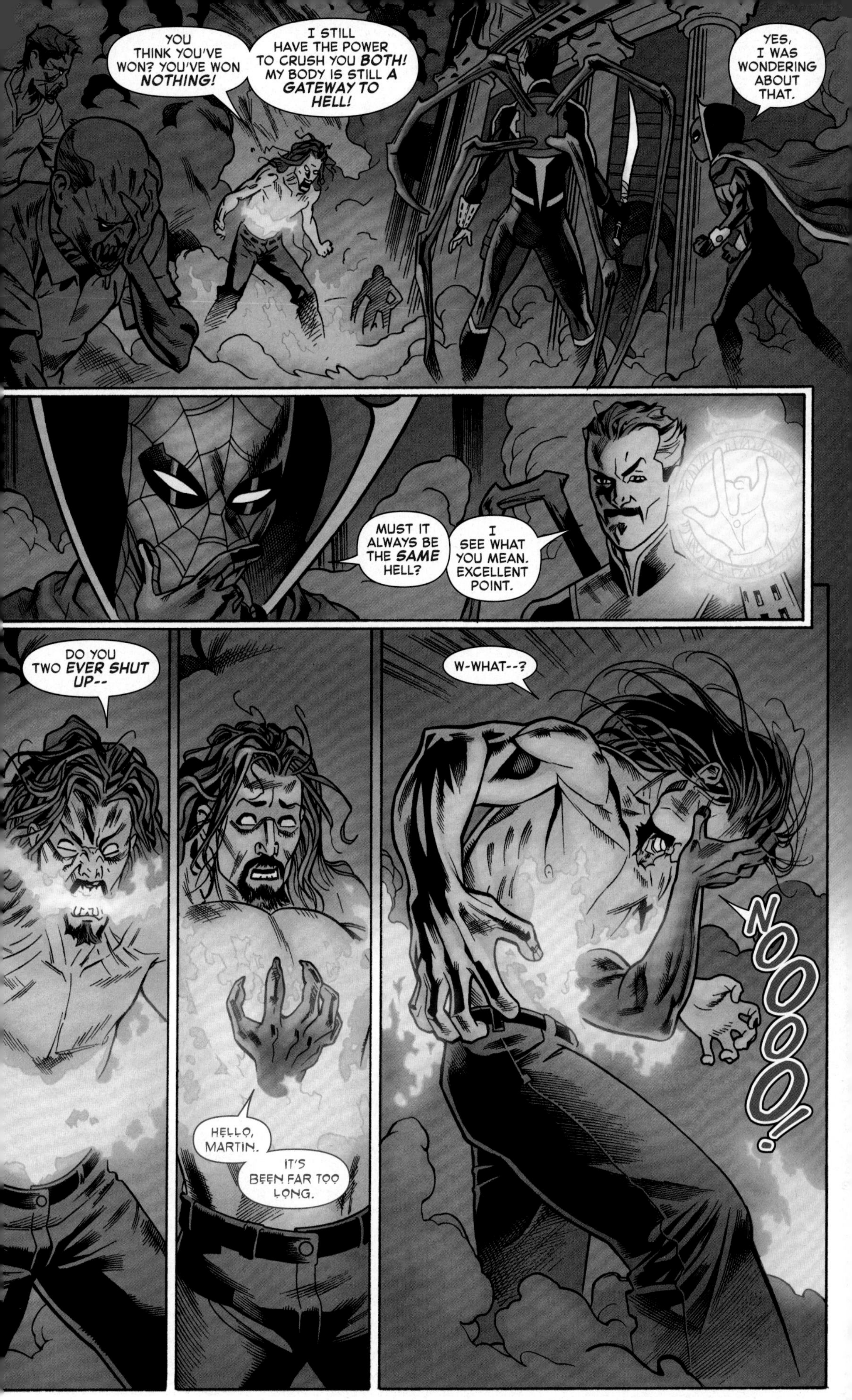
YOU THINK YOU'VE WON? YOU'VE WON NOTHING!
I STILL HAVE THE POWER TO CRUSH YOU BOTH! MY BODY IS STILL A GATEWAY TO HELL!
YES, I WAS WONDERING ABOUT THAT.
MUST IT ALWAYS BE THE SAME HELL?
I SEE WHAT YOU MEAN. EXCELLENT POINT.
DO YOU TWO EVER SHUT UP--
HELLO, MARTIN.
IT'S BEEN FAR TOO LONG.
W-WHAT--?
NOOOOO!

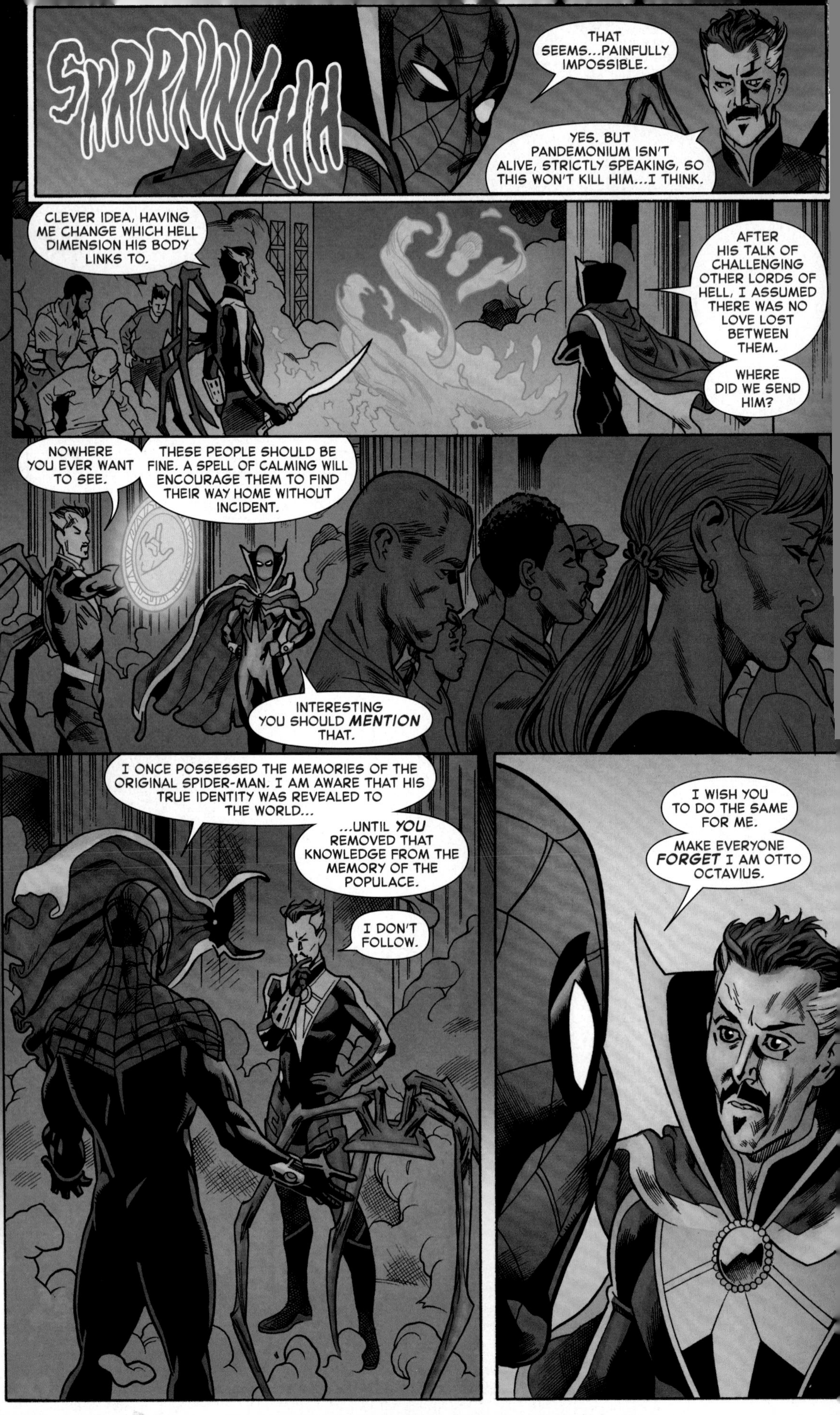

SKRRNNCHH
THAT SEEMS...PAINFULLY IMPOSSIBLE.
YES. BUT PANDEMONIUM ISN'T ALIVE, STRICTLY SPEAKING, SO THIS WON'T KILL HIM...I THINK.
CLEVER IDEA, HAVING ME CHANGE WHICH HELL DIMENSION HIS BODY LINKS TO.
AFTER HIS TALK OF CHALLENGING OTHER LORDS OF HELL, I ASSUMED THERE WAS NO LOVE LOST BETWEEN THEM.
WHERE DID WE SEND HIM?
NOWHERE YOU EVER WANT TO SEE.
THESE PEOPLE SHOULD BE FINE. A SPELL OF CALMING WILL ENCOURAGE THEM TO FIND THEIR WAY HOME WITHOUT INCIDENT.
INTERESTING YOU SHOULD *MENTION* THAT.
I ONCE POSSESSED THE MEMORIES OF THE ORIGINAL SPIDER-MAN. I AM AWARE THAT HIS TRUE IDENTITY WAS REVEALED TO THE WORLD...
...UNTIL *YOU* REMOVED THAT KNOWLEDGE FROM THE MEMORY OF THE POPULACE.
I DON'T FOLLOW.
I WISH YOU TO DO THE SAME FOR ME.
MAKE EVERYONE *FORGET* I AM OTTO OCTAVIUS.

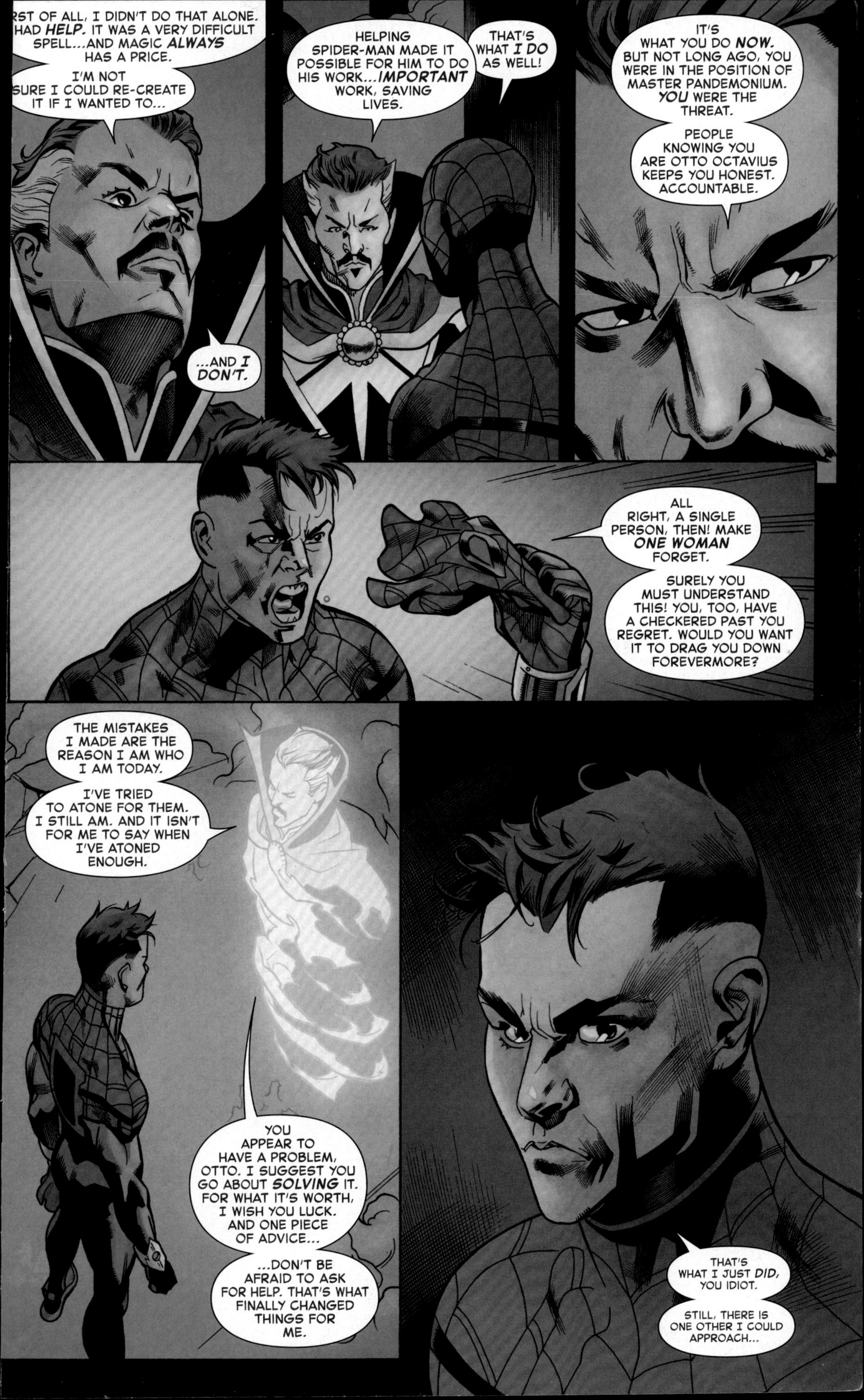
RST OF ALL, I DIDN'T DO THAT ALONE. HAD HELP. IT WAS A VERY DIFFICULT SPELL...AND MAGIC ALWAYS HAS A PRICE.
I'M NOT SURE I COULD RE-CREATE IT IF I WANTED TO...
...AND I DON'T.
HELPING SPIDER-MAN MADE IT POSSIBLE FOR HIM TO DO HIS WORK...IMPORTANT WORK, SAVING LIVES.
THAT'S WHAT I DO AS WELL!
IT'S WHAT YOU DO NOW. BUT NOT LONG AGO, YOU WERE IN THE POSITION OF MASTER PANDEMONIUM. YOU WERE THE THREAT.
PEOPLE KNOWING YOU ARE OTTO OCTAVIUS KEEPS YOU HONEST. ACCOUNTABLE.
ALL RIGHT, A SINGLE PERSON, THEN! MAKE ONE WOMAN FORGET.
SURELY YOU MUST UNDERSTAND THIS! YOU, TOO, HAVE A CHECKERED PAST YOU REGRET. WOULD YOU WANT IT TO DRAG YOU DOWN FOREVERMORE?
THE MISTAKES I MADE ARE THE REASON I AM WHO I AM TODAY.
I'VE TRIED TO ATONE FOR THEM. I STILL AM. AND IT ISN'T FOR ME TO SAY WHEN I'VE ATONED ENOUGH.
YOU APPEAR TO HAVE A PROBLEM, OTTO. I SUGGEST YOU GO ABOUT SOLVING IT. FOR WHAT IT'S WORTH, I WISH YOU LUCK. AND ONE PIECE OF ADVICE...
...DON'T BE AFRAID TO ASK FOR HELP. THAT'S WHAT FINALLY CHANGED THINGS FOR ME.
THAT'S WHAT I JUST DID, YOU IDIOT.
STILL, THERE IS ONE OTHER I COULD APPROACH...

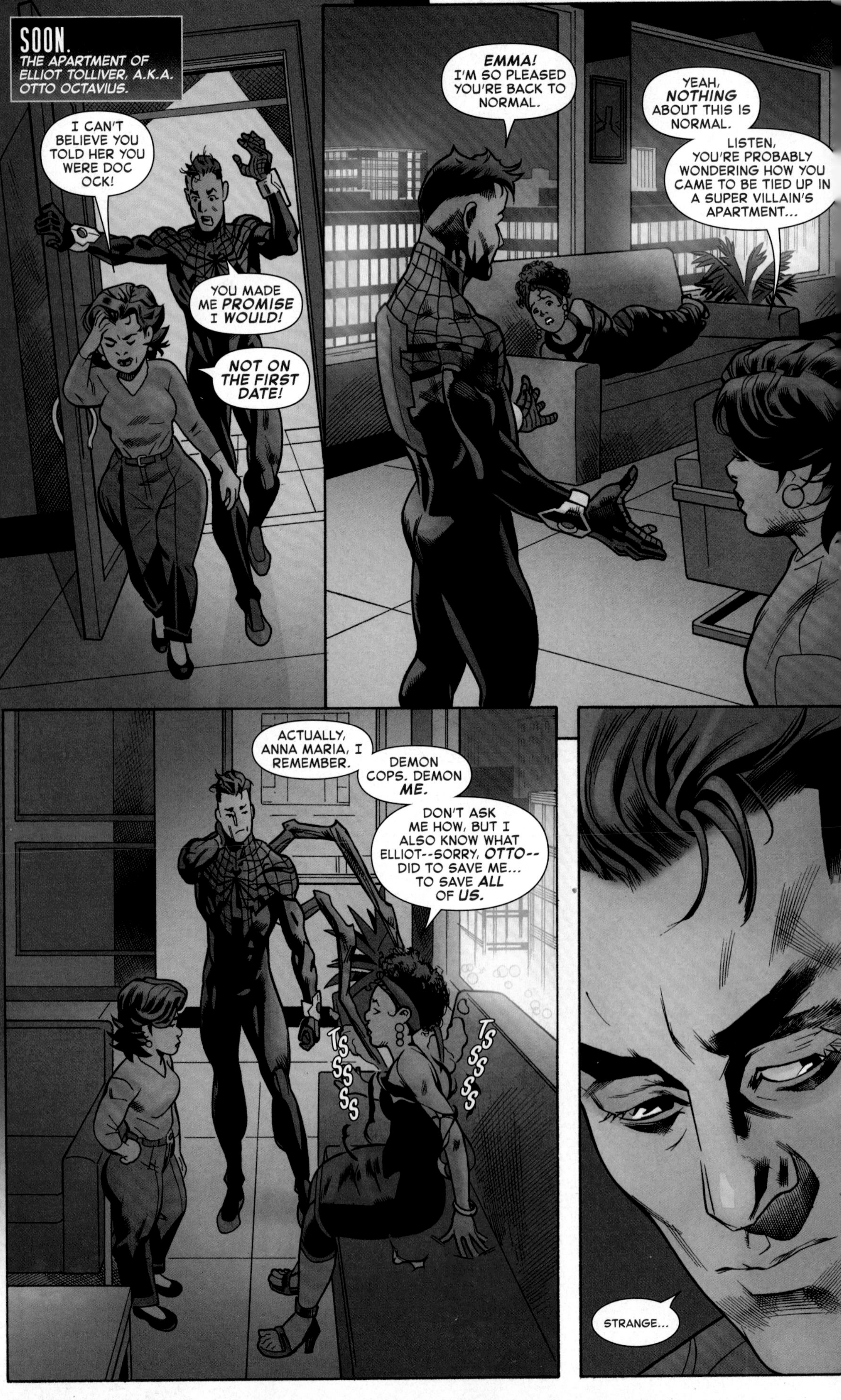
SOON.
THE APARTMENT OF ELLIOT TOLLIVER, A.K.A. OTTO OCTAVIUS.
I CAN'T BELIEVE YOU TOLD HER YOU WERE DOC OCK!
YOU MADE ME PROMISE I WOULD!
NOT ON THE FIRST DATE!
EMMA! I'M SO PLEASED YOU'RE BACK TO NORMAL.
YEAH, NOTHING ABOUT THIS IS NORMAL.
LISTEN, YOU'RE PROBABLY WONDERING HOW YOU CAME TO BE TIED UP IN A SUPER VILLAIN'S APARTMENT...
ACTUALLY, ANNA MARIA, I REMEMBER.
DEMON COPS. DEMON ME.
DON'T ASK ME HOW, BUT I ALSO KNOW WHAT ELLIOT--SORRY, OTTO--DID TO SAVE ME... TO SAVE ALL OF US.
TSSSSS
TSSSSS
STRANGE...

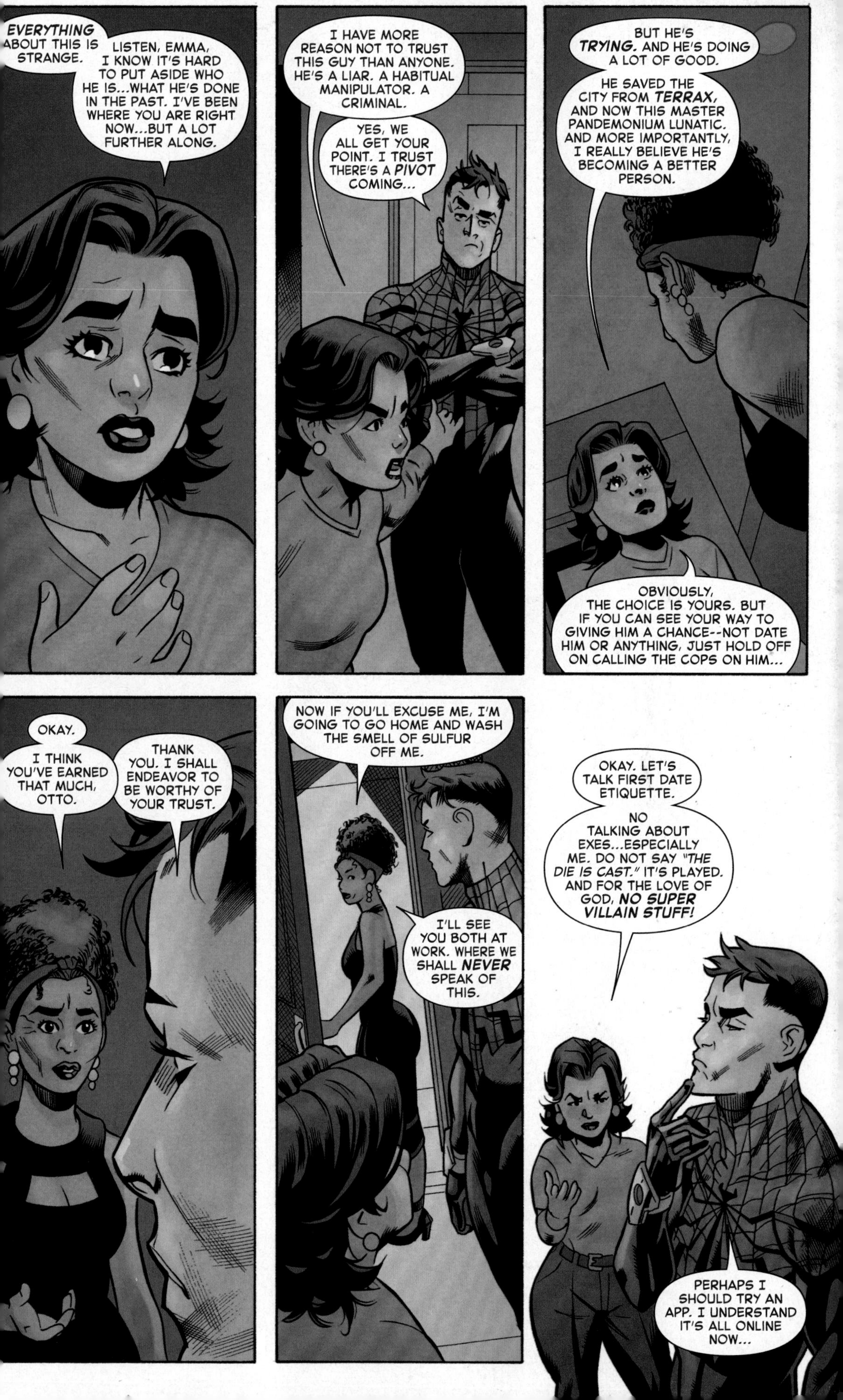
EVERYTHING ABOUT THIS IS STRANGE.
LISTEN, EMMA, I KNOW IT'S HARD TO PUT ASIDE WHO HE IS...WHAT HE'S DONE IN THE PAST. I'VE BEEN WHERE YOU ARE RIGHT NOW...BUT A LOT FURTHER ALONG.
I HAVE MORE REASON NOT TO TRUST THIS GUY THAN ANYONE. HE'S A LIAR. A HABITUAL MANIPULATOR. A CRIMINAL.
YES, WE ALL GET YOUR POINT. I TRUST THERE'S A PIVOT COMING...
BUT HE'S TRYING. AND HE'S DOING A LOT OF GOOD.
HE SAVED THE CITY FROM TERRAX, AND NOW THIS MASTER PANDEMONIUM LUNATIC. AND MORE IMPORTANTLY, I REALLY BELIEVE HE'S BECOMING A BETTER PERSON.
OBVIOUSLY, THE CHOICE IS YOURS. BUT IF YOU CAN SEE YOUR WAY TO GIVING HIM A CHANCE--NOT DATE HIM OR ANYTHING, JUST HOLD OFF ON CALLING THE COPS ON HIM...
OKAY.
I THINK YOU'VE EARNED THAT MUCH, OTTO.
THANK YOU. I SHALL ENDEAVOR TO BE WORTHY OF YOUR TRUST.
NOW IF YOU'LL EXCUSE ME, I'M GOING TO GO HOME AND WASH THE SMELL OF SULFUR OFF ME.
I'LL SEE YOU BOTH AT WORK. WHERE WE SHALL NEVER SPEAK OF THIS.
OKAY. LET'S TALK FIRST DATE ETIQUETTE.
NO TALKING ABOUT EXES...ESPECIALLY ME. DO NOT SAY "THE DIE IS CAST." IT'S PLAYED. AND FOR THE LOVE OF GOD, NO SUPER VILLAIN STUFF!
PERHAPS I SHOULD TRY AN APP. I UNDERSTAND IT'S ALL ONLINE NOW...

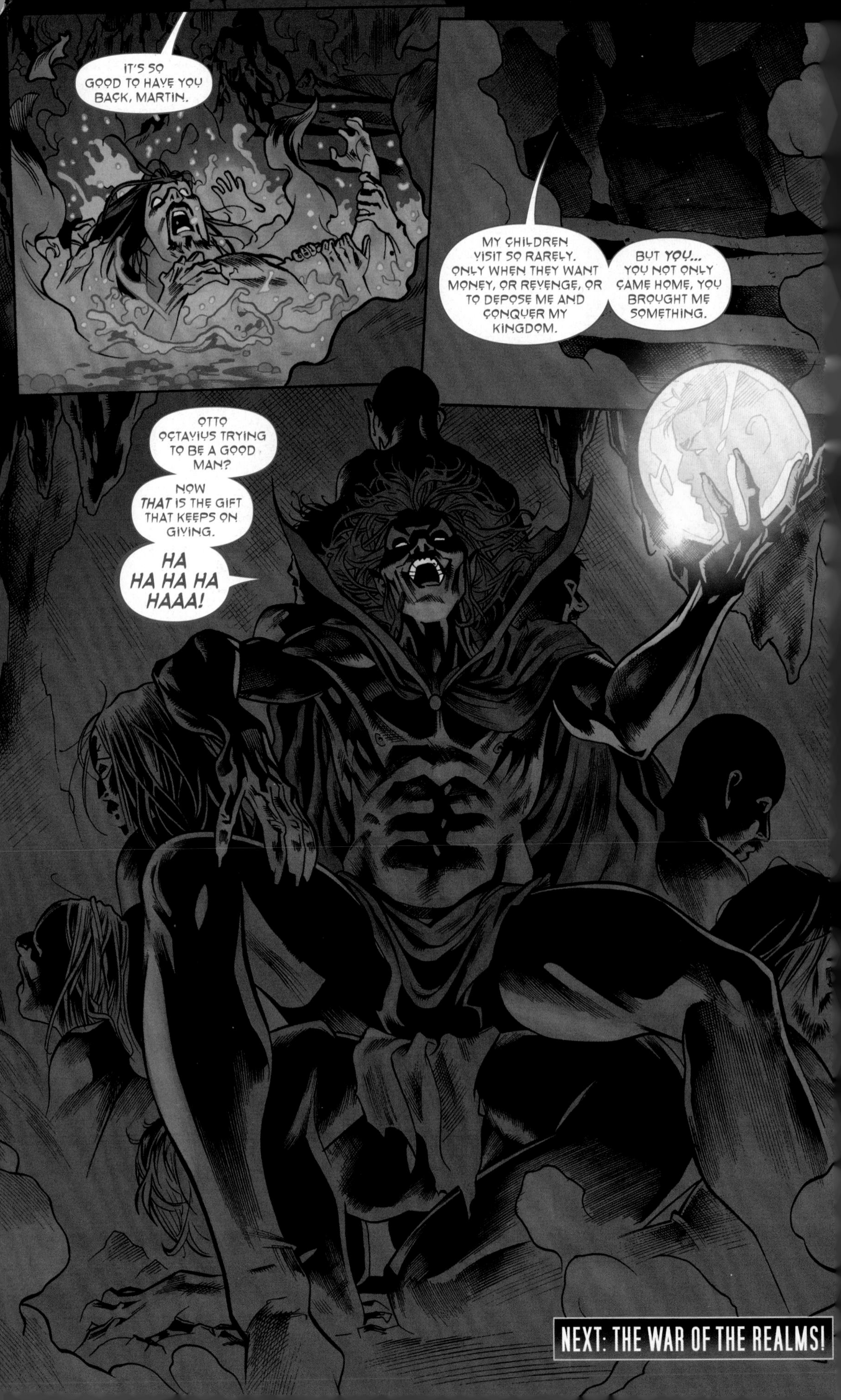
IT'S SO GOOD TO HAVE YOU BACK, MARTIN.
MY CHILDREN VISIT SO RARELY. ONLY WHEN THEY WANT MONEY, OR REVENGE, OR TO DEPOSE ME AND CONQUER MY KINGDOM.
BUT YOU... YOU NOT ONLY CAME HOME, YOU BROUGHT ME SOMETHING.
OTTO OCTAVIUS TRYING TO BE A GOOD MAN?
NOW THAT IS THE GIFT THAT KEEPS ON GIVING.
HA HA HA HA HAAA!
NEXT: THE WAR OF THE REALMS!

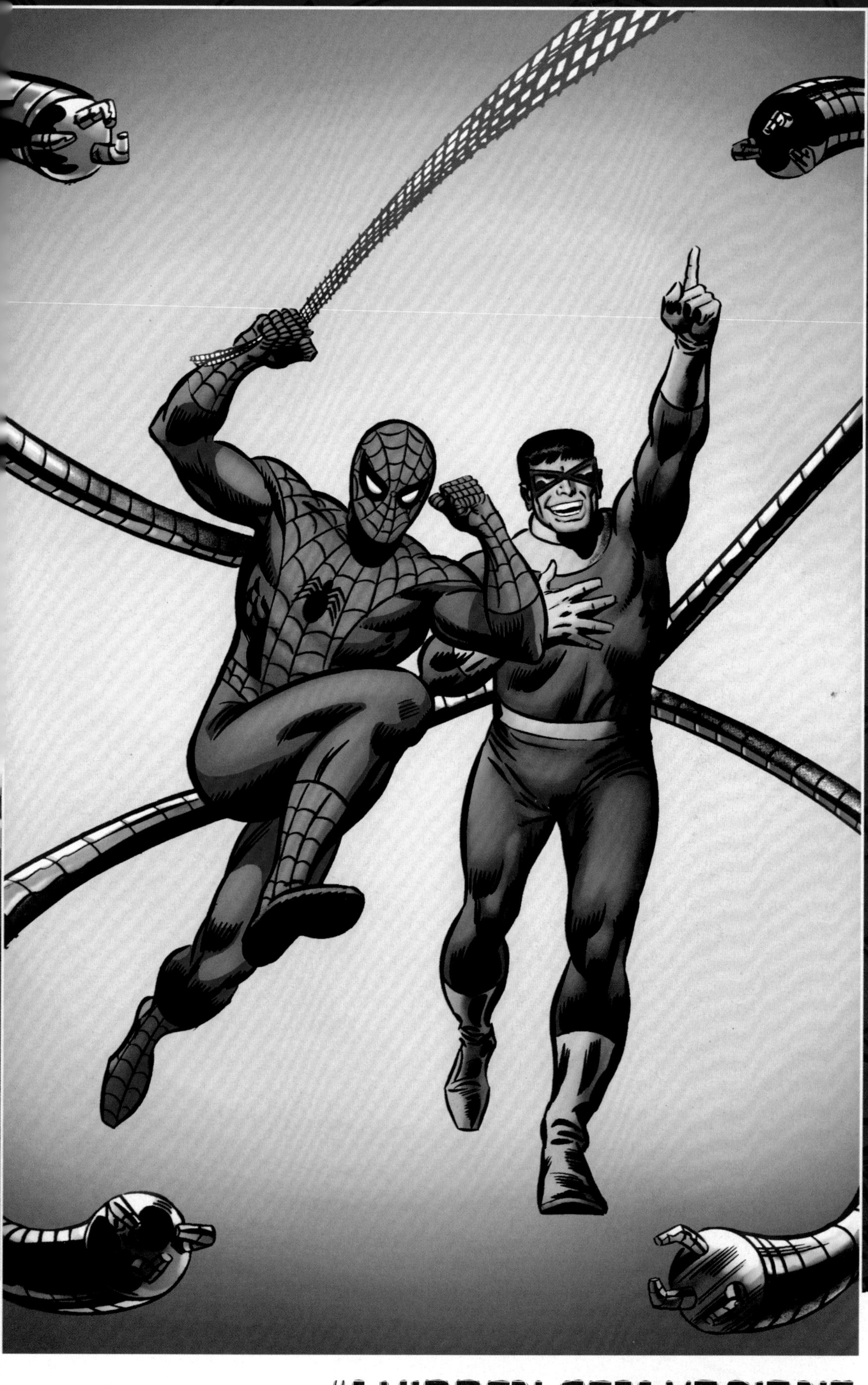

#1 HIDDEN GEM VARIANT
BY JOHN BUSCEMA & JASON KEITH

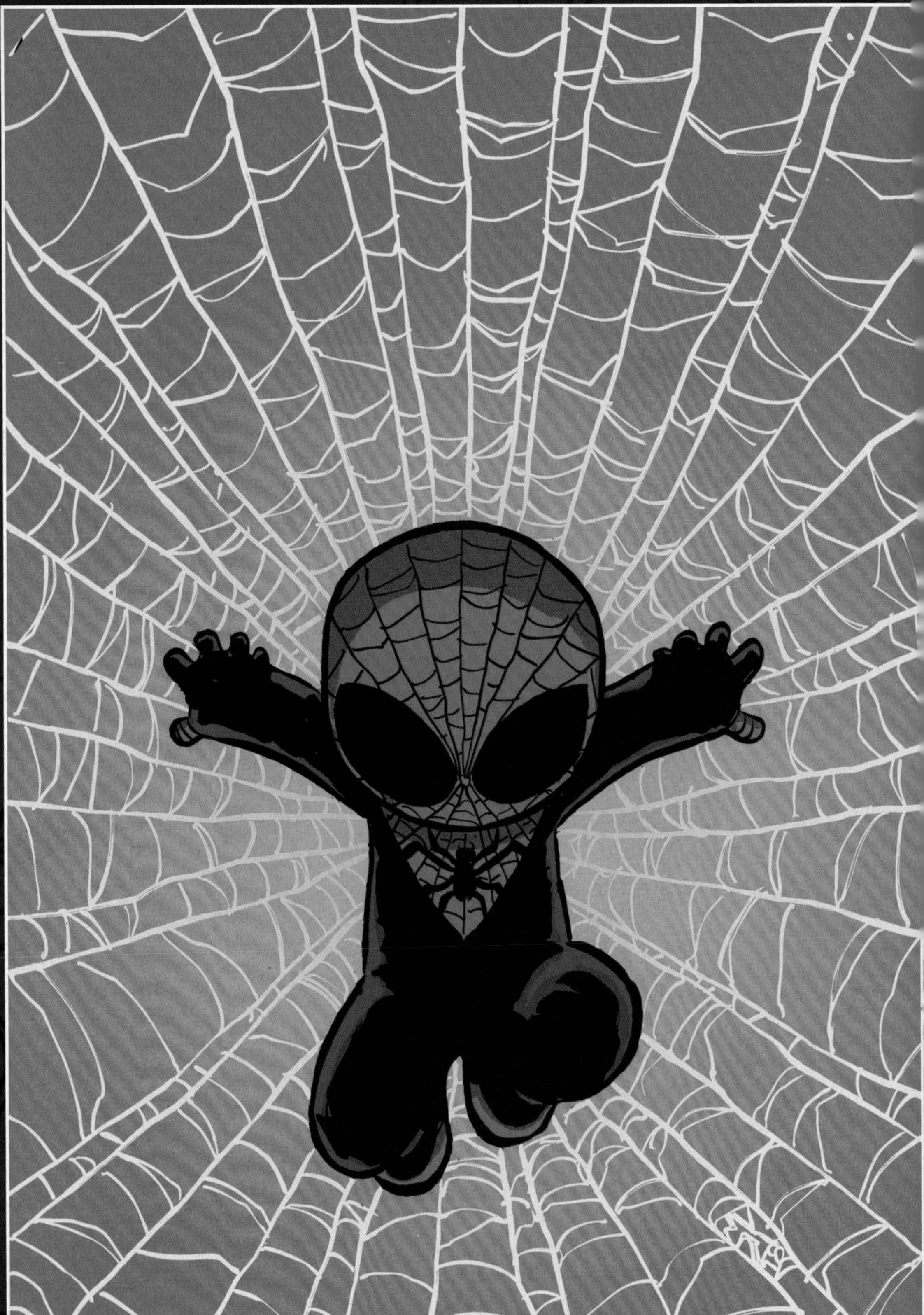

#1 VARIANT
BY SKOTTIE YOUNG

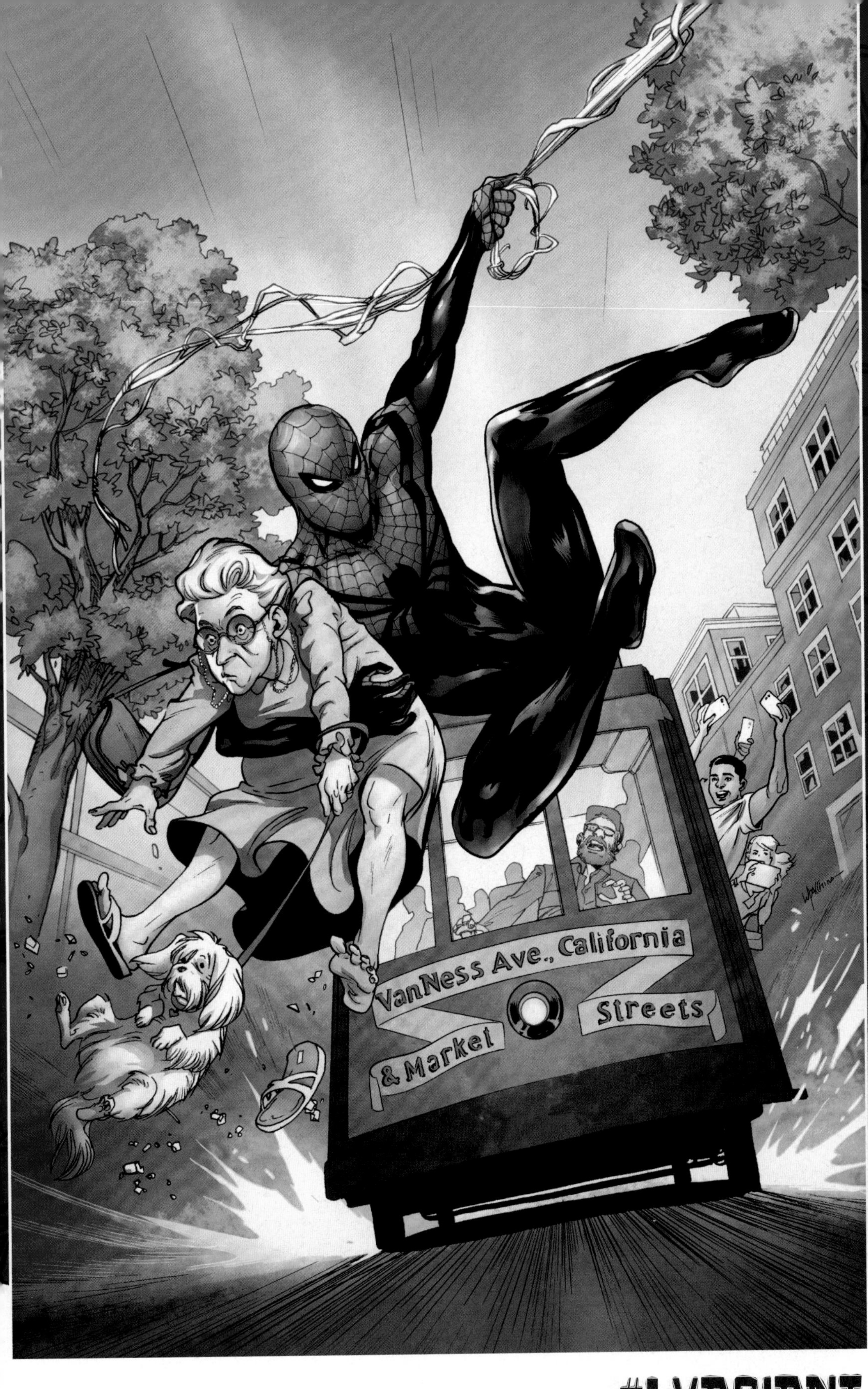
VanNess Ave., California
Streets
& Market

#1 VARIANT

BY EMA LUPACCHINO & JASON KEITH

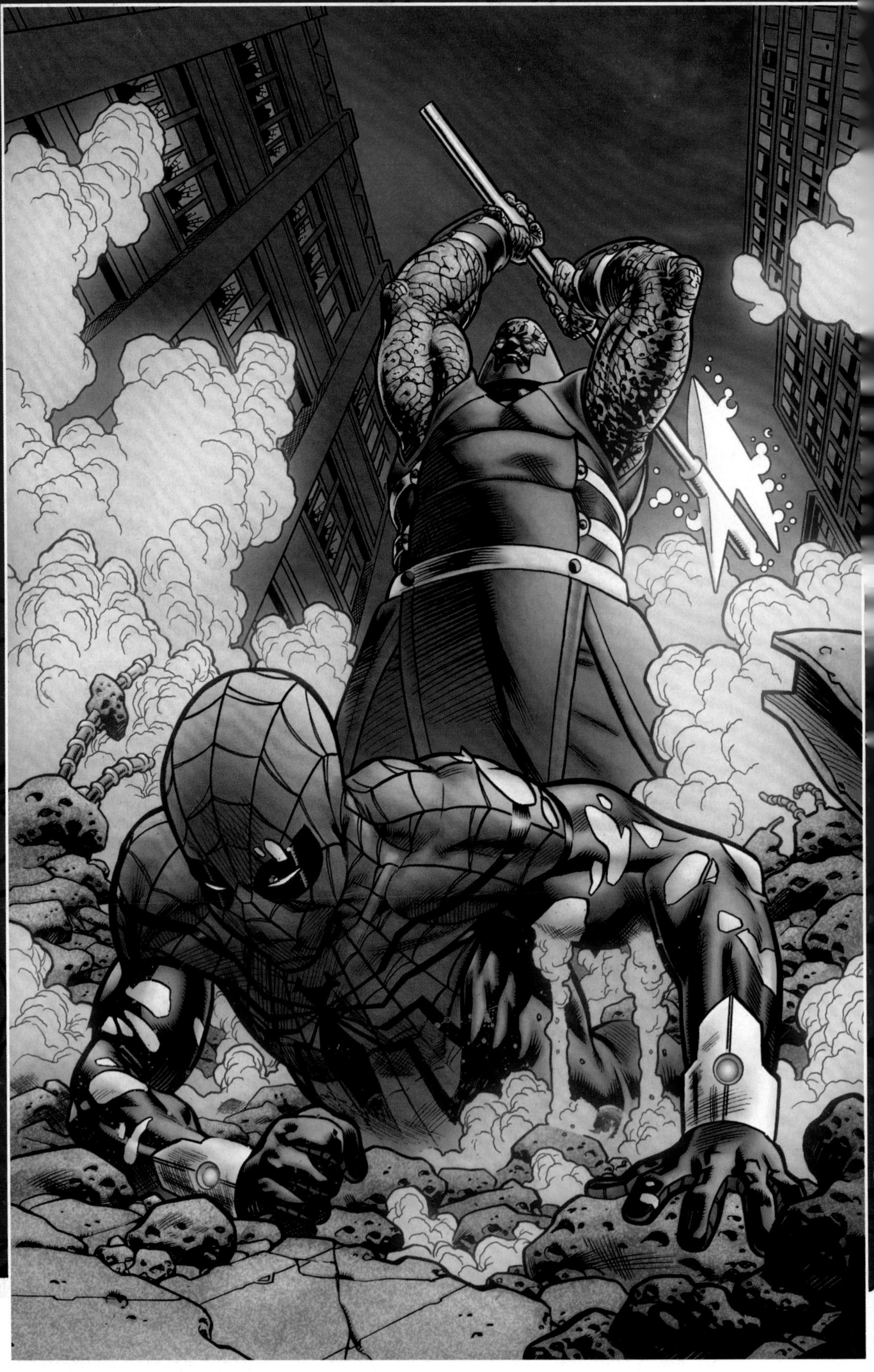

#2 VARIANT
BY MIKE HAWTHORNE & MORRY HOLLOWELL

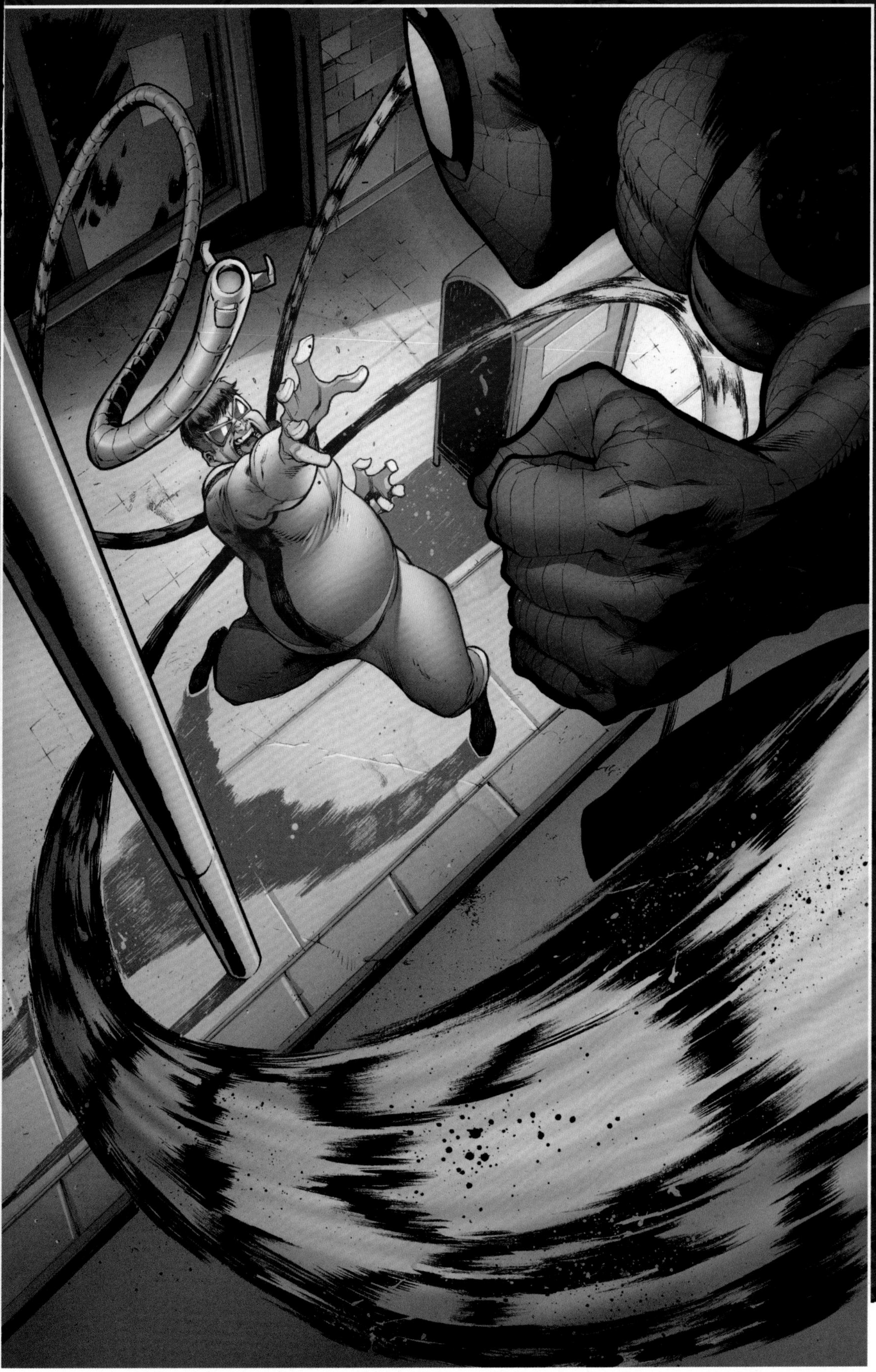

#4 SPIDER-MAN VILLAINS VARIANT
BY IBAN COELLO & MARTE GRACIA

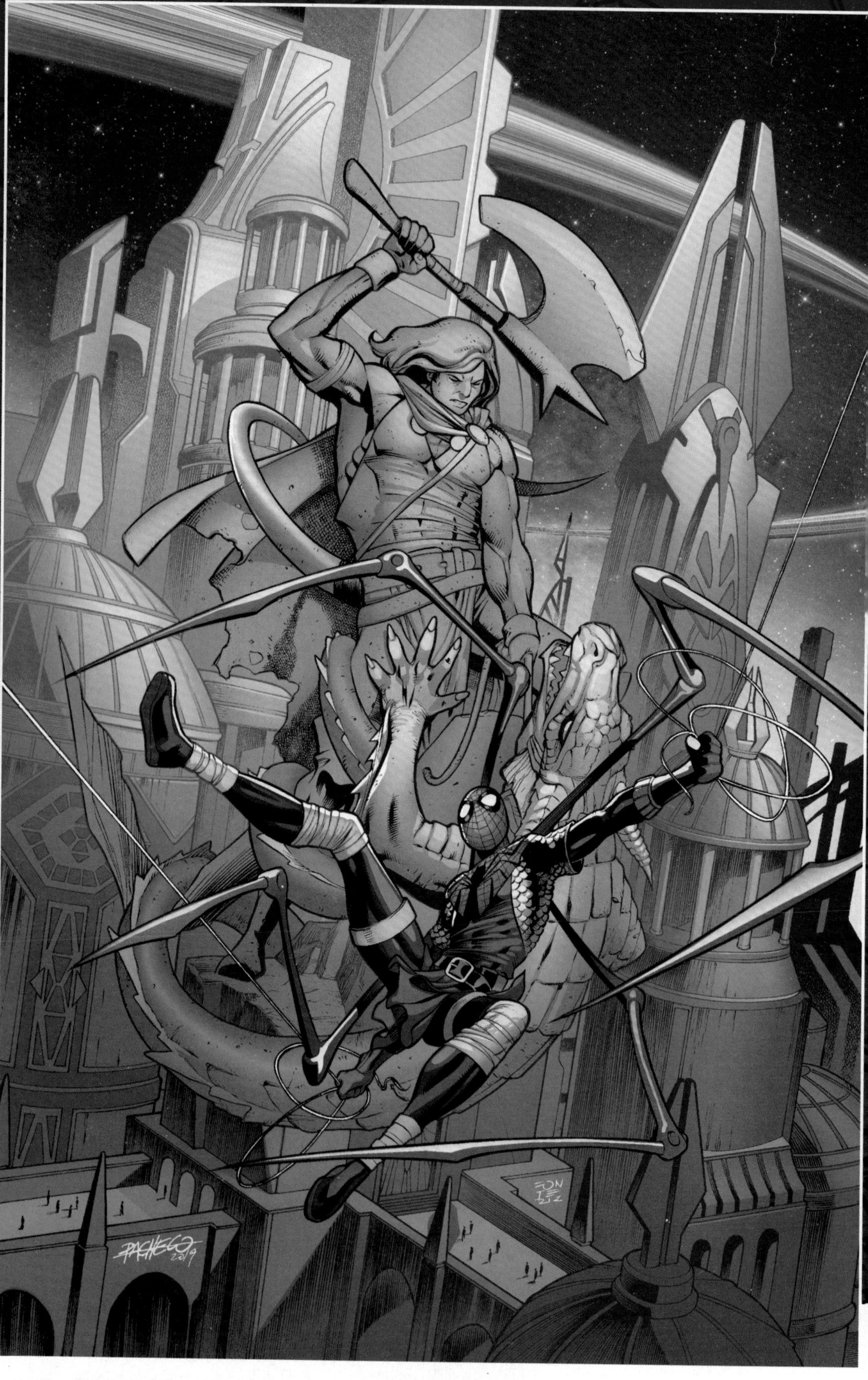

#5 ASGARDIAN VARIANT

BY CARLOS PACHECO, RAFAEL FONTERIZ & MARTE GRACIA